In̲st̲ ... Letters
of
England's
Queens

MARGARET SANDERS

First published 1957

This edition first published 2014

Amberley Publishing
The Hill, Stroud
Gloucestershire, GL5 4EP

www.amberley-books.com

British Library Cataloguing in Publication Data.
A catalogue record for this book is available from the British Library.

ISBN 978 1 4456 3807 2 (paperback)
ISBN 978 1 4456 2027 5 (ebook)

Typeset in 10pt on 12pt Sabon.
Typesetting and Origination by Amberley Publishing.
Printed in the UK.

Contents

Preface

This selection of intimate letters of England's queens, regnant and consort, has been made with a view to interesting and entertaining the general reader. For that reason, the letters have been chosen for their human and romantic appeal, rather than for their historic importance or their direct influence on the trend of national events.

To the student of history, many of the letters will be familiar. The chief aim in making this compilation has been to portray for the general reader aspects of the personality of each royal lady concerned, showing how 'human' were the queens, despite the exigencies of their high calling.

In review they pass across the stage of England's history with the vividness of living actresses. They fascinate by their contrasting personalities; they intrigue by their varying interpretations of the part they have to play. Each made her own individual contribution, in greater or lesser degree, to the immortal annals of England.

The study of the lives of these queens, as presented by historians, is apt to produce the feeling that one has attended a 'Conference of International Biographers of Royalty' and has come away with a mass of confused and contradictory reports and impressions. Historians must inevitably be prejudiced, either from religious, political, or personal attitudes. On the other hand, anyone scanning the correspondence of these royal ladies feels that they have been permitted to unlock their secret bureaux, there to discover their intimate thoughts and emotions. The letters throw light – sometimes glaring, sometimes mere candle-glow – on unsuspected aspects of the writer's life, and of her disposition.

In order to maintain the solely personal angle, which is an object of this compilation, where necessary only excerpts of an intimate nature from the queens' letters have been used. Care has been taken not to give the reader a misleading impression of the writer's true intent by such abridgements.

As to the connecting precis matter, this has been limited to brief biographical details, and to essential facts relating to the circumstances in which the letter was written. It is intended for the reader's guidance only. Although the compiler has been unable to refrain, in many instances, from making comment in the precis, it will be appreciated that this is but an expression of personal opinion. In this connection, it is suggested that the reader might gain no little stimulus in perusal of the letters by ignoring such comment and criticism, where thought fit, and forming an independent view as to what tendencies and characteristics the writer reveals. The deed, and the spoken word, can be subject to misinterpretation or misunderstanding. Letters, however, are written with the intention of their being read. The penned word is, perhaps, the most conclusive evidence of a person's trend of thought and character. It permits of little equivocation on the part of the writer.

It is not improbable that the reader may have the same difficulty as the compiler (whose ideal has been complete impartiality in dealing with the queens) and find it impossible to be quite unbiased. In any event, the letters of these royal scribes provide useful, if exacting, material for anyone seeking – if only as a recreation – to form independent and unprejudiced judgment.

The queens' letters in this collection begin with those of Catherine of Aragon (1485–1536), first wife of Henry VIII, and conclude with a limited selection from those of Queen Victoria (1819–1901), thus covering a period of some 400 years. Letters of certain queens prior to the consorts of Henry VIII are extant, but they would be of interest today only to historians.

As the Tudor period begins with the accession of Henry VII, this collection, if adhering to strict conformability, should open with a letter which his consort, Elizabeth of York, wrote to Isabella, queen of Ferdinand of Aragon and Castile, in 1497[1] The letter was written on the occasion of the betrothal of Elizabeth of York's eldest son, Arthur, Prince of Wales, to Queen Isabella's daughter, Catherine of Aragon. It is, however, not of an intimate nature, and is couched in such stilted, though elegant, phraseology that it would serve as a misleading introductory sample of the letters of the queens selected for this collection. For that reason it has been made the subject of an appendix.

In conclusion, the compiler would add that the collecting together into one volume of personal letters of England's queens (a work not hitherto attempted, as far as the compiler has been able to trace), and providing a thumbnail sketch of the life of each, has proved an edifying and engaging pastime rather than an arduous labour. It is hoped that the reader will gain not only some fresh knowledge and insight but also pleasure from the result.

Margaret Sanders
Scotsgrove, near Thame, Oxon.

1

Catherine of Aragon

(1485–1536), First Queen Consort of Henry VIII

When Princess of Wales, to her father, King Ferdinand of Aragon, 1505

From earliest times the arranged marriage was the normal custom in Europe. This convention was established by the royal houses, and the linking of their families for reasons of state was taken for granted.

Catherine of Aragon, youngest daughter of the powerful and wealthy King Ferdinand of Aragon and Queen Isabella of Castile, was a very eligible bride; and her marriage to Prince Arthur, Henry VII's eldest son and heir, was approved by both royal families. Prince Arthur, however, died of a prevailing epidemic, 'sweating sickness', within a few months of the marriage, and with an avaricious eye on her more-than handsome dowry, Henry VII deliberately detained his daughter-in-law in England. He had no intention that such a rich prize should be lost, and on the death of his consort, Elizabeth of York, at the early age of thirty-seven, even contemplated the idea of marrying Catherine himself. The suggestion, however, was loathsome to Catherine, and equally distasteful to her mother.

In the meantime, this young widow of an unconsummated marriage found herself practically penniless in a strange country, owing to the plotting and the miserly propensities of her father-in-law, Henry VII. In her youth and ignorance, she attributed her troubles to the Spanish ambassador Dr de Puebla, who was merely a willing pawn in Henry VII's game.

Most high and most puissant Lord,

Hitherto I have not wished to let Your Highness know the affairs here, that I might not give you annoyance, and also thinking that they would improve; but it appears that the contrary is the case, and that each day my troubles increase; and all this on account of the doctor de Puebla, to whom it has not sufficed that from the beginning he transacted a thousand falsities against the service of Your Highness, but now he has given me new trouble; and because I believe that Your Highness will think that I complain without reason, I desire to tell you all that has passed.

Your Highness shall know, as I have often written to you, that since I came to England I have not had a single maravedi, except a certain sum that was given to me for food, and this is such a sum, that it did not suffice without my having many debts in London; and that which troubles me more is, to see my servants and maidens so at a loss, and that they have not wherewithal to get clothes. This I believe is all done by the hand of the doctor, who, notwithstanding Your Highness has written, sending him word that he should have money from the King of England, my lord, that their costs should be given them; yet, in order not to trouble him, will rather intrench upon and neglect the service of Your Highness.

Now, my lord, a few days ago donna Elvira de Manuel[1] asked my leave to go to Flanders, to get cured of a complaint that has come into her eyes, so that she lost the sight of one of them, and there is a physician in Flanders who cured the infanta Isabella of the same disease with which she is afflicted. She laboured to bring him here, so as not to leave me, but could never succeed with him; and I, since if she were blind she could not serve me, durst not hinder her journey. I begged the King of England, my lord, that until our donna Elvira should return his highness would command that I should have as a companion an old English lady, or that he should take me to his Court; and I imparted all this to the doctor, thinking to make of the rogue a true man; but it did not avail me because he not only drew me to Court (in which I have some pleasure, because I had supplicated the King for an asylum), but he[2] negotiated that the King should dismiss all my household, and take away my chamber,[3] and place it in a house of his own, so that I should not in any way be mistress of it ...

My lord, I had forgotten to remind Your Highness how you know that it was agreed that you were to give, as a certain part of my dowry, the plate and jewels that I brought; and yet I am certain that the King of England, my lord, will not receive anything of plate nor of jewels which I have used; because he told me himself that he was indignant that they should say in his kingdom that he took away from me my ornaments. And as little may Your Highness expect that he will take them in account and will return them to me; because I am certain that he will not do so, nor is any such thing customary here. In like wise, the jewels which I brought came from thence [Spain] valued at a great sum.[4] The King would not take them in the half of the value, because here all these things are esteemed much cheaper, and the King has so many jewels that he rather desires money than them. I write thus to Your Highness because I know that there will be great embarrassment if he will not receive them, except at less price. It appears to me that it would be better that Your Highness should take them for yourself, and should give to the King of England, my lord, his money. Your Highness will see what would serve you best, and with this I shall be most content.

The humble servant of Your Highness,
who kisses your hands,
The Princess of Wales

To her father, King Ferdinand of Aragon, *c.* 1506

Henry VII eventually decided that Catherine should marry his second son and heir, Prince Henry, and used this as an excuse for keeping, for his own purposes, Catherine even more without money than before. With what must have been the courage of desperation, she wrote urgently to her father King Ferdinand of her debts and pressing needs.

That a princess of Wales should be brought so low financially that she had nothing for chemises, and should have to sell jewellery to prevent herself from going, as she says, 'all but naked', seems incredible. Incidentally, it is doubtful whether King Ferdinand ever received this appeal for aid, as Henry VII was intercepting his daughter-in-law's letters.

My Lord,

... I have written many times to Your Highness, supplicating you to order a remedy for my extreme necessity, of which [letters] I have never had an answer. Now I supplicate Your Highness, for the love of Our Lord, that you consider how I am your daughter, and that after Him (our Saviour) I have no other good nor remedy, except in Your Highness; and how I am in debt in London, and this not for extravagant things, nor yet by relieving my own people,[5] who greatly need it, but only [for] food; and how the King of England, my lord, will not cause them[6] to be satisfied, although I myself spoke to him and all those of his Council, and that with tears: but he said, that he is not bound to give me anything, and that even the food he gives me is of his good will; because Your Highness has not kept promise with him in the money of my marriage-portion. I told him that I believed that in time to come Your Highness would discharge it. He told me that was yet to see, and that he did not know it. So that, my lord, I am in the greatest trouble and anguish in the world. On the one part, seeing all my people that they are ready to ask alms; on the other, the debts that I have in London.

About my own person I have nothing for chemises; wherefore, by Your Highness' life, I have now sold some bracelets to get a dress of black velvet, for I was all but naked; for since I departed thence[7] I have had nothing but two new dresses, for till now, those I brought from thence have lasted me. Although now I have got nothing but dresses of brocade ... Calderon, who brings this letter, has served me very well. He is now going to be married. I have not wherewith to recompense him. I supplicate Your Highness to do me so great a favour as to command him to be paid there,[8] and have him recommended; for I have such care for him, that any favour that Your Highness may do him I should receive as most signal. Our Lord guard the life and royal estate of Your Highness, and increase it as I desire.

From Richmond, the 22nd of April.
The humble servant of Your Highness,
who kisses your hands,
The Princess of Wales

When queen consort to Henry VIII, 1513

Before his death in 1509, Henry VII had arranged the betrothal of his son, Prince Henry, to Catherine of Aragon; immediately upon his accession Henry VIII married her.

Three years later Henry went to war with France and Scotland, and on leaving England to lead his army in France, he entrusted the government and the captaincy of his forces in this country to Catherine. During his absence, led by their king, James IV, the Scots invaded, and while preparing to go on a pilgrimage to a shrine in Norfolk, Catherine received the news that the Scots had been defeated at the battle of Flodden Field, and their king killed.

That her duties as unofficial regent had been successful no doubt gave Catherine the satisfaction of trusts fulfilled, but one wonders how much her gentle and pious character suffered at the need for these happenings.

In spite of the formal opening, the affectionate tone of the following letter is remarkable.

Sir,

My lord Havard[9] hath sent me a letter open to Your Grace within one of mine own, by which you shall see the great victory that Our Lord hath sent your subjects in your absence and for this cause it is no need herein to trouble Your Grace with long writing but to my thinking, this battle hath been to Your Grace, and all your realm, the greatest honour that could be, and more than should you win all the crown of France. Thanked be God for it, and I am sure Your Grace forgetteth not to do this; which shall be cause to send you many more such victories as, I trust, he shall do.

My husband, – For hastiness with Rouge-Crosse [the pursuivant-at-arms] I could not send Your Grace the piece of the King of Scott's coat, which John Glyn now bringeth. In this Your Grace shall see how I can keep my promise, sending you for your banners a king's coat. I thought to send himself to you, but our Englishmen would not suffer It. It should have been better for him to have been in peace, than to have this reward. All that God sendeth is for the best. My lord of Surrey[10] my Henry, would fain know your pleasure in burying the King of Scott's body; for he hath written to me so. With the next. messenger, Your Grace's pleasure may be herein known; and with this I make an end, praying God to send you home shortly; for without this, no joy here can be accomplished, and for the same I pray.

And now I go to Our Lady at Walsingham,[11] that I promised so long ago to see. At Woburn, 16th of September.

I send Your Grace herein a *bill* [a note], found in a Scottish man's purse, of such things as the French King sent to the said King of Scott's to make war against you. Beseeching you to send Matthew hither, as soon as this messenger cometh to bring me tidings from Your Grace,

Your humble wife and true servant,

Katharine [*sic*]

To her daughter, Mary, later to become first (acknowledged) Queen Regnant of England, *c.* 1529

On the surface, the marriage of Henry VIII and Catherine of Aragon continued successfully for some years.

In 1511 Catherine gave birth to a son, but the child died within a month. Two years later another son was born, but died just as quickly. Only a daughter, Mary, born in 1516, lived.

Eventually, disappointment at Catherine's failure to produce a male heir, combined with what we now know was a licentious temperament, influenced Henry to seek grounds for divorcing her.

Meanwhile, Catherine's love for her only surviving child can be imagined. A fine linguist, she did all she could to assist in the education of her daughter, and was Mary's principal tutor in Latin. In the following letter she recommends Mary's attentions to her studies under the guidance of a Dr Featherstone.

Daughter,

I pray you think not that forgetfulness has caused me to keep Charles so long here, and answered not your good letter, in which I perceive ye would know how I do. I am in that case, that the absence of the King and you troubleth me. My health is metely good; and I trust in God that He, who sent it me, doth it to the best, and will shortly turn all to come with good effect. And in the meantime, I am very glad to hear from you, especially when they shew me that ye be well amended. I pray God to continue it to His pleasure.

As for your writing in Latin, I am glad that ye shall change from me to Maister Federston, for that shall do you much good to learn from him to write right; but yet sometimes I would be glad, when ye do write to Maister Federston of your own inditing, when he hath read it that I may see it, for it shall be a great comfort for me to see you keep your Latin, and fair writing and all. And so I pray to recommend me to My Lady of Salisbury.[12] At Woburn, this Friday night.

> Your loving Mother.
> Katharine the Qwene [*sic*]

To her daughter, Mary, *c*. 1533

The ingenuity and trickery employed and the numbers of people whom Henry VIII involved in his determination to rid himself of Catherine of Aragon are well-known facts. Although Henry succeeded in his aim, Catherine, to the day of her death, refused to recognise the legality of the annulment of their marriage.

The annulment proceedings, however, were duly put into operation, in order that Henry might be free to make Lady Anne Boleyn – his presiding mistress, and one of Catherine's maids-of-honour – his new consort.

During this time Catherine was cut off from all contact with the court, and from her daughter, whom Henry VIII had also dismissed from his presence. Later, for political reasons, he was to send for Mary to be present at the birth of his first child by Anne Boleyn. On hearing rumours to this effect, Catherine wrote to her daughter a letter which expresses her hopes and fears as to the outcome of this royal command. The letter is particularly touching in its counsel of patience and humility during the continuing crisis in the life of both mother and daughter.

Daughter,

I have heard such tidings this day, that I do perceive (if it be true) the time is very near when Almighty God will provide for you, and I am very glad of it; for I trust that He doth handle you with a good love. I beseech you agree to His pleasure with a merry[13] heart, and be sure that, without fail, He will not suffer you to perish if you be aware to offend Him.[14] I pray God that you, good daughter, offer yourself to Him. If any pangs come over you, shrive yourself; first make you clean, take heed of His commandments, and keep them as near as He will give you grace to do, for there you are sure armed. And if *this lady* do come to you, as it is spoken; if she bring you a letter from the King, I am sure in the self-same letter you will be commanded what to do.

Answer with very few words, obeying the King your father in everything – save only that you will not offend God, and lose your soul, and go no further with learning and disputation in the matter. And wheresoever, and in whatsoever company, you shall come obey the King's commandments, speak few words, and meddle nothing.

I will send you two books in Latin; one shall be *De Vita Christi* with the declarations of the Gospels; and the other, the epistles of St. Jerome, that he did write to Paula and Eustochium, and in them, I trust, you will see good things.

Sometimes, for your recreation, use your virginals or lute, if you have any.

But one thing specially I desire you, for the love you owe to God and unto me – to keep your heart with a chaste mind, and your person from all ill and wanton company, not thinking or desiring of any husband, for Christ's Passion; neither determine yourself to any manner of living, until this troublesome time be past.

For I do make you sure you shall see a very good end, and better than you can desire.

I would God, good daughter, that you did know with how good a heart I write this letter unto you. I never did one with a better, for I perceive very well that God loveth you. I beseech Him, of His goodness, to continue it.

I think it best you *keep your keys yourself,*[15] for whosoever it is[16] shall be done as shall please them. And now you shall begin, and by likelihood I shall follow. I set not a rush by it, for when they have done the utmost they can, then I am sure of amendment.

I pray you recommend me unto my good Lady of Salisbury,[17] and pray her to have a good heart, for we never come to the Kingdom of Heaven but by troubles.

Daughter, *wheresoever* you come, take no pain to send to me, for if I may, I will send to you.

> By your loving mother,
> Katharine the Quene [*sic*]

To an unnamed friend, 1535

The actual date of the separation of Catherine of Aragon from her daughter is not known; but what grief the parting caused them both needs little speculation. Once the separation had taken place Catherine was prevented by Henry VIII from ever seeing Mary again.

Years spent in ill health, and latterly sorrow and loneliness, culminated in a fatal disease. Catherine, on the brink of death, entreated Henry in vain that she might see her daughter once more. Mary also made equally fruitless appeals. Such last consolation to the dying mother, however, was sternly refused.

The following letter was written by Catherine to a friend who had tried to intercede on her behalf.

Mine especial friend,

You have greatly bound me with the pains that you have taken in speaking with the King my lord concerning the coming of my daughter unto me. The reward you shall trust to have of God; for (as you know) in me there is no power to gratify that you have done, but only with my good will. As touching the answer which hath been made you, that His Highness is contented to send her[18] to some place nigh me, so as I do not see her, I pray you vouchsafe to give unto His Highness mine effectual thanks for the goodness which he showeth unto his daughter and mine, and for the comfort that I have thereby received; and as to my seeing of her, you shall certify that, if she were within one mile of me, I would not see her. For the time permitteth not that I should go about sights, and be it that I would, I could not, because I lack provision therefor.

Howbeit, you shall always say unto His Highness that the thing which I desired was to send her where I am; being assured that a little comfort and mirth, which she should take with me, should undoubtedly be half a health unto her. I have proved the like by experience, being diseased of the same infirmity, and know how much good it may do that I say. And, since I desired a thing so just and reasonable, and [that] so much touched the honour and conscience of the King my lord, I thought not it should have been denied me.

Let not, for my love, to do what you may that this may be yet done. Here have I, among others, heard that he had some suspicion of the surety of her. I cannot believe that a thing so far from reason should pass from the royal heart of His Highness; neither can I think that he hath so little confidence in me. If any such matter[19] chance to be communed of, I pray you say unto His Highness that I am determined to die (without doubt) in this realm; and that I, from henceforth, offer mine own person for surety, to the intent that, if any such thing should be attempted, that then he do Justice of me, as of the most evil woman that ever was born.

The residue I remit to your good wisdom and judgment, as unto a trusty friend, to whom I pray God give health.

To Dr John Forest, 1535

Even the solace of her confessor, Father John Forest, was denied to Catherine.

At an early stage in the annulment proceedings Dr Forest was imprisoned with criminals in Newgate for his allegiance to his queen and his faith; and not long afterwards was put to death. Catherine, powerless to help, felt herself to be responsible for his sufferings; but even in the fear that should her letter be intercepted it might do him greater harm, wrote of her gratitude and faith in him. She was to have the comfort of learning from the ageing priest that 'in justification of her cause he was content to suffer all things,' to which assurance he added, 'Would it become, lady mine, an old man to be appalled with childish fears, who has seen sixty-four years of life, and forty of those has worn the habit of the glorious St. Francis?'

It must have meant much to Catherine to receive such an answer to the following letter.

My Revered Father,

Since you have ever been wont in dubious cases to give good counsel to others, you will necessarily know all the better what is needed for yourself, being called to combat for the love of Christ and the truth of the Catholic Faith. If you will bear up under these few and short pains of your torments which are prepared for you, you will receive, as you well know, eternal reward, which, whoever will basely lose for some tribulation of this present life, I verily esteem him wanting both in sense and reason.

But O happy you, my father, to whom it has been graciously granted that you should experience this more fully than other men; and that none otherwise than by these bonds, by this imprisonment, by these torments, and finally by a most cruel death, for Christ's sake, you should happily fulfil the course of your most holy life and fruitful labours.

But woe to me, your poor and wretched daughter, who, in the time of this my solitude and the extreme anguish of my soul, shall be deprived of such a corrector and father, so loved by me in the bowels of Christ. And truly, if it were lawful for me freely to confess what is my most ardent desire in reference to this, to your paternity, to whom I have always revealed (as was my duty) all the secrets of my heart and conscience, I confess to you that I am consumed by a very great desire to be able to die, either together with you or before you; which I should always seek, and would purchase by any amount of the most hearty and infinite torments of whatsoever sort, provided it were not a thing repugnant to the Divine Will, to which I always willingly submit all my life and my every affection and desire; so much do I dislike, and so greatly would it displease me, to allow myself any joy in this miserable and unhappy world, those being removed of whom the world is not worthy.

But perhaps I have spoken as a foolish woman. Therefore, since it appears that God has thus ordained, go you, my father, first with joy and fortitude, and by your prayers plead with Jesus Christ for me, that I may speedily and intrepidly follow you through the same wearisome and difficult journey; and, meanwhile, that I may be able to share your holy labours, your torments, punishments, and struggles. I shall have all this by your last blessing in this life, but when you have fought the battle and obtained the Crown, I shall expect to receive more abundant grace from heaven by your means.

As to the rest, I think it would be an extravagant thing in me to extort you to desire above all other things that immortal reward, and to seek to acquire and gain possession of it, at whatever expense or pain in this life, you being of such noble birth, gifted with such excellent knowledge of divine things, and (what I ought to mention first) brought up from your youth in a religion so holy and in the profession of the most glorious father St. Francis. Nevertheless, since this is a very principal and supreme good bestowed by God on mortals, that for His sake they may endure grevious pains, I shall always supplicate His Divine Majesty with continual prayers, with passionate weeping, and with assiduous penitence, that you may happily end your course, and arrive at the incorruptible crown of eternal life.

Farewell, my revered Father, and on earth and in heaven always have me in remembrance before God.

Your very sad and afflicted daughter,
Katharine

To Henry VIII, 1535

The last line of this last letter written, or rather dictated, by Catherine of Aragon to Henry VIII gives the amazing impression that in the face of all that she had suffered at his hands, she retained her affection for the king to the hour of her death.

It is to be expected that a letter written while dying would show the magnanimity and devoutness of her character, but does it not also contain the suggestion that Catherine, in spite of all, still loved that scandalous but obviously attractive man?

Although Catherine addresses Henry as 'Husband,' which in her own eyes and according to the tenets of her religion he remained, she was buried at Peterborough Abbey as the widow of his brother, Prince Arthur, and not as his own one-time wife and consort.

My Lord and Dear Husband,

I commend me unto you. The hour of my death draweth fast on, and my case being such, the tender love I owe you forceth me, with a few words, to put you in remembrance of the health and safeguard of your soul, which you ought to prefer before all worldly matters, and before the care and tendering of your own body, for the which you have cast me into many miseries and yourself into many cares.

For my part I do pardon you all, yea, I do wish and devoutly pray God that He will also pardon you.

For the rest I commend unto you Mary, our daughter, beseeching you to be a good father unto her, as I heretofore desired. I entreat you also, on behalf of my maids, to give them marriage-portions, which is not much, they being but three. For all my other servants, I solicit a year's pay more than their due, lest they should be unprovoked for.

Lastly, do I vow, that mine eyes desire you above all things.

2

Anne Boleyn

(*c.* 1507–1536), Second Queen Consort of Henry VIII

To her father, Sir Thomas Boleyn, *c.* 1514

Reputedly a lineal descendant of Adelicia of Louvaine[1] (known as 'The Fair Maid of Brabant') by Adelicia's second marriage with William de Albini, Anne Boleyn was the younger daughter of Sir Thomas Boleyn, ambassador to the court of France, and Lady Elizabeth Boleyn, a beauty at Catherine of Aragon's court who had died when Anne was still a child.

The following letter was written in French by Anne Boleyn to her father, when, as a girl in her teens, he sent for her to come to London from Hever Castle, in Kent, where she resided with her French governess, to be presented at court.

Sir,

I find by your letter, that you wish me to appear at Court in a manner becoming a respectable female; and likewise that the Queen will condescend to enter into conversation with me. At this I rejoice, as I do think that conversing with so sensible and elegant a Princess will make me even more desirous of continuing to speak and to write good French; the more as it is by your earnest advice, which (I acquaint you by this present writing) I shall follow to the best of my ability.

Sir, I entreat you to excuse me if this letter is badly written. I can assure you the spelling proceeds entirely from my own head, while the other letters were the work of my hands alone; and Semmonet[2] tells me she has left the letter to be composed by myself, that nobody else may know what I am writing to you. I therefore pray you do not suffer your superior knowledge to conquer the inclination which (you say) you have to advance me. As to myself, rest assured that I shall not ungratefully look upon this fatherly office as one that might be dispensed with; nor will it tend to diminish the affection you are in quest of, resolved as I am to lead as holy a life as you may please to desire of me; indeed my love for you is founded on so firm a basis, that it can never be impaired. I put an end to this my lucubration, after having very humbly craved your goodwill and affection. Written at Hever, by

Your very humble and obedient daughter,
Anna de Boullan [*sic*]

To Henry VIII, *c.* 1527

While still a young woman, Anne Boleyn was appointed a maid-of-honour to Henry VIII's young sister, Mary, married to Louis XII of France. Some years later Anne returned to this country, and in due course became a maid-of-honour to Henry's consort, Catherine of Aragon.

Considered a woman of intelligence, was she also, even at an early age, the accomplished and unscrupulous schemer that history has proclaimed her? Certainly, in the following (undated) letter, she flatters King Henry unreservedly, and one is tempted to read into it her hope of even greater royal favours to follow the immediate appointment to which she refers.

Sire,

It belongs only to the august mind of a great King to whom Nature has given a heart full of generosity towards the sex, to repay by favours so extraordinary an artless and short conversation with a girl. Inexhaustible as is the treasury of Your Majesty's bounties, I pray [you] to consider that it cannot be sufficient to your generosity; for if you recompense so slight a conversation by gifts so great, what will you be able to do for those who are ready to consecrate their entire obedience to your desires? How great soever may be the bounties I have received, the joy that I feel in being loved by a King whom I adore, and to whom I would with pleasure make a sacrifice of my heart, if fortune had rendered it worthy of being offered to him, will ever be infinitely greater.

The warrant of maid of honour to the Queen[3] induces me to think that Your Majesty has some regard for me, since it gives me the means of seeing you oftener, and of assuring you by my own lips (which I shall do on the first opportunity) that I am,

Your Majesty's very obliged and very obedient servant

without reserve,

Anne Boleyn

The Lady Anne Boleyn, to Cardinal Wolsey, *c.* 1529

Obviously Anne Boleyn's main purpose was to allure the king, and this in turn produced the ambition to supplant Catherine of Aragon as his consort. Not only wiles, but strategies were needed to attain her ends. The powerful chancellor Cardinal Wolsey was one whose connivance, willing or unwilling, was essential to Anne Boleyn's schemes at this juncture.

While her hopes were high, she wrote to Cardinal Wolsey with hypocritical subserviency.

My Lord,

After my most humble recommendations, this shall be to give unto Your Grace, as I am most bound, my humble thanks for the pain and travail that Your Grace doth take in studying, by your wisdom and great diligence, how to bring to pass honourably the greatest wealth that is possible to come to any creature living, and in especial remembering how wretched and unworthy I am in comparing to his highness.

And for you, I do know myself never to have deserved by my deserts that you should take this great pain for me; yet daily of your goodness I do perceive by all my friends, and though that I had not knowledge of them, the daily proof of your deeds doth declare your words and writing toward me to be true.

Now, good my lord, your discretion may consider as yet how little it is in my power to recompense you, but all only with my good will, the which I assure you, that after this matter is brought to pass you shall find me, as I am bound in the meantime, to owe you my service, and then look what thing in this world I can imagine to do you pleasure in, you shall find me the gladdest woman in the world to do it, And next unto the King's Grace, of one thing I make you full promise to be assured to have it, and that is my hearty love unfeignedly during my life; and being fully determined, with God's Grace, never to change this purpose, I make an end of this my rude and true-meaning letter, praying Our Lord to send you much increase of honour, with long life.

Written with the hand of her that beseeches Your Grace to accept this letter as proceeding from, one that is most bound to be

Your humble and obedient servant,

Anne Boleyn

To Cardinal Wolsey, *c.* 1529

On Anne Boleyn realising, at a later stage, that Cardinal Wolsey was no longer willing to aid her in her determined aspirations, she did not hesitate to show bitter anger.

Once aware that Wolsey was inclined to favour the cause of Catherine of Aragon, Anne's vengeance pursued him relentlessly, and brought about the cardinal's downfall. A woman of vast ambition, she seems to have pinned her hopes of becoming queen on her own abilities.

The letter which follows is of special interest in the contrast it displays between her character and that of Catherine of Aragon.

My lord,

Though you are a man of great understanding, you cannot avoid being censured by everybody for having drawn on yourself the hatred of a King who has raised you to the highest degree to which the greatest ambition of a man seeking his fortune can aspire. I cannot comprehend, and the King still less, how your reverend Lordship after having allured us by so many fine promises about divorce, can have repented of your purpose, and how you could have done what you have, in order to hinder the consummation of it. What, then, is your mode of proceeding?

You quarrelled with the Queen to favour me at the time when I was less advanced in the King's good graces; and after having therein given me the strongest marks of your affection, your Lordship abandons my interests to embrace those of the Queen. I acknowledge that I have put much confidence in your professions and promises, in which I find myself deceived.

But for the future I shall rely on nothing but the protection of Heaven and the love of my dear King, which alone will be able to set right again those plans which you have broken and spoiled, and to place me in that happy station which God wills, the King so much wishes, and which will be entirely to the advantage of the Kingdom.

The wrong you have done me has caused me much sorrow; but I feel infinitely more in seeing myself betrayed by a man who pretended to enter into my interests only to discover the secrets of my heart. I acknowledge that, believing you sincere, I have been too precipitate in my confidence; it is this which has induced, and still induces me, to keep more moderation in avenging myself, not being able to forget that I *have* been

Your servant,
Anne Boleyn

When queen consort, to Henry VIII, 1536

Anne Boleyn succeeded in her object of becoming crowned consort of Henry VIII. Once more, however, Henry was disappointed in his desire for a male heir; for on 7 September 1533, Anne gave birth to a female child. This infant, after many vicissitudes, and surprising developments in the story of the succession, was to become Queen Elizabeth I, the greatest independent monarch that England has known.

Later, Anne gave birth to a son, but the boy was stillborn, owing – so it is said – to the shock she sustained on unexpectedly witnessing Henry's amorous advances to Jane Seymour, one of her maids-of-honour. Did the memory of her own like conduct while maid-of-honour to Catherine of Aragon sharpen the impact of the situation? Certainly, the disappointment of the premature birth, combined with the advent of a dangerous rival, warned Anne that her star was setting where Henry's affections were concerned. She was too intelligent a woman not to realise, by this time, the character of her royal husband; but, all too quickly, he found means to send Anne Boleyn to the Tower on the charges of unfaithfulness, of incest, and of conspiring against the life of the king.

From her 'doleful prison' she wrote the following tragic, but, one might be tempted to consider, all too clever letter[4] to Henry, displaying as it does humbleness, arrogance, and failure to refrain from insinuations with regard to the king's character, yet ending on a note which unquestionably was of genuine entreaty for her alleged lovers in jeopardy with her.

It should be mentioned that Strickland, author of *Lives of the Queens of England*, was a staunch believer in Anne Boleyn's innocence. She quotes as authority the historian, Lord Bacon, who said that Queen Anne protested her innocence with undaunted greatness of mind at the time of her death. Bacon continues: 'By a messenger, faithful and generous as she supposed, who was one of the King's privy chamber, she, just before she went to execution, sent this message to the

King: "Commend me to His Majesty, and tell him he hath been ever constant in his career of advancing me; from a private gentlewoman he made me a marchioness,[5] from a marchioness a queen, and now he hath left no higher degree of honour, he gives my innocency the crown of martyrdom".'

Her appeal to Henry VIII was unavailing, and Anne, the 'Queen of a Thousand Days', was executed in the Tower on 19 May 1536, within a few months of the death of Catherine of Aragon.

Your Grace's displeasure and my imprisonment are things so strange unto me, that what to write, or what to excuse, I am altogether ignorant. Whereas you send to me (willing me to confess a truth, and so obtain your favour) by such a one, whom you know to be mine ancient professed enemy, I no sooner received this message by him, than I rightly conceived your meaning; and if, as you say, confessing a truth indeed may procure my safety, I shall, with all willingness and duty, perform your command. But let not Your Grace ever imagine that your poor wife will ever be brought to acknowledge a fault, where not so much as a thought ever proceeded. And to speak a truth, never a prince had wife more loyal in all duty, and in all true affection, than you have ever found in Anne Bulen – with which name and place I could willingly have contented myself, if God and Your Grace's pleasure had been so pleased. Neither did I at any time so far forget myself in my exaltation or received queen ship, but that I always looked for such alteration as I now find; for the ground of my preferment being on no surer foundation than Your Grace's fancy, the least alteration was fit and sufficient (I knew) to draw that fancy to some other subject.

You have chosen me from a low estate to be your Queen and companion, far beyond my desert or desire; if, then, you found me worthy of such honour, Good your Grace, let not any light fancy or bad counsel of my enemies withdraw your princely favour from me; neither let that stain – that unworthy stain – of a disloyal heart towards your good grace ever cast so foul a blot on me, and on the infant Princess your daughter.

Try me, good King, but let me have a lawful trial, and let not my sworn enemies sit as my accusers and as my judges; Yea, let me receive an open trial, for my truth shall fear no open shames. Then shall you see either my innocency cleared, your suspicions and conscience satisfied, the ignominy and slander of the world stopped, or my guilt openly declared. So that, whatever God may determine of, Your Grace may be freed from an open censure; and mine offence being so lawfully proved, Your Grace may be at liberty, both before God and man, not only to execute worthy punishment on me as an unfaithful Wife, but to follow your affection already settled on that party,[6] for those sake I am now as I am, whose name I could some good while since, have pointed unto – Your Grace being not ignorant of my suspicion therein. But if you have already determined of me and that not only my death, but an infamous slander must bring you the joying of your desired happiness, then I desire of God that He will pardon your great sin herein, and likewise my enemies the instruments thereof; and that He will not call you to a strait account for your unprincely and cruel usage of me at His general judgment-seat, where both you and myself must shortly appear; and in whose judgment, I doubt not (whatsoever the world may think of me), mine innocency shall be openly known and sufficiently cleared.

My last and only request shall be, that myself may only bear the burden of Your Grace's displeasure, and that it may not touch the innocent souls of those poor gentlemen[7] whom as I understand are likewise in strait imprisonment for my sake.

If ever I have found favour in your sight – if ever the name of Anne Bulen have been pleasing in your ears – then let me obtain this request; and so I will leave to trouble Your Grace any further, with mine earnest prayer to the Trinity to have Your Grace in good keeping, and to direct you m all your actions.

From my doleful prison in the Tower, the 6th of May:

Anne Bulen [*sic*]

Endorsed: 'To the King, from the Ladye in the Tower.'

Jane Seymour

(*c.* 1510–1537), Third Queen
Consort of Henry VIII

If Anne Boleyn was personally ambitious, Henry VIII's third wife, Jane Seymour – whom he married within twenty-four hours of Anne's execution – seems to have been the tool, willing or otherwise, of an ambitious family. The eldest daughter of eight children of a country gentleman, Sir John Seymour, Jane attained the unlikely summit of queen consort by a series of nefarious manoeuvres engineered by her relations, coupled with the lustful appetites of a king already beginning to be discredited as a reliable husband.

She maintained her position as queen consort, although she was never crowned – the coronation having to be postponed owing to a plague that had broken out, and later, her pregnancy – for eighteen months, dying on the birth of her son, afterwards Edward VI. She was buried in St George's Chapel at Windsor.

Apart from being the means of flagrant nepotism, by which her uncles, brothers, sisters and cousins came to fill lucrative offices at court, Jane seems to have passed her brief spell of royal life without uttering or doing anything of significance, with the exception of bearing a male heir. The only act of her queenship of which documentary evidence appears to have been preserved was an order to a park keeper at Havering-atte-Bower to 'deliver to her well-beloved gentlemen of her sovereign lord the King's Chapel Royal, two bucks of high season'.

Shortage of time may, perhaps, have been in her favour, but it can at least be said that Jane Seymour's title as wife and queen of Henry VIII were never disputed by the king or his subjects. This, however, did not prevent universal rumour that Henry's three wives had all come by unfair deaths – Catherine of Aragon by poison, Anne Boleyn by the block, and Jane Seymour by neglect and want of proper care in childbirth.

Undeterred, the royal widower wasted little time before seeking yet another wife. He found himself, however, so greatly at a discount among the princesses of Europe that he was forced to remain without prospect of a consort for upwards of two years.

Anne of Cleves

(1516–1557), Fourth Queen Consort of Henry VIII

When queen consort, to the king, 1540

Anne of Cleves was the second daughter of John, Duke of Cleves. In contrast to the 'commoner' ancestors of Anne Boleyn and of Jane Seymour, the powerful family of this ancient duchy of Germany were of sufficient quality to warrant the betrothal of a princess of their house to the English king.

It is unnecessary here to describe the state-, or other craft, that lay behind the arrangements for this marriage. On the personal side, the reader will no doubt be familiar with the fact that Henry VIII's first introduction to his fourth consort took the form of a flattering portrait (a miniature by Holbein) specially painted to mislead the king.

In spite of Henry's being more than twice Anne of Cleve's age, and by this time obese and diseased, he did not hesitate to show his fury, at their first meeting, on finding his bride-to-be what he described as 'no better than a Flanders mare', and made no secret of his disgust with her appearance and demeanour.[1] Most women would surely have been appalled at such a situation, in view of the fate of Henry's previous wives. Anne of Cleves, however, kept her head in more ways than one. Realising that Henry was determined to be rid of her, she unprotestingly acquiesced to an annulment of her marriage, which was based on the accusation, among other things, of her not having been a virgin at the time of the betrothal.

A woman of unusual common sense, she most likely considered herself to have made little or no sacrifice in exchanging the role of wife for that of sister; that being the proposal made to her by Henry VIII, his lords and council. These last were apparently present at the writing of Anne of Cleves's letter to the king which follows. In fact, the stiff, almost legal phraseology, and careful coverage of all essential points, suggest that it was in all probability dictated for Anne of Cleves to sign.

Pleaseth your most excellent Majesty to understand that, whereas, at sundry times heretofore, I have been informed and perceived by certain Lords and others of Your Grace's Council, of the doubts and questions which have been moved and found in our marriage; and how hath petition thereupon been made to Your Highness by your Nobles and Commons, that the same might be examined and determined by the Holy Clergy of this realm; to testify to Your Highness by my writing, that which I have before promised by my word and will, that is to say, that the matter should be examined and determined by the said Clergy; it may please Your Majesty to know that, though this case must needs be most hard and sorrowful unto me, for the great love which I bear to your most noble person, yet, having more regard to God and His truth than to any worldly affection, as it beseemed me, at the beginning, to submit me to such examination and determination of the said Clergy, whom I have and do accept for judges competent in that behalf.

So now being ascertained how the same Clergy hath therein given their judgment and sentence, I knowledge myself hereby to accept and approve the same, wholly and entirely putting myself, for my state and condition, to Your Highness' goodness and pleasure; most humbly beseeching Your Majesty that, though it be determined that the pretended matrimony between us is void and of none effect, whereby I neither can nor will repute myself Your Grace's wife, considering this sentence (whereunto I stand) and Your Majesty's clean and pure living with me, yet it will please you to take me for one of your most humble servants, and so to determine me, as I may sometimes have the fruition of your most noble presence; which I shall esteem for a great benefit, so, my Lords and others of Your Majesty's Council, now being with me, have put me in comfort thereof; and that Your Highness will take me for Your sister; for the which I most humbly thank you accordingly.

Thus, most gracious Prince, I beseech our Lord God to send Your Majesty long life and good health, to God's Glory, your own honour, and the wealth of this noble realm.

From Richmond, the 11th day of July, the 32nd year of Your Majesty's most noble reign.

Your Majesty's most humble sister and servant,
Anne, the daughter of Cleves

As the Lady Anne of Cleves to her brother, the Duke of Cleves, *c.* 1540

Thus the marriage of Anne of Cleves to Henry VIII was dissolved within six months; but it was still necessary for her to steer a steady course among the intersecting currents of those critical times. She was well aware that Henry VIII was determined to hold her as a hostage in England, in case her brother, now Duke of Cleves, should seek reprisals for the insults and ill-treatment that had been meted out to his sister. Tempers, especially with regard to any actual or fancied slight upon the honour of a royal house, were apt to run very short, and Anne knew all too well that a hasty gesture on the part of her brother, however well-intentioned, might easily cost her her life.

With this much in mind, she wrote post-haste to the Duke of Cleves, who was preparing to take violent action on her behalf.

The following letter may well have averted a minor war, and undoubtedly helped Anne of Cleves to attain the kind of life which she would seem to have desired, and which she succeeded in enjoying until her death seventeen years later.

Viewed against the grasping and covetous behaviour of her contemporaries, her methods may appear to have had a negative quality; but history could ill spare such characters as Anne of Cleves, and surely would have been much the worse for their absence. Even in the highest circles the personal aspirations of those involved will naturally differ. For Anne of Cleves they apparently consisted in a desire for an ordered private life, and this she achieved without injury to anyone.

Following the dissolution of her marriage, she gave her attention and care to the English property from which she derived her income, and maintained, at Henry VIII's instigation, the precedence of first lady at court, after his queen and daughters, which he had ensured for her. This precedence no member of the royal family ever attempted to dispute.

My Dear and Well-Beloved Brother,

... After my most hearty commendation: Whereas, by your letters of the 13th of this month, which I have seen, written to the King's Majesty of England, my most dear and most kind brother I do perceive you take the matter lately moved and determined between him and me somewhat to heart. Forasmuch as I had rather ye knew the truth by mine advertisement, than for want thereof ye should be deceived by vain reports, I thought meet to write these present letters to you; by the which it shall please you to understand, how the Nobles and Commons of this realm desired the King's Highness to commit the examination of the matter of the marriage between His Majesty and me to the determination of the Holy Clergy of this realm.

I did then willingly consent thereto; and since their determination made, have also, upon intimation of their proceedings allowed approved, and agreed to the same ... God willing I purpose to lead my life in this realm.

> Anna, duchess born of Cleves, Gulick, Geldre,
> and Berg, and your loving sister

To Queen Mary I, 1554

During her retirement, Anne of Cleves was to witness many changes at the English court: the marriage of Henry VIII to two further consorts, his death, the accession of Edward VI (son of Jane Seymour) and his death, the alleged usurpation of the throne by the Lady Jane Grey, and finally the accession of Mary, daughter of Henry VIII by his first consort, Catherine of Aragon.

After the marriage of Mary I to Philip of Spain, Anne of Cleves wrote to the royal bride a letter of congratulation, in which it will be noticed that she rings the changes on the titles of majesty, highness, and grace in an amusing manner, a not surprising confusion of terms, however, when one realises that Mary was the first Queen Regnant of England as from Tudor times.

To The Queen's Majesty.

After my humble commendations unto Your Majesty, with thanks for you: loving favour showed to me in my last suit, and praying of Your Highness your loving continuance, it may please Your Highness to understand that I am informed of Your Grace's return to London again; and being desirous to do my duty to see Your Majesty, and the King, if It may so stand with Your Highness' pleasure, and that I may know when and where I shall wait on Your Majesty and his.

Wishing you both much joy and felicity, with increase of children to God's Glory, and to the preservation of your prosperous estates, long to continue with honour in all godly virtue.

   From my poor house at Hever, the 4th of August,

                        Your Highness' to command,

                        Anna, the daughter of Cleves

Endorsed: 'The Lady Anne of Cleves to the Queen's Majesty, August, 1554.'

The clear-minded and unassuming character of Anne of Cleves won for her both respect and affection, and on her death in 1557, Queen Mary I directed that she should be buried near the high altar in Westminster Abbey.[2] Anne of Cleves thereby secured an honoured burial place unusual for Henry VIII's wives.

But we must return to events that occurred before the death of Anne of Cleves, and which took place after she had been adopted by Henry's royal edict as his sister.

5

Catherine Howard

(1520–1542), Fifth Queen Consort of Henry VIII

Within a matter of days, if not hours, of the annulment of his marriage to Anne of Cleves, Henry VIII made Catherine Howard his next consort, although his finances were so low at the time that he could afford for her neither a public wedding nor a coronation. As events were shortly to turn out, this was perhaps just as well.

Catherine Howard was a full cousin of Anne Boleyn, and the second daughter of Lord Edmund Howard, one of the victors of Flodden Field, who had fallen upon hard times. Although she might appear to have been little more than a highly placed courtesan, there was regal blood in her veins as a descendant of the imperial race of Charles the Great, king of the Franks.

Catherine was the third private gentlewoman whom Henry VIII had elevated to the dignity of queenship, which spurious position the unfortunate bride held for less than two years. Her promiscuous temperament was known to many people, her first 'affair' reputedly having taken place when she was twelve years of age.[1] His passion, however, seems to have blinded the king to any such propensities in Lady Catherine, until she was accused by her enemies of introducing into her household, as gentleman-in-waiting, a former lover.

Ageing, ill, and torn with opposing emotions, Henry VIII had the young Catherine sent to the Tower, from whence she swiftly went to her execution, without so much as the option of a trial.

Two of her supposed lovers had already gone to their deaths, and Lady Rochford,[2] charged with being an accomplice, was beheaded at the same time as the queen consort.

As a consequence of Catherine Howard's private indiscretions before she entered on her brief and luckless marriage to the king, a memorable Act of Parliament was passed, making it 'high treason for any person to know of a flaw in the character of any lady whom the king might propose to marry, without revealing it; and subjecting the lady to the penalty of death, if she presumed to deceive her Sovereign on this point'.

Without doubt Catherine Howard wrote letters, and without doubt they were of an intimate nature. Unfortunately, none of them are available.

It throws some light on the morals of the court at that time that, after the passing of the Act of Parliament referred to, there would appear to have been no more youthful spinster candidates anxious for wedlock with Henry VIII. As a result, his choice perforce fell upon Catherine Parr, to give her her maiden name, who had already been the wife of two elderly widowers before she married the king.

6

Catherine Parr

(*c.* 1512–1548), Sixth Queen Consort of Henry VIII

When queen consort, to the king, *c.* 1544

The marriage between Henry VIII and Catherine Parr was to last three years, six months, and fourteen days, during which time Catherine Parr acted with prudence and discretion, except for on one occasion, after they had been married for three years. The trouble arose over a strong difference of opinion on a theological matter,[1] and to her dismay Catherine Parr found herself in imminent danger of the Tower. Only her woman's wit, and the retraction of her views, saved her. All the same, it is to be questioned whether Catherine Parr would have successfully maintained her position as queen consort any more than her predecessors had not the king died shortly after this incident.

That she was an astute woman, with a good brain, is unquestionable, and it may have been Henry's recognition of these qualities in her that made him have officially conferred upon Catherine Parr the title of 'Quene-Regent of England and Ireland', the highest title borne by a woman in this country up to that time. She signed herself 'Kateryn, the Quene-Regent, K. P.' on all letters and state documents. The initials 'K. P.' are interesting. Although claiming only the rank of a private gentlewoman (she was the daughter of Sir Thomas Parr, a distinguished knight), Catherine Parr was descended, on her father's side, from Anglo-Saxon kings, and neither her queenship nor her elevation to the position of queen regent could lessen her pride in her own paternal origin.

Being a woman of sagacity, she was able to subdue this pride sufficiently for it not to affect a tactful and dutiful attitude towards the king, as is evidenced by the following (undated) letter written to Henry VIII during an expedition undertaken by him to Calais and Boulogne in 1544.

Although the distance of time and account of days neither is long nor many of Your Majesty's absence, yet the want of your presence, so much desired and beloved by me, maketh me that I cannot quietly pleasure in anything until I hear from Your Majesty. The time, therefore, seemeth to me very long, with a great desire to know how Your Highness hath done since your departing hence, whose prosperity and health I desire more than mine own. And whereas I know Your Majesty's absence is never without great need, yet love and affection compel me to desire your presence.

Again, the same zeal and affection forceth me to be best content with that which is your will and pleasure. Thus love maketh me in all things to set apart mine own convenience and pleasure, and to embrace most joyfully his will and pleasure whom I love. God, the knower of secrets, can judge these words not to be written only with ink, but most truly impressed on the heart. Much more I omit, lest it be thought I go about to praise myself, or crave a thank; which thing to do I mind nothing less, but a plain simple relation of the love and zeal I bear Your Majesty, proceeding from the abundance of the heart. Wherein I must confess I desire no commendation, having such just occasion to do the same.

I make like account with Your Majesty as I do with God for His benefits and gifts heaped upon me daily, acknowledging myself a great debtor to Him, not being able to recompense the least of His benefits; in which state I am certain and sure to die, yet I hope in His gracious acceptation of my good will. Even such confidence have I in Your Majesty's gentleness, knowing myself never to have done my duty as were requisite and meet for such a noble prince, at whose hands I have found and received so much love and goodness that with words I cannot express it.

Lest I should be too tedious to Your Majesty, I finish this my scribbled letter, committing you to the governance of the Lord with long and prosperous life here, and after this life to enjoy the Kingdom of His elect.

From Greenwich, by Your Majesty's humble and obedient servant,

> Kateryn the Quene, K. P. [*sic*]

When queen dowager, to Admiral Sir Thomas Seymour, 1547

On the death of Henry VIII, Catherine Parr found herself in her mid-thirties, and a widow for the third time. She had survived the difficult and dangerous, though politic, advantage of being the king's consort, and was now free to contemplate marriage with Sir Thomas Seymour, a brother of Jane Seymour, with whom she had long been in love. There was, however, still need for discretion. The burial of the king had only just taken place.

It is probable that Catherine Parr was aware of Seymour's character, and that he was playing the common role of political schemer would have been no surprise to her. In marrying Henry VIII, she had doubtless played a like part herself; and from this knowledge may come the note of caution that she sounds in the following letter, sent in reply to a plea from Seymour for their immediate marriage.

My Lord,
... Whereas ye charge me with a promise, written with mine own hand, to change the two years into two months, I think

ye have no such plain sentence written with my hand. I know not whether ye be a paraphraser or not. If ye be learned in that science, it is possible ye may of one word make a whole sentence, and yet not at all times alter the true meaning, of the writer, as it appeareth by this your exposition upon my writing.

When it shall be your pleasure to repair hither, ye must take some pain to come early in the morning, that ye may be gone again by seven o'clock; and so I suppose ye may come without suspect.

I pray you let me have knowledge overnight at what hour ye will come, that your portress may wait at the gate of the fields for you. And thus, with my most humble and hearty commendations I take my leave of you for this time, giving you like thanks for your coming to Court when I was there.

From Chelsea.

P.S. By her that is, and shall be, your humble, true and loving wife during her life.

Kateryn the Quene, K. P. [*sic*]

To her husband, Thomas Seymour, Baron of Sudeley, 1547

Catherine Parr's desire for caution was ruthlessly overruled by Thomas Seymour (who had been created Baron of Sudeley), and, on this occasion, her heart overcame her head, for she secretly married Seymour almost at once. The result was strong disapproval and censure from all those in high places struggling for power.

Particularly did the marriage receive the disapprobation of her brother-in-law, the Protector, Edward Seymour, Duke of Somerset, who feared – and no doubt, rightly – that by marrying the dowager queen, his brother, Thomas Seymour, might well be aiming to supplant himself as guardian of the young king.

Whatever the truth of this, Somerset, regarding himself as having full authority of the Crown, withheld from Catherine Parr all the jewels that had been given her by Henry VIII (under the pretext that they were Crown heirlooms) and then proceeded to deprive her of her favourite manor of Fausterne. In defiance of her attempt to retain the property, he handed over the lease to a tenant of his own choice.

In the following spirited letter to her husband, Catherine expresses her wrath at Somerset's autocratic behaviour and her intention to approach the king.

My Lord,

This shall be to advertise you, that my lord your brother hath this afternoon made me a little warm. It was fortunate we were so much distant, for I suppose else I should have bitten him.

What cause have they to fear having such a wife?

To-morrow, or else upon Saturday, at three o'clock in the afternoon, I will see the King[2] when I intend to utter all my choler to my lord your brother, if you shall not give me advice to the contrary for I would be loath to do anything to hinder your matter.

I will declare to you how my lord hath used me concerning Fausterne; and after, I shall most humbly desire you to direct mine answer to him in that behalf. It liked him to-day to send my Chancellor to me, willing him to declare to me that he had brought Master Long's lease, and that he doubted not but I would let him enjoy the same to his commodity, wherein I should do to his succession no small pleasure, nothing considering his honour which this matter toucheth not a little; for-so-much as I at sundry times declared unto him that the only cause of my repair into those parts was for the commodity of the park, which else I would not have done, he, notwithstanding hath so used the matter with giving Master Long such courage, that he refuseth to receive such cattle as are brought here for the provision of my house; and so, in the meantime, I am forced to commit them to farmers.

My Lord, I beseech you send me word with speed how I shall order myself to my new brother. And thus I take my leave, with my most humble and hearty commendations, wishing you all your godly desires, and so well to do as I would myself, and better.

From Chelsea, in great haste.

By your humble, true, and loving wife in her heart,

Kateryn the Quene, K. P. [*sic*]

On Henry VIII's marriage to Catherine Parr, he had made a will by which, in the event of his son and heir Edward having no children, the Crown should 'come to the heirs of our beloved wife, Queen Kateryn [Parr] that now is, or any other lawful wife that we shall hereafter marry'. This clause needs little comment, beyond the fact that Catherine Parr, having failed to bear Henry a child in over three years of married life, might have found herself in a very dangerous position had Henry VIII remained alive much longer. The more interesting part of this same will, however, is that in which he includes in the line of succession – without making any mention of their restoration to legitimacy – Mary, daughter of Catherine of Aragon, and Elizabeth, daughter of Anne Boleyn, respectively, in the absence of heirs by himself or his son. There then followed in the king's will a placing of descendants as heirs presumptive that served to encourage the ambitions of the ever-intriguing courtiers, and subsequently led to a series of astonishing happenings in the story of the succession.

After Mary and Elizabeth,[3] Henry VIII had nominated as heirs presumptive the descendants of his young sister, Mary – not, however, her children, but her grandchildren. This sister Mary had been married successively to Louis XII of France and, after his death, to Charles Brandon. By Charles Brandon she had two daughters, the eldest of whom married Henry Grey (later created Duke of Suffolk), and in her turn gave birth to a daughter – the Lady Jane Grey.

Catherine Parr, after her marriage to Thomas Seymour, had had the Lady Jane Grey under her guardianship, and took special pains in tutoring her, in the same way that she had directed the education of Edward and Elizabeth. There are clear indications that Catherine Parr connived in the schemes afoot on Edward VI's accession to marry him to his cousin, the Lady Jane; but while such plans were in preparation, Catherine Parr died in giving birth to a daughter by Thomas Seymour, having outlived Henry VIII by only eighteen months.

There is no doubt of her qualities as a consort to Henry VIII, and in his more reasonable moods he had been the first to recognise Catherine Parr's value as a wife and queen. From their correspondence with their last stepmother, there is little question but that her influence on the royal children under her guardianship was of a high order, and they must have felt the loss of a sincere and wise friend by her death.

Catherine Parr was buried in the chapel at Sudeley Castle, Gloucestershire. On her coffin lid appeared the following (modernised) inscription: 'K. P. Here lies Queen Catherine, Sixth Wife of Henry VIII. And after, Wife of Thomas, Lord of Sudeley, High Admiral of England, and Uncle of Edward VI. She died September 1548.'

When Edward, son of Jane Seymour, ascended the throne in his tenth year, his uncle, Somerset, became Protector and self-appointed guardian to the young king.

Within two years, however, John Dudley, Duke of Northumberland, succeeded in supplanting Somerset in power, and was first among those who brought influence to bear in persuading Edward VI to make a will nominating the Lady Jane Grey as his successor. The young Edward was ailing. The next in line was his elder stepsister, Mary, daughter of Catherine of Aragon. Her ardent Catholicism, however, angered and frightened him; this, coupled with the activities of a faction anxious to prevent Roman Catholicism from becoming once more the dominant creed in England, persuaded Edward VI to exclude Mary from the succession, contrary to the intentions of his father.

The succession of the Lady Jane Grey having thus been secured by Edward's will, the moment it was obvious that the boy king was dying, the Duke of Northumberland hastily married his own son, Lord Guildford Dudley, to the Lady Jane Grey. Promptly upon the death of Edward VI, Northumberland and his satellites proclaimed the Lady Jane (grand-niece of Henry VIII) queen. So occurred the 'nine days' wonder' of her reign.

7

Lady Jane Grey

(1537–1554)

To Mary I, 1553

The Lady Jane Grey, eldest daughter of Henry Grey, Duke of Suffolk and Lady Frances Brandon, niece of Henry VIII, was sixteen years of age when she was married to the Duke of Northumberland's son, Lord Guildford Dudley. Of a studious and retiring nature, this child was the helpless and bewildered victim of the ambitions of her father-in-law and of her own parents in the jostling for power that took place shortly before Edward VI's death. Merciless and greedy statesmen, playing for high stakes, exhibited no pity for Jane Grey's youth and innocence when they sought to thrust her on to the throne to serve their own ends. Nor did they care, apparently, that if they failed in their plans, her life must inevitably be in jeopardy.

The populace received her proclamation as queen with apathy, having strong views as to hereditary rights, which, in their opinion, were being peremptorily swept aside. In addition, her father-in-law, Northumberland, was unpopular. The cause of Mary – disinherited by Edward VI's will – was strongly supported by the nobility and gentry, and in her claim to the right to succession, Mary, when she raised her standard, quickly found herself at the head of an army of 30,000 men. Realising that the forces against them were too strong, Northumberland

and his followers finally surrendered to Mary, and the Lady Jane 'resigned' the throne in Mary's favour.

As a result of the conspiracy against her succession Mary had three people only – one of them Northumberland – put to death: an instance of clemency, considering all the circumstances, not to be equalled in the history of those times. Against the advice of her counsellors, she spared the life of the Lady Jane and of her husband, Lord Guildford Dudley, but had them sent to the Tower as state prisoners.

It was from the Tower that the Lady Jane Grey wrote to Mary I the following letter – or rather, statement, since it bears neither address nor signature – outlining in simple detail, obviously in her own wording, the leading incidents of the short-lived regality of 'Queen Jane'. It is indeed a moving and pathetic tale that the unfortunate child pours out to Mary, and doubtless one to which Mary I gave full credence.

[Undated]

Although my fault be such that, but for the goodness and clemency of the Queen, I can have no hope of finding pardon, nor in craving forgiveness, having given ear to those who at that time appeared, not only to myself, but also to a great part of this realm, to be wise, and now have manifested themselves the contrary, not only to my and their great detriment, but with the common disgrace and blame of all, they having with such shameful boldness made so blamable and dishonorable an attempt to give to others that which was not theirs, neither did it become me to accept (wherefore rightly and justly am I ashamed to ask pardon for such a crime). Nevertheless, I trust in God that as now I know and confess my want of prudence, for which I deserve heavy punishment, except for the very great mercy of Your Majesty, I can still on many grounds conceive hope of your infinite clemency, it being known that the error imputed to me has not been altogether caused by myself. Because, although my fault may be great, and I confess it to be so, nevertheless I am charged and esteemed guilty more than I have deserved. For whereas I might take upon me that of which I was not worthy, yet no one can ever say either that I sought it as my own, or that I was pleased with it or ever accepted it.

For when it was publicly reported that there was no more hope of the King's life, as the Duchess of Northumberland had before promised that I should remain in the house with my mother, so she, having understood this soon after from her husband, who was the first that told it to me, did not wish me to leave my house, saying to me that if God should have willed to call the King to His Mercy, of whose life there was no longer any hope, it would be needful for me to go immediately to the Tower, I being made by His Majesty heir of his realm. Which words being spoken to me thus unexpectedly, put me in great perturbation, and greatly disturbed my mind, as yet soon after they oppressed me much more. But I, nevertheless, making little account of these words, delayed not to go from my mother. So that the Duchess of Northumberland was angry with me and with the Duchess my mother. Saying that, if she had resolved to keep me in the house, she should have kept her son, my husband, near her, to whom she thought I would certainly have gone, and she would have been free from the charge of me. And, in truth, I remained in her house two or three nights, but at length obtained leave to go to Chelsea, for my recreation, where soon after; being sick, I was summoned by the Council, giving me to understand that I must go that same night to Sion, to receive that which had been ordered for me by the King. And she who brought me this news was the Lady Sidney, my sister-in-law, the daughter of the Duke of Northumberland, who told me with extraordinary seriousness that it was necessary for me to go with her, which I did.

When we arrived there, we found no one, but soon after came the Duke of Northumberland, the Marquis of Northampton, the Earl of Arundel, the Earl of Huntingdon, and the Earl of Pembroke. By which Lords I was long held in conversation, before they announced to me the death of the King, especially by the Earls of Huntingdon and Pembroke, who, with unwonted caresses and pleasantness, did me such reverence as was not at all suitable to my state, kneeling down before me on the ground, and in many other ways making semblance of honouring me. And acknowledging me as their Sovereign Lady (so that they made me blush with infinite confusion), at length they brought to me the Duchess Frances my mother, the Duchess of Northumberland, and the Marchioness of Northampton. The Duke of Northumberland, as President of the Council, announced the death of King Edward, shewing afterward what cause we all had to rejoice for the virtuous and praiseworthy life that he had led, as also for his very good death. Furthermore, he pretended to comfort himself and the by-standers by praising much his prudence and goodness, for the very great care that he had taken of his Kingdom at the very close of his life, having prayed God to defend it from the Popish Faith and to deliver it from the rule of his evil sisters.

He then said that His Majesty had well weighed an Act of Parliament, wherein it was already resolved that whoever should acknowledge the most serene Mary, that is Your most serene Majesty, or the Lady Elizabeth, and receive them as true heirs of the Crown of England, these should be held all for traitors, one of them having been formerly disobedient to her father, Henry the Eighth, and also to himself, concerning the truth of religion, and afterwards also capital enemies of the Word of God, and both bastards. Wherefore in no manner did he wish that they should be heirs of him and of that Crown, he being able in every way to disinherit them. And therefore before his death, he gave order to the Council that, for the honour they owed to him, and for the love they bare to the realm and for the affection that was due to their country, they should obey this his last will.

The Duke then added that I was the heir named by His Majesty to succeed to the Crown, and that my sisters should likewise succeed me in case of my default of issue. At which words all the Lords of the Council kneeled down before me, telling me that they rendered to me the honour that was due to my person, I being, of true and direct lineage, heir to that Crown, and that it became them in the best manner to observe that which, with deliberate mind, they had promised to the King, even to shed their blood, exposing their own lives to death. Which things, as soon as I had heard, with infinite grief of mind how I was beside myself stupefied and troubled, I will leave it to those Lords who were present to testify, who saw me, overcome by sudden and unexpected grief, fall on the ground, weeping very bitterly; and then declaring to them my insufficiency, I greatly bewailed myself for the death of so noble a prince, and at the same time turned myself to God, humbly praying and beseeching Him, that if what was given to me was rightly and lawfully mine, His Divine Majesty would grant me such grace and spirit that I might govern it to His glory and service and to the advantage of this realm.

On the day following (as is known to everyone) I was conducted to the Tower, and shortly afterwards were presented to me by the Marquis of Winchester, Lord High Treasurer, the jewels, with which he also brought me the Crown, although it had never been demanded from him by me or by anyone in my name; and he further wished me to put it on my head, to try whether it really became me well or no. The which, although with many excuses, I refused to do, he nevertheless added that I might take it without fear, and that another also should be made to crown my husband with me. Which thing I for my part, heard truly with a troubled mind, and with ill will, even with infinite grief and displeasure of heart. And, after the said Lord was gone, and I was reasoning of many things with my husband, he assented that if he were to be made King, he would be made so by me by Act of Parliament. But afterwards I sent for the Earls of Arundel and Pembroke, and said to them that, if the Crown belonged to me I should be content to make my husband a Duke, but would never consent to make him a King. Which resolution of mine gave his mother (this my opinion being related to her) great cause for anger and disdain, so that she, being very angry with me and greatly displeased persuaded her son not to sleep with me any longer as he was wont to do, affirming to me moreover that he did not wish in any wise to be a Duke but a King. So that I was constrained to send to him the Earls of Arundel and Pembroke, who had negotiated with him to come, from me, otherwise I knew that the next morning he would have gone to Sion.[1]

And thus in truth was I deceived by the Duke and the Council, and ill treated by my husband and his mother. Moreover, (as Sir John Gates has confessed) he [the Duke] was the first to persuade King Edward to make me his heir. As to the rest, for my part, I know not what the Council may have determined to do, but I know for certain that, twice during this time, poison was given to me, first in the house of the Duchess of Northumberland, and afterwards here in the Tower, as I have the best and most certain testimony, besides that since that time all my hair has fallen off. And all these things I have wished to say for the witness of my innocence and the disburdening of my conscience.

To her father, Henry Grey, Duke of Suffolk, 1554

After her coronation, Mary I announced her intention of marrying her cousin, the Roman Catholic Philip of Spain. As a result, serious insurrections broke out in the country, and an attempt was made by one faction of the insurrectionists to reinstate the imprisoned Lady Jane Grey. The faction was headed by her father, the Duke of Suffolk, to whom, incidentally, Mary I had granted a free pardon at the time of Northumberland's execution.

The queen, in grave danger of her life, had no alternative but to submit at last to the advice of her counsellors, and have the

Lady Jane and her husband, Guildford Dudley, put to death. On 12 February 1554, Jane Grey was beheaded in the Tower, at the age of seventeen years.

On the day of her execution, she wrote the following brief note to her father,[2] whose wilful and ill-considered behaviour had been instrumental in bringing about her tragic fate.

The Lord comfort Your Grace, and that in His word, wherein all creatures only are to be comforted. And though it has pleased God to take away two of your children, yet think not, I most humbly beseech Your Grace, that you have lost them, but trust that we, by leaving this mortal life have won an immortal life.

And I, for my part, as I have honoured Your Grace in this life, will pray for you in another life.

8

Mary I

(1516–1558)

When princess, to Cardinal Wolsey, *c.* 1528

Mary I, only surviving child of Catherine of Aragon and Henry VIII, might reasonably be regarded as an historic example of a deeply unhappy adolescence. Up to the age of twelve years all augured well for her. She enjoyed the care and the love of both of her parents; she was educated by the best tutors available so that she could take her place with the highest in the land, and, on her mother's instructions, those in charge of the little princess were counselled strictly as to her physical welfare.[1]

Then, slowly, the gathering cloud of divorce began to shadow Mary's horizon, and from that time all the promise of her life was changed. It is probable that over-education at an early age may have helped to lay the foundation of her melancholy temperament; but the ill health that she suffered throughout her days was due, undoubtedly, to the anxiety and distress to which she was subjected as a consequence of Henry VIII's callous treatment of her mother and herself. Her pathetic efforts to win back her father's love, and be permitted to see the mother from whom she had been banished, make sad reading.

From earliest years she had conducted herself with dignity and courtesy in all she undertook; and this is borne out by her correspondence.

The following letter (possibly the first of Princess Mary's in existence) was addressed to Cardinal Wolsey, who was her godfather, at a time when, owing to the epidemic known as 'sweating sickness', Mary went to stay with her parents at the palace of Ampthill, Wolsey himself being absent from the court suffering from this complaint.

The original letter was written in Latin, in which Mary was proficient, although she was only twelve years of age at the time.

To the right revered Lord the Legate, and my godfather, greeting worthy of so great and holy a father premised.

I confess myself much indebted to your right revered sanctity, both for your welcome letters delivered to me at the palace of Ampthill, and more especially that it is by your late intercession that I have been allowed for a month to enjoy, to my supreme delight, the society of the King and Queen my parents: the health of both of whom may the great Sovereign of kings crown with enduring felicity.

One thing has, however, meanwhile vexed me, while in other respects most happy, namely, the opportunity denied me of visiting you, most holy father. If this had been granted to my wishes, I would, having humbly sought your most sacred benediction, have repaid, as far as might be, by personal thanks, your frequent favours vouchsafed to me and mine. That which now remains for me to do, since what I so much desired to obtain before I did not then achieve, is, most meekly imploring your blessing (which is to be named but with profound reverence), to conjure your Highness, in my best manner, that you will ever show as candid mind towards me as you have hitherto done; so shall I pray more earnestly, as for many other reasons I ought to do, that the great and good God may ever prolong your health, for the Realm's common good, more than for my own.

At Hartlebury (Worcestershire)

Your spiritual daughter,
Mary, Princess

To her father, Henry VIII, *c.* 1534

Brought up in her mother's faith as a strict Roman Catholic, the Reformation was to Mary nothing less than a catastrophe, which she never attempted to nor could understand at any time in her life.

Henry VIII waited until the birth of Anne Boleyn's child before disinheriting his eldest daughter as heir to the throne. She was then removed from Beaulieu, and her father withdrew from her her royal title of Princess.

In the face of this impending degradation, Mary wrote the following letter to Henry VIII.

In most humble wise I beseech Your Grace of your daily blessing. Pleaseth the same to be advertised, that this morning my chamberlain came and showed me that he had received a letter from Sir William Paulet, Comptroller of your Household; the effect whereof was, that I should, with all diligence, remove to the castle of Hertford. Whereupon I desired him to see that letter, which he showed me, wherein was written that 'the Lady Mary, the King's daughter, should remove to the place aforesaid' – leaving out in the same the name of Princess. Which when I heard, I could not a little marvel, trusting verily that Your Grace was not privy to the same letter, as concerning the leaving out of the name of Princess, forasmuch as I doubt not that Your Grace doth take me for your lawful daughter, born in true matrimony. Wherefore, if I were to say to the contrary, I should in my conscience run into the displeasure of God, which I hope assuredly that Your Grace would not that I should do.

And in all other things Your Grace shall have me, always, as humble and obedient daughter and handmaid as ever was child to the father, which my duty bindeth me to, as knoweth Our Lord, who have Your Grace in His most holy tuition, with much honour and long life to His pleasure.

From your Manor of Beaulieu, October 2.

By your most humble daughter,
Mary, Princess

When the Lady Mary, to Thomas Cromwell, Chancellor, 1536

Shortly after the execution of Anne Boleyn, Mary, who had been living in absolute seclusion for two years, wrote to Thomas Cromwell,[2] Chancellor of the Exchequer and First Secretary to the king, asking him to intercede for her with her father. Henry VIII had forbidden Mary to write to him, and she was not even permitted to have any writing materials at this time. These were eventually provided, however, by Lady Kingston,[3] who is mentioned in the following letter.

Lady Kingston was visiting Mary to bring her a last message from the woman who had displaced her own mother as consort of Henry VIII. Anne Boleyn asked forgiveness for past wrongs she had done to Mary. The death of Anne Boleyn encouraged Mary to write to the powerful chancellor in the hope that her relationship with her father might now be restored.

Master Secretary,

I would have been a suitor to you before this time, to have been a means for me to the King's Grace, my father, to have obtained His Grace's blessing and favour, but I perceived that nobody durst speak for me as long as that woman lived which is now gone (whom I pray God of His Mercy to forgive). Wherefore, now she *is* gone, I am bolder to write to you, as one which taketh you for one of my chief friends. And therefore I desire you for the Love of God to be a suitor to me of the King's Grace, to have his blessing and licence to write unto His Grace, which shall be of great comfort to me, as God knoweth who have you evermore in His holy keeping.

Moreover, I must desire you to accept mine evil writing, for I have not done so much for this two years or more, nor could have had the means to do it at this time, but My Lady Kingston's being here.

At Hunsdon, 26th of May.

By your loving friend,
Mary

To Henry VIII, 1536

In view of Mary's strong religious convictions, she must have sustained a grievous shock when the king put aside his marriage with her mother in order to wed Anne Boleyn. What, then, must have been her feelings when, Anne Boleyn's head only just having fallen from the block, Mary was to learn of her father's marriage to Jane Seymour?

In the following letter Mary, permitted at last to write to the king, makes an attempt to congratulate her father, but at what cost to her personal feelings, however well disguised, it is hard to conceive. Her aspirations seem always to have been concerned with her faith rather than things temporal. Even in this difficult letter she wishes her father the blessings of a male issue, regardless of her own prospects.

In the lowest manner that I can, I beseech Your Grace to accept me your humble daughter, who doth not a little rejoice to hear the comfortable tidings (not only to me, but to all Your Grace's realm) concerning the marriage which is between Your Grace and the Queen,[4] now being Your Grace's wife and my mother-in-law [*sic*]. The hearing thereof caused Nature to constrain me to be an humble suitor to Your Grace, to be so good and gracious lord and father to me as to give me leave to wait upon the Queen, and to do Her Grace such service as shall please her to command me which my heart shall be as ready and obedient to fulfil (next unto Your Grace) as the most humble servant that she hath.

Trusting to Your Grace's mercy to come into your presence, which ever hath and ever shall be the greatest comfort that I can have within this world, having also a full hope in Your Grace's natural pity, which you have always used as much, or more, than any Prince christened, that Your Grace will show the same unto me, your most humble and obedient daughter, which daily prayeth to God to have Your Grace in His holy keeping, with long life and as much honour as ever had king; and to send Your Grace shortly a prince, whereof no creature living shall more rejoice or heartlier pray for continually than I, as my duty bindeth me.

From Hunsdon, the 1st day of June

By your grace's most humble and obedient daughter and handmaid,

Mary

To Henry VIII, 1536

Although Mary wrote, humbly and beseechingly, to him on several occasions, Henry VIII neither replied nor permitted her to see him, until he had forced her to accept his ruling, in the assumption of his being supreme and absolute Head of the Church, that her mother's marriage to him was illegal, and therefore Mary herself illegitimate. That Mary was finally persuaded – at least outwardly – was probably due to the fact that she believed that if she could come into her father's presence once more she would win back his love for her as a daughter.

She wrote the following letter to Henry VIII from Hunsdon, where Elizabeth, whom Henry had likewise disowned, was also housed. Towards the end of the letter Mary puts in a word for her rejected half-sister, which shows her kindliness and moral courage, and also that Anne Boleyn's plea for forgiveness had reached Mary's heart, at least where Anne's child was concerned.

My bounden duty most humbly remembered to your most excellent Majesty. Whereas I am unable and insufficient to render and express to your Highness those most hearty and humble thanks for your gracious mercy and fatherly pity (surmounting mine offences at this time) extended towards me, I shall lie prostrate at your noble feet humbly, and with the very bottom of my heart beseech Your Grace to repute that in me (which in my poor heart, remaining in your most noble hand, I have conceived and professed towards Your Grace) whiles the breath shall remain in my body. That is that as I am in such merciful sort recovered, being almost lost in mine own folly, that Your Majesty may as well accept me, justly your bounden slave by redemption, as your most humble and obedient child and subject.

My sister Elizabeth is in good health (thanks to Our Lord), and such a child toward, as I doubt not but Your Highness shall have cause to rejoice of in time coming (as knoweth Almighty God), who send Your Grace, with the Queen,[5] my good mother health with the accomplishment of your desires. From Hunsdon: the 21st day of July.

Your Highness's most humble daughter and faithful subject,

Mary

When princess, to the Duchess of Somerset, 1547

After Henry VIII's death, and the accession of his son by Jane Seymour, Edward VI, in 1547, Mary was still living a life of retirement. She writes from one of her retreats to the wife of Edward Seymour, Duke of Somerset, and now Protector, to enlist that lady's aid in securing the welfare of certain old servants of her mother, Catherine of Aragon.

That she concerned herself with the needs of these old retainers of her mother's time shows Mary not only as a dutiful daughter but as one anxious for the preservation of a past regime.

My Good Gossip,[6]

After my very hearty commendations to you, with like desire to hear of the amendment and increase of your good health, these shall be put to you in remembrance of mine old suit concerning Richard Wood who was my mother's servant when *you were one of Her Grace's maids.* As you know, by his application, he hath sustained great loss, almost to his utter undoing, without any recompense hitherto which forced me to trouble you with his suit before, whereof (I thank you) I had a very good answer, and desire you now to renew the same to My Lord your husband, for I consider it impossible for him to remember such matters; having such a heap of business as he hath. Wherefore I heartily require you to go forward in this suit till you have brought it to an honest end, for the poor man is notable long to abide in the City.

And thus, my good Nann, I trouble you with myself and all mine; thanking you with all my heart for your earnest gentleness towards me in all my suits hitherto, reckoning myself out of doubt of the continuance of the same. Wherefore, once again I must trouble you with my poor George Brickhouse, who was an officer of my mother's wardrobe and beds from the time of the King my father's coronation, whose only desire is to be one of the Knights of Windsor, if all the rooms be not filled; and if they be, to have the next reversion in obtaining, whereof (in mine opinion) you shall do a charitable deed, as knoweth Almighty God, who send you good health, and us shortly meet, to His pleasure. From St. John's, this Sunday in the afternoon, being the 24th of April.

Your loving friend during my life,

Mary

To Admiral Thomas Seymour, Baron of Sudeley, 1547

One of the many situations in which Mary was called upon to form a judgment was no less than that of the marriage of her fifth and last stepmother, Catherine Parr, to Thomas Seymour.

Only the rumours and politics of that time could supply the reason for Seymour's desire for Mary's approval. Her answer contains much that we have come to understand about her. It would appear she did not wish to be involved in this 'worldly' affair, and while still loving her father, feared for the soul of one who had rejected the Catholic faith.

My Lord,

... I received your letter, wherein as me thinketh, I perceive strange news concerning a suit you have in hand to the Queen, for marriage, for the sooner obtaining whereof you seem to think that my letters might do you a favour.

My Lord, in this case, I trust your wisdom doth consider, that if it were for my nearest kinsman and dearest friend alive of all other creatures in the world it standeth least with my poor honour to be a meddler in this matter, considering whose wife Her Grace was of late; and besides that, if she be minded to grant your suit, my letters shall do you but small pleasure.

On the other side, if the remembrance of the King's Majesty my father (whose soul God pardon!) will not suffer her to grant your suit, I am nothing able to persuade her to forget the loss of him who is, as yet, very rife in mine own remembrance. Therefore I shall most earnestly require you (the premises considered) to think none unkindness in me though I refuse to be a meddler in any ways in this matter assuring you that, wooing matters set apart, wherein being a maid, I am nothing cunning, if otherways it shall lie in my power to do you pleasure, I shall be as glad to do it as you to require it, both for his bloods sake that you be of,[7] and also for the gentleness which I have always found in you, as knoweth Almighty God, to whose tuition I commit you.

From Wanstead, this Saturday, at night, being the fourth of June.

Your assured friend, to my power,

Marye [*sic*]

To the Dowager Queen Catherine Parr, 1548

While privately disapproving of the hasty marriage of the dowager queen, Catherine Parr, to Thomas Seymour, Mary maintained friendly correspondence with her stepmother. A firm affection and friendship had always existed between these two women (who were much of an age), despite their opposing religious convictions.

As all her life Mary suffered from delicate health, this perhaps contributed to her quick sympathies in others' sickness. She was also very fond of children, and on learning that Catherine Parr was expecting a child, wrote the following letter to her before the dowager queen's confinement.

Madame,

Although I have troubled Your Highness lately with sundry letters, yet that, notwithstanding, seeing my Lord Marquis,[8] who hath taken the pains to come to me at this present, intendeth to see Your Grace shortly, I could not be satisfied without writing to the same, and especially because I purpose to-morrow (with the help of God) to begin my journey towards Norfolk, where I shall be farther from Your Grace; which journey I have intended since Whitsuntide, but lack of health hath stayed me all the while; which, altho' it be as yet unstable nevertheless I am enforced to remove for a time, hoping, with God's Grace, to return again about Michaelmas, at which time, or shortly after, I trust to hear good success of Your Grace's condition; and in the mean time shall desire much to hear of your health, which I pray Almighty God to continue and increase to His pleasure, as much as your own heart can desire.

And thus, with my most humble commendations to Your Highness, I take my leave of the same, desiring Your Grace to take the pain to make my commendations to my Lord Admiral.

From Beaulieu, the 9th of August.

Your Highness's humble and assured loving daughter,

Marye [*sic*]

To Edward VI, *c.* 1551

All possible efforts were made by the Protestant counsellors of Edward VI to prevent Mary from observing her own religious rites, even if only privately. They met with signal failure, but Mary's staunch determination to abide by her faith, eventually, as we know, gave the young king's advisers the opportunity they desired of persuading Edward VI to make the Lady Jane Grey his heir, as a Protestant successor to the throne.

The following strong, reasoned letter, written by a woman in her mid-thirties, who had endured so much for her beliefs, to a youth who, as Mary herself says, had not reached the years to 'be a judge in matters of religion', bears out the previous evidence that Mary put her faith before everything – even her life.

My duty most humbly remembered to Your Majesty.

It may please you to be advertised that I have by my servants received your most honourable letter, the contents whereof do not a little trouble me; and so much the more, for that any of my servants should move or trouble me in matters touching my soul, which I think the meanest subject in your realm could evil bear at their servants' hand, having, for my part, utterly refused heretofore to talk with them in such matters, and of all other persons least regarded them therein. To them I have declared what I think, as she which trusteth Your Majesty would have suffered me, your poor humble sister and beadswoman, to have used the accustomed Mass which the King, your father and mine, with all his predecessors evermore used, wherein also I have been brought up from my youth; and thereunto my conscience doth not only bind me (which will by no means suffer me to think one thing and do *another*), but also the promise made to the Emperor[9] by Your Majesty's Council was an assurance to me, that in so doing I should not break the laws, although they seem now to qualify and deny the thing.

And at my last waiting on Your Highness I was so bold as to declare my mind and conscience, and desired Your Highness, rather than constrain it, *to take my life*; whereunto Your Majesty made me a *very gentle answer*.

And now I beseech Your Highness to give me leave to write what I think touching Your Majesty's letters. Indeed, they may be signed with your own hand, and nevertheless, in my opinion, not Your Majesty's in effect; because it is well known, and heretofore I have declared in the presence of Your Highness that, though (Our Lord be praised) Your Majesty hath far more knowledge and greater gifts than others of your years, yet it is not possible that Your Highness can at these years be a judge in matters of religion; and therefore I take it that the matter proceedeth from such as do wish those things to take place which be most agreeable to themselves, by whose doings, Your Majesty not offended, I mean not to rule my conscience.

And thus, without molesting Your Highness any further, I humbly beseech the same ever, for God's sake, to bear with me, as you have done; and not to think that by my doings or example any inconvenience might grow to Your Majesty, or to your realm, for I use it not after any such sort, having no doubt but in time to come, whether I live or die, Your Majesty shall perceive mine intent is grounded upon a true love towards you; whose royal estate I beseech Almighty God long to continue which is and shall be my prayer, according to my duty.

And after pardon craved of Your Majesty for this rude and bold letter, if, neither at my humble suit nor for regard of the promise made to the Emperor, you will suffer and bear with me as you have done, till Your Majesty may be a judge herein yourself, and right understand their proceeding (of which yet I despair not), rather than to offend God and my conscience I offer my body at your will, *and death shall be more welcome than life* with a troubled conscience.

Most humbly beseeching Your Majesty to pardon my slowness in answering your letters, for my old disease would not suffer me to write any sooner. And thus I pray Almighty God to keep Your Majesty in all virtue, and honour, and long life, at His pleasure.

From my poor house at Copped-hall (Essex), the 19th of August.

Your Majesty's most humble sister,
Mary

To Edward VI, 1553

Mary's genuine affection for her young half-brother (she was also his godmother) must have been severely tested after Edward VI's accession to the throne, owing to the machinations of his counsellors – whose schemes Mary doubtless divined. She was, however, unmoved, either in her religious views or her devotion to her half-brother. His health was fast declining, but on hearing – falsely, as it proved – that he was in better health, she wrote the following congratulatory letter to him.

This was the last communication that passed between Mary and Edward VI, for he died within two months. His real condition had been deliberately misrepresented to Mary, who had kept herself free from the court as much as possible. His death was actually concealed from her for two days, while efforts were made to lure her up to London on the pretence that Edward wanted to see her, but with the real object of throwing her into the Tower and proclaiming the Lady Jane Grey as queen in her stead. Mary set out to go to Edward, but was secretly advised of the trap laid for her in time to prevent its being put into effect.

My duty most humbly presented to Your Majesty. It may please the same to be advertised, that as hearing of Your Highness's late rheum and cough was as much grief as ever was any worldly thing, even so the hope which I have conceived since I received Your Majesty's last token by my servant hath not been a little to my comfort, praying Almighty God, according to my most bounden duty, to give Your Majesty perfect health and strength, with long continuance in prosperity to reign, beseeching Your Highness to pardon my bold and rude writing, and if in the same I do trouble Your Majesty at this present (which I hope I do not), that my humble duty and nature which enforceth me thereunto, may excuse my default.

Thus most humbly taking my leave of Your Majesty, I do, and shall, daily pray for the prosperous preservation of your royal estate as, of all others, I am most bound.

From Beaulieu (Newhall), the 16th of May, scribbled with a rude hand.

Your Majesty's most humble sister,

Mary

When queen regnant, to Princess Elizabeth, 1554

Mary succeeded to the throne after the brief reign of the Lady Jane Grey, as first acknowledged Queen Regnant of England. As mentioned earlier, the insurrections that broke out in different parts of the country on her announcing, after her coronation in 1553, that she intended to marry Philip of Spain, and the consequent intrigues afoot to bring back the Lady Jane, or to place Elizabeth on the throne, culminated in Mary's life being in danger.

Whether or not Elizabeth gave countenance to the plot for Mary's dethronement can only be conjectured, but it is unlikely, especially in view of the letter she wrote to the Duke of Northumberland on learning of the design to disinherit Mary and herself.

In reply to the following letter from Mary at this critical time in the history of both of them, Elizabeth pleaded that she was too sick to travel. She probably 'sensed' that her own enemies were stronger, for the time being, than Mary's faith in Elizabeth's loyalty. The letter which Elizabeth wrote to Mary, shortly afterwards, seems to support this view. As a result, Mary had to enforce her command, and Elizabeth was borne to the queen's presence on a litter.

Right dearly and entirely beloved sister, we greet you well.

And whereas certain ill-disposed persons, minding more the satisfaction of their malicious minds than their duty of allegiance towards us, have, of late, spread divers untrue rumours; and by that means, and other devilish practices, do travail to induce our good and loving subjects to an unnatural rebellion against God and us, and the common tranquillity of our Realm: We, tendering the surety of your person, which might chance to come to some peril if any sudden tumult should arise, either where you now be,[10] or about Donnington (whither we understand you are bound shortly to remove), do therefore think it expedient you should put yourself in good readiness, with all convenient speed, to make your repair hither to us, which we pray you will not fail to do, assuring you that you will be most heartily welcome to us. Of your mind herein, we pray you return answer by this messenger. And thus we pray God to have you in His holy keeping.

Given under our signet, at our Manor of St. James, the 26th day of January, the first of our Reign.

Your loving sister,
Mary the Queen

To Philip of Spain, 1554

The rebellion – that cost the Lady Jane Grey her life, and was to send Elizabeth to the Tower – was subdued, but Mary's determination in regard to her choice of husband and consort was as strong as ever. Her unswerving allegiance to the Roman Catholic faith, and her deep affection for the country of her mother's birth, undoubtedly had great influence in forming her resolution to 'wed no other man than Philip', despite the opposition of her parliament, and the extreme repugnance manifested by her subjects to the alliance.

Twelve years younger than his bride-to-be, Philip, for his part, entertained the marriage solely from ambition, as the ill-fated Mary was soon to discover to her sorrow.

In those days, it was not unusual to conduct courtship almost entirely by proxy. As will be seen in the following letter, proposals – even protestations of affection or love – were often addressed through an ambassador or a representative of the court. Unthinkable as it may be to us today, the custom does not seem to have prevented Mary from expressing feelings of love, or at least strong affection, for Philip of Spain,[11] and it would be difficult to interpret the following as anything else than a love letter.

It was entrusted to Mary's Lord Privy Seal, who negotiated the marriage, which took place in July, 1554.

Sir, my good and constant Ally:

Knowing that the Ambassador of the Emperor, my Lord and good father, resident at my Court, was despatching the bearer hereof to Your Highness; although you have not privately written to me since our alliance has been negotiated, so it is that, feeling myself so much obliged by the sincere and true affection which you bear me, which you have as much confirmed by deeds, as by the letters written to the said Ambassador and by the negotiation which the Sieur d'Egmont[12] and others, and the Ambassador of my said Lord have managed, I could not omit signifying to you my good wishes and duty which I have ever to communicate with you; and I thank you very humbly for so many good offices, and apprise you at the same time that the

Parliament, which represents the estates of my kingdom, has heard the articles of our marriage without opposition, inasmuch as they find the conditions thereof honourable, advantageous, and more than reasonable, which puts me in entire confidence, that your coming hither will be certain and agreeable.

And, hoping shortly to supply the remainder verbally, I will make an end at present, praying the Creator to grant you, my good and constant Ally, to make your journey hither in prosperity and health, commending myself very affectionately and humbly to Your Highness.

At London, 20th April.

Your entirely assured and most obliged Ally,

Mary

To Philip of Spain, *c.* 1557

Philip of Spain, having conceived a plan to wed Princess Elizabeth to his friend, the Prince of Savoy, did all in his power to force Mary to give her consent to this marriage. Had such an alliance taken place, one wonders what the effect would have been on England's history. Mary, however, insisted that her parliament would never give permission for her half-sister to leave the kingdom, thereby tacitly confirming that Elizabeth was next in the line of succession.

In reply to an angry letter from her husband, Mary wrote in a self-denying and humble style, but making distinct avowal of her determination to act in this matter only as her parliament should decree. This was the principle which (apart from her marriage) governed her throughout her regal life.

In maintaining this view, Mary makes a proper distinction between the duty of a wife and the duties of an English sovereign, as the following extract from her letter to Philip clearly shows. It will be remembered, however, this was long before the days of constitutional monarchy.

... In my last letter to Your Highness, I made an offer to agree to the marriage, *provided I have the consent of this Realm*, and so I will; but without such consent, I fear that neither Your Highness nor the Realm will be well served on this occasion.

For Your Highness will remember, that once I procured of myself, an opportunity of listening to Your Highness' friars, but they, and Alphonso,[13] propounded questions so obscure that, to my simple understanding, there was no comprehending them: as, for instance, 'Who was King in Adam's days?' and said, withal, 'That I was bound to conclude this marriage by an article in my creed'...

Meantime, Your Highness has written in the said letters, that, if a Parliament shall go contrary, Your Highness will impute the fault to me.

I beg, in all humility, that Your Highness will defer this matter till your return, and then it will be manifest whether I am culpable or not. Otherwise, I shall live in apprehension of Your Highness' displeasure, which would be worse to me than death; for I have already begun to taste it too much, to my regret ...

Wherefore, Monseigneur, in as humble wise as it is possible for me (being your very loyal and very obedient wife, which to be I confess myself justly obliged, and in my opinion more than any other woman, having such a husband as Your Highness is, without speaking of the multitude of your kingdoms, for which that is not my principal motive), I entreat Your Highness that we both pray to God, and put our first confidence in Him, that we may meet and live together. And that same God, in whose hand is the direction of the hearts of Kings, will, I hope, without fail enlighten us in such manner, that all at last shall tend to His glory and your satisfaction.

To the Lord Admiral, 1558

It was apparent, very soon after their marriage, that Philip of Spain had no intention of playing consort to Mary I, or of residing permanently in England.

Mary continued to hope, however, and did everything possible to induce her husband to stay at her side, but after his departure in 1557, Mary was never to see Philip of Spain again.

In the following letter to her Lord Admiral, Mary eagerly anticipates the possibility of her husband's return, but it did not take place.

A very sick, sad, and a childless woman, Mary died six months after this letter was written.

By the Queen.

Right trusty and well-beloved, we greet you well.

And whereas of late we were advertised that our dearest Lord and Husband, the King, intended to make his repair to this realm, for which cause we willed you to go to sea, and to make such provision of ships, and other things necessary, as for the transportation of His Highness shall seem convenient: we let you wit that we have now received advertisement from His Highness, whereby we perceive that his affairs and weighty business be such, and the enemy in such readiness to annoy that country, that His Highness can in no wise accomplish his former intent, whereof we have thought good to give you knowledge: and farther to will you, that with all expedition you land in some convenient place of that coast, and so repair to our said dearest lord and husband, not only to see His Highness, but also to understand his farther pleasure in anything that he shall say unto you: taking such order for disposing our ships in the meantime as to your wisdom shall seem best: which we commit wholly to your discretion.

Given under our signet, at our Manor of Greenwich, the 17th day of May, the fourth and fifth years of our Reign.

A last request to Philip of Spain, 1558

The following codicil to Mary I's will is included in this collection because it shows that, in addition to her high religious principles, Mary had concern for the prosperity of her country. It also hints at the queen's desire that there shall be peace and harmony between her husband and her half-sister Elizabeth. Females at this time were called 'heirs', the word 'heiress' being then unknown. Mary obviously means Elizabeth by 'heir and successor', as she calls Philip 'brother' of the realm, not 'heir'.

> For the ancient amity sake that hath always been between our noble progenitors, and between this my realm and the Low Countries, whereof His Majesty King Philip is now inheritor, as God shall reward him (I hope, among the elect servants of God), I pray that it may please His Majesty to show himself as a father in his care, or as a brother of this realm in his love and favour, and as a most assured and undoubted friend in his power and strength, to my heir and successor.

This first Queen Regnant of England is, perhaps, remembered chiefly for her intolerance with regard to the Reformation, but she had had a hard struggle against adversity, and without doubt had been sorely embittered, if not warped in outlook, by the cruel treatment meted out to her devout mother, Catherine of Aragon. There were other English monarchs who, acting from far lower principles, might equally have been styled by the prefix 'Bloody', probably more justifiably.

Queen Mary was buried in Henry VII's Chapel at Westminster Abbey, with all ceremonial and royal array, although she had asked to be buried as a poor *religieuse*, and that 'no semblance of the Crown, which had pressed so heavily upon her brow in life, might encumber her corpse in death'.

9

Elizabeth I

(1533–1603)

When the Lady Elizabeth, to the queen consort, Anne of Cleves, 1540

Elizabeth I is reputed to have shown exceptional understanding from childhood, and, it is said, comported herself at times with the gravity of a middle-aged woman. She had a predilection for learning, particularly the scriptures, languages, and science, although she could resort to her lute or her needlework with equal pleasure.

Left motherless before the age of three years, and branded as illegitimate, is it possible that Elizabeth was in some way early aware, even in the years of her banishment, of the part she was eventually to play in history? Fortunately enough, in early youth she came under the guardianship of Lady Margaret Bryan, wife of Sir Thomas Bryan who was a kinsman of her mother, Anne Boleyn. Lady Bryan had been governess-in-ordinary, also, to Mary I and Edward VI, and it is said that her influence on Elizabeth, combined with early adversities, helped in no small measure to form this great Tudor sovereign's character.

Elizabeth's love of language makes many of her letters – especially those written in later life – pedantic and austere in composition. She seemed to prefer the fine phrase and obscure quotation to a simply worded expression of her feelings.

The following (undated) letter is probably the first that Elizabeth wrote. She was seven years of age at the time, and it was addressed to the queen consort, her new stepmother, Anne of Cleves, for whom she developed a sincere and lasting affection. The little princess had been very anxious to meet her new stepmother, but the king – already scheming for divorce – would not permit it. Later, when a meeting occurred, Anne of Cleves was so attracted by her stepdaughter that, after her divorce, she asked permission to see Elizabeth as much as possible; this Henry VIII granted.

Madame,

I am struggling between two contending wishes; one is, my impatient desire to see Your Majesty, the other that of rendering the obedience l owe to the commands of the King my father, which prevent me from leaving my house till he has given me full permission to do so. But I hope that I shall be able shortly to gratify both these desires. In the meantime, I entreat Your Majesty to permit me to show, by this billet, the zeal with which I devote my respect to you as my Queen, and my entire obedience to you as my mother.

I am too young and feeble to have power to do more than to felicitate you with all my heart in this commencement of your marriage. I hope that Your Majesty will have as much good-will for me, as I have zeal for your service.

When princess, to the queen consort, Catherine Parr, 1544

After Catherine Parr's marriage to Henry VIII, Elizabeth, then in her eleventh year, managed to incur the anger and disfavour of her royal father, to the extent that she was banished from the court for a whole year. What her offence was is unknown, but Henry VIII's ire was such that Elizabeth was afraid to write to him.

Her new and fourth stepmother, Catherine Parr, however, had consideration and regard for the exiled Elizabeth, and took upon herself the office of peacemaker between father and daughter.

The following letter[1] was written by Elizabeth to the queen consort a few days after Henry VIII had sailed for France. As a result of Catherine Parr's intercession, Henry sent a message of 'hearty blessing' to all his children, in which Elizabeth was seemingly included.

Inimical fortune, envious of all good and ever revolving human affairs, has deprived me for a whole year of your most illustrious presence; and not thus content, has yet again robbed me of the same good, which thing would be intolerable to me did I not hope to enjoy it very soon. And in this my exile I well know that the clemency of Your Highness has had as much care and solicitude for my health, as the King's Majesty himself. By which thing I am not only bound to serve you, but also to revere you with filial love since I understand that your most illustrious Highness has not forgotten me every time you have written to the King's Majesty, which, indeed, it was my duty to have requested from you. For heretofore I have not dared to write to him.

Wherefore I now humbly pray your excellent Highness that, when you write to His Majesty, you will condescend to recommend me to him, praying ever for his sweet benediction, and similarly entreating our Lord God to send him best success and the obtaining victory over his enemies, so that Your Highness and I may as soon as possible rejoice in his happy return.

No less I pray God that He would preserve your most illustrious Highness; to whose grace, humbly kissing your hands, I offer and recommend myself.

From St. James's this 31st of July.

Your most obedient daughter, and most faithful servant,

Elizabeth

To Thomas Seymour, Baron of Sudeley, 1547

Thomas Seymour, the lady-killer, had boundless covetousness and a great conceit of himself. His ambition was to marry one of the highest ladies in the land. He did not propose to Princess Mary, doubtless because of her religious views, which in his opinion made her chances of succeeding to the throne somewhat meagre. He did, however, propose to Elizabeth, when she was fourteen years of age.

The following letter shows her definite refusal to his suit.

In consequence, that same year, as already recorded, he married the queen dowager, Catherine Parr, as the one offering the next-best chance to the attainment of his ambitions and designs.

My Lord Admiral,

The letter you have written to me is the most obliging and at the same time the most eloquent in the world. And as I do not feel myself competent to reply to so many courteous expressions, I shall content myself with unfolding to you, in a few words, my real sentiments. I confess to you that your letter, all elegant as it is, has very much surprised me; for, besides that neither my age nor my inclination allows me to think of marriage, I never could have believed that any one would have spoken to me of nuptials, at a time when I ought to think of nothing but sorrow for the death of my father. And to him I owe so much, that I must have two years at least to mourn for his loss. And how can I make up my mind to become a wife before I shall have enjoyed for some years my virgin state, and arrived at years of discretion?

Permit me, then, my Lord Admiral, to tell you frankly that, as there is no one in the world who more esteems your merit than myself, or who sees you with more pleasure as a disinterested person, so would I preserve to myself the privilege of recognizing you as such, without entering into that strict bond of matrimony, which often causes one to forget the possession of true merit. Let Your Highness be well persuaded that, though I decline the happiness of becoming your wife, I shall never cease to interest myself in all that can crown your merit with glory, and shall ever feel the greatest pleasure in being your servant, and good friend,

Elizabeth

27th February.

To Princess Mary, 1547

Elizabeth's skill at dissimulation and ability to steer a middle course in her own interests speak for themselves in the following letter, which she wrote to her half-sister, Mary, on the occasion of the premature marriage of the queen dowager, Catherine Parr, and Thomas Seymour. The letter also displays unusual foresight and tact in a delicate situation.

Princess, and very dear sister,

You are very right in saying, in your most acceptable letters, which you have done me the honour of writing to me, that, our interests being common, the just grief we feel in seeing the ashes, or rather the scarcely cold body of the King, our father, so shamefully dishonoured by the Queen, our step-mother, ought to be common to us also. I cannot express to you, my dear Princess, how much affliction I suffered when I was first informed of this marriage, and no other comfort can I find than that of the necessity of submitting ourselves to the decrees of Heaven; since neither you nor I, dearest sister, are in such condition as to offer any obstacle thereto, without running heavy risk of making our own lot much worse than it is; at least, so I think.

We have to deal with too powerful a party, who have got all the authority into their hands, while we, deprived of power, cut a very poor figure at Court. I think, then, that the best course we can take is that of dissimulation, that the mortification may fall upon those who commit the fault. For we may rest assured that the memory of the King, our father, being so glorious in itself, cannot be subject to those stains which can only defile the persons who have wrought them. Let us console ourselves by making the best of what we cannot remedy. If our silence do us no honour, at least it will not draw down upon us such disasters as our lamentations might induce.

These are my sentiments, which the little reason I have dictates and which guides my respectful reply to your agreeable letter. With regard to returning of visits, I do not see that you who are the elder are obliged to this; but the position in which I stand obliges me to take other measures; the Queen having shown me so great affection and done me so many kind offices, that I must use much tact in manoeuvring with her, for fear of appearing ungrateful for her benefits. I shall not, however, be in any hurry to visit her lest I should be charged with approving what I ought to censure.

However, I shall always pay much deference to your instructions and commands, in all which you shall think convenient or serviceable to you, as being Your Highness's &c. &c.

To the dowager queen, Catherine Parr, 1548

After Catherine Parr's marriage to Thomas Seymour, Elizabeth stayed with the newly wedded pair for a while at their household in Chelsea.

Catherine had reason to object to the unbecoming behaviour of Elizabeth, who was under her charge, and her husband; the so-called 'friendly romps'[2] being a matter for Catherine Parr's concern, whether or not she was aware that Thomas Seymour had previously proposed to Elizabeth. As a result, Elizabeth was forced to remove herself to Cheston, where she was established in her own household with her governess, Kate Ashley.

In the following letter to Catherine Parr, Elizabeth refers to the dowager queen's care for Elizabeth's reputation, which care indicates that Catherine Parr's motive in bringing about the separation was with a view to safeguarding Elizabeth's good name as the king's sister. There is no suggestion that Catherine Parr had displayed any feelings of jealousy, and she and Elizabeth had obviously parted as friends.

Although I could not be plentiful in giving thanks, for the manifold kindnesses at Your Highness's hand, at my departure, yet I am something to be borne withal, for truly I was replete with sorrow to depart from Your Highness, especially seeing you undoubtful of health, and albeit I answered little. I weighed it more deeper when you said – 'You would warn me of all evilnesses that you should hear of me,' for if Your Grace had not a good opinion of me, you would not have offered friendship to me that way at all – meaning the contrary. But what may I more say than thank God for providing such friends for me, desiring God to enrich me with their long life, and me grace to be in the heart no less thankful to receive it than I am now made glad in writing to shew it? And although I have plenty of matter here, I will stay, for I know you are not quick to rede.[3] From Cheston, this present Saturday.

Your Highness's humble daughter,
Elizabeth

To the dowager queen, Catherine Parr, 1548

From the playful and friendly tone in which Elizabeth writes to Catherine Parr in the following letter, any awkwardness that may have been experienced in their relationship while at Chelsea has clearly been dispelled.

Catherine Parr, too ill to write herself to Elizabeth, got her husband Seymour to do so.

This was the last communication they were to have with each other, for Catherine Parr was fated to die shortly after the birth of her child six weeks later.[4]

Although Your Highness's letter be most joyful to me in absence, yet, considering what pain it is for you to write, Your Grace being so sickly, your commendations were enough in my lord's letter.

I much rejoice at your health, with the well liking of the country, with my humble thanks that Your Grace wished me with you till I were weary of that country. Your Highness were like to be cumbered, if I should not depart till I were weary of being with you; although it were the worst soil in the world, your presence would make it pleasant. I cannot reprove my lord for not doing your commendations in his letter, for he did it; and although he had not, yet I will not complain on him, for he shall be diligent to give me knowledge from time to time how his busy child doth; and if I were at his birth, no doubt I would see him beaten, for the trouble he hath put you to.

Master Denny and my lady, with humble thanks, prayeth most entirely for Your Grace, praying the Almighty God to send you a most lucky deliverance; and my mistress[5] wisheth no less, giving Your Highness most humble thanks for her commendations.

Written, with very little leisure, this last day of July,

Your humble daughter,
Elizabeth

To the Protector, Edward Seymour, Duke of Somerset, 1549

Shortly after Catherine Parr's death, the bereaved Thomas Seymour – still indefatigable in his ambitions – schemed once more to bring about his marriage with Elizabeth. While she was probably attracted by him, one cannot lose sight of the fact that

Elizabeth, from her early beginnings, showed unusual caution in her dealings with others. She was a past master in the art of self-navigation, and as her subsequent history shows guided herself like a ship through whatever storms and shoals prevailed.

Seymour was in due course arrested for high treason (for which he was eventually executed), and Elizabeth found herself sorely implicated, as one of the charges against Seymour was that he had sought to marry the young king's sister.

In consequence of an attempt to extract a confession from her, or at least to obtain sufficient evidence to incriminate her governess, 'Kat' Ashley, and her husband, Elizabeth was constrained to write the following letter to Seymour's brother, the Protector Somerset, from Hatfield, where she was held under the care of Sir Robert Tyrwhitt. When it is remembered that Elizabeth was only sixteen years of age at that time, the strategic skill of her admissions is impressive. There is, however, an oddly childlike simplicity about her letter, which bears the stamp of truth.

January 28

My Lord

Whereas your lordship willeth and counselleth me as an earnest friend to declare what I know in this matter, and also to write what I have declared to Master Tyrwhitt, I shall most willingly do it.

I declared unto him, first, that after the cofferer had declared unto me what my lord Admiral answered, for Allen's matter,[6] and for Durham-place,[7] he told me that my lord Admiral did offer me his house for my time being with the King's Majesty; and further said and asked me, 'If the Council did consent that I should have my lord Admiral, whether I would consent to it, or no?' I answered, 'That I would not tell him what my mind was;' and I further inquired of him, 'What he meant by asking me that question, or who bade him say so?' He answered me, and said, 'Nobody bade him say so, but that he perceived, as he thought, by my lord Admiral inquiring whether my patent were sealed or no, and debating what he spent in his house, and inquiring what was spent in my house, that he was given that way rather than otherwise.'

And as concerning Kat Ashley,[8] she never advised me to it, but said always, when any talked of my marriage, 'That she would never have me marry, neither in England nor out of England, without the consent of the King's Majesty, Your Grace's, and the Council's.'

And after the Queen was departed,[9] when I asked her 'What news she heard from London?' she answered merrily, 'They say Your Grace shall have my lord Admiral, and that he will shortly come to woo you. And, moreover, I said unto him, that the cofferer sent a letter hither, that My Lord said he would come this way as he went down into the country.' Then I bade her write as she thought best, and bade her show it to me when she had done: so she wrote 'That she thought it not best[10] for fear of suspicion.'

And the lord Admiral, after he had heard that asked the cofferer 'Why he might not come to me as well as to my sister?' and then I desired Kat Ashley to write again (lest My Lord might think that she knew more in it than he) that she knew nothing, but only suspected; and I also told Master Tyrwhitt that, to the effect of the matter I never consented to any such thing without the Council's consent thereto. And as for Kat Ashley and the cofferer, they never told me that they would practise it.[11]

These be the things which I declared to Master Tyrwhitt, and also whereof my conscience beareth me to witness which I would not for all earthly things offend in anything, for I know I have a soul to be saved as well as other folks have; wherefore I will above all things have respect unto this same.

If there be any more things which I can remember I will either write it myself, or cause Master Tyrwhitt to write it.

Master Tyrwhitt and others have told me 'That there goeth rumours abroad which be greatly both against my honour and honesty,' which above all things I esteem 'which be these that I am in the Tower, and with child by my lord Admiral.' My lord, these are shameful slanders, for the which, beside the great desire I have to see the King's Majesty, I shall most heartily desire your Lordship that I may come to Court after your first determination that I may show myself there as I am.

Elizabeth

To the Protector, Edward Seymour, Duke of Somerset, 1549

Scandalous rumours regarding Elizabeth's intimate relationship with Thomas Seymour had been afloat for some time and reached a climax for Elizabeth when it was publicly reported that she had actually had a child by him, which had been 'miserably destroyed'.

In the following carefully worded but justly indignant letter, Elizabeth demands that the Protector and his council shall take requisite steps to put a stop to slanders so injurious to the character of a sister of the reigning monarch.[12]

As a result of her protest, the council offered to punish any and all persons Elizabeth could name as instigators of the malicious rumours. This she declined to do, saying that if she showed 'she were glad to punish', she would incur the ill will of the people. This prudent policy, so early exhibited by Elizabeth, she adopted through life, thereby ensuring the respect and affection of her English subjects.

My Lord,

Having received Your Lordship's letters, I perceive in them your goodwill towards me, because you declare to me plainly your mind in this thing; and again, for that you would not wish that I should do anything that should not seem good unto the Council, for the which thing I give you most hearty thanks...

But if it might seem good to Your Lordship, and the rest of the Council, to send forth a proclamation into the counties that they refrain their tongues, declaring how the tales be but lies, it should make both the people think that you and the Council have great regard that no such rumours should be spread of any of the King's Majesty's sisters (as I am, though unworthy), and also that I should think myself to receive such friendship at your hands as you have promised me, although Your Lordship hath showed me great already.

Howbeit, I am ashamed to ask it any more, because I see you are not so well-minded thereunto. And as concerning that you say that I give folks occasion to think, in refusing the good to uphold the evil, I am not of so simple understanding, nor I would that Your Grace should have so evil an opinion of me that I have so little respect of my own honesty, that I would maintain it if I had sufficient promise of the same, and so Your Grace shall prove me when it comes to the point.

And thus I bid you farewell, desiring God always to assist you in all your affairs. Written in haste. From Hatfield, this 21st of February.

Your assured friend to my little power,
Elizabeth

To the Protector, Edward Seymour, Duke of Somerset, 1549

Mrs Ashley, Elizabeth's governess, had been sent to the Tower with her husband as suspected of confederacy in Thomas Seymour's plot to marry Elizabeth. Elizabeth immediately took up the cudgels on 'Kat' Ashley's behalf.

A nature having less fearlessness and sense of gratitude might have thought it advisable, in view of the difficult circumstances, to leave the Ashleys to their fate. This, however, was not Elizabeth's way. The following (undated) letter to the Protector shows her loyalty in friendship, a quality exhibited on so many occasions in later life.

My Lord,

I have a request to make unto Your Grace which fear has made me omit till this time for two causes; the one because I saw that my request for the rumours which were spread abroad of me took so little place, which thing, when I considered, I thought I should little profit in any other suit; howbeit, now I understand that there is a proclamation for them (for the which I give Your Grace and the rest of the Council most humble thanks), I am the bolder to speak for another thing; and the other was, because, peradventure Your Lordship and the rest of the Council will think that I favour her evil doing for whom I shall speak, which is Kateryn Ashley, that it would please Your Grace and the rest of the Council to be good unto her. Which thing I do, not to favour her in any evil (for that I would be sorry to do), but for these considerations that follow, the which hope doth teach me in saying, that I ought not to doubt Your Grace and the rest of the Council will think I do it for other considerations.

First, because that she hath been with me a long time and many years, and hath taken great labour and pain in bringing me up in learning and honesty; and therefore I ought of very duty speak for her, for Saint Gregorie sayeth, 'That we are more bound to them that bringeth us up well than to our parents, for our parents do that which is natural for them that bringeth us into the world, but our bringers-up are a cause to make us live well in it.'

The second is, because I think that whatsoever she hath done in my lord Admiral's matter, as concerning the marrying of me, she did it because, knowing him to be one of the Council, she thought he would not go about any such thing without he had the Council's consent thereunto; for I have heard her many times say 'That she would never have me marry in any place without Your Grace's and the Council's consent.'

The third cause is, because that it shall and doth make men think that I am not clear of the deed myself, but that it is pardoned to me because of my youth, because that she I loved so well is in such a place.

Thus hope, prevailing more with me than fear, hath won the battle, and I have at this time gone forth with it, which I pray God be taken no otherwise than it is meant. Written in haste. From Hatfield, this 7th day of March.

Also, if I may be so bold, not offending, I beseech Your Grace and the rest of the Council to be good to Master Ashley, her husband, which, because he is my kinsman, I would be glad he should do well.

Your assured friend to my little power,
Elizabeth
To my very good lord, my Lord Protector.

To John Dudley, Duke of Northumberland, 1553

Immediately she learned of the intention to place the Lady Jane Grey on the throne, Elizabeth entered battle with Northumberland, who, it will be remembered, had succeeded Somerset.

Her wisdom and policy in preferring a straightforward path as the safest, is borne out in the following letter, in which she does not mince her views. It provides an example of how Elizabeth could use her pen not as a goose-quill but with rapier-like effect when she chose.

When, later, Elizabeth was offered by Northumberland a large sum of money and considerable grant of lands, if she would voluntarily renounce her right to the succession, her reply was 'That they[13] must first make their agreement with her elder sister, during whose life-time she herself had no claim or title to resign'.

My Lord Duke,

My sister and I were, some days ago, apprized of the plots and cabals which your ambition for the advancement of your own house has led you to form, in order to exclude us both from the succession to the Crown. We were not, however, willing to give credit to these reports; because we could not conceive that a gentleman of your merit, of whom we hold so good an opinion and who evinced, when you took the reins of government of this kingdom, such ardour and zeal in the defence of laws and justice, was capable of doing one of the most scandalous acts of injustice – that of inducing and even forcing an innocent king, when in the languor of bodily infirmity, to exclude, under foolish suspicions and ill-founded pretexts, by a surreptitious and violent will, the lawful heirs of the Crown – those who have been so recognized by will[14] and by a legitimate act of open Parliament.

Now, why do us this injustice? Is it to call to the inheritance of the Crown persons more remotely allied, of other blood, and other name, merely because they are your relations? Is this the fair renown that the King, our dear brother and sovereign lord, will, through your mad passion, leave behind, if God should take him from us? Is this the mighty honour Your Lordship will gain – to make use of your present power, only to exclude from the succession the rightful daughters of King Henry our father, and the sisters on the father's side of King Edward, to bring in the daughter of the Duke of Suffolk, who has had no other claim than that of having married one of our aunts? Is this the illustrious glory that you are to acquire among foreign nations, when they shall know that, by your passion and ambition, are violated and broken the most sacred laws of this kingdom and the legitimate rights of the succession to the throne?

However, we console ourselves in the hope, that that Heaven which is adverse to wrongs done upon earth, will restore health to our royal brother[15] and give him time to discover that he has been over-reached and ill-counselled; and to Your Lordship time for repentance for your machinations against the glory of the

King, the tranquillity of the Kingdom, the laws of the State, the rights of the Crown, and *our* individual interests. But if God wills otherwise, we hope that He, the guardian of justice, will take in hand our cause, so trampled upon by Your Lordship; and that the Parliament and the judges, who are the defenders of the laws and of the Crown, will draw us out of that oppression into which your ambition has cast us. I remain, meanwhile, in that state in which you have placed me,

Elizabeth

To Queen Mary I, 1554

During the insurrections that broke out when Mary I announced her intended marriage with Philip of Spain, Elizabeth was to find herself under the black cloud of sedition, as already mentioned. The supposed plot, where she was concerned, was to prevent the Catholic marriage, put Queen Mary to death, and place Elizabeth, as Protestant queen, on the throne.

Mary, incredulous and in great distress of mind, was persuaded to have Elizabeth formally charged, placed under guard, and threatened with imprisonment in the Tower.

The following letter, eloquent in its despair, was penned by the distraught Elizabeth to her half-sister. It has every appearance of having been written on the spur of the moment, and, as an example of Elizabeth's letters, it possesses more lucidity and feeling than perhaps any other compositions from her pen. She obviously had had no time, or inclination, to indulge in artificial sentences, lofty quotations, or ambiguity of any kind. She is pleading for her life in right good earnest, and in straightforward language appeals boldly and sincerely to Mary I's natural affections in the face of the rulings of a hostile privy council.

If any ever did try this old saying 'That a King's word was more than another man's oath,' I most humbly beseech Your Majesty to verify it to me, and to remember your last promise and my last demand[16] that I be not condemned without answer and due proof, which it seems that I now am; for without cause proved, I am by your Council from you commanded to go to the Tower, a place more wanted for a false traitor than a true subject, which though I know I deserve it not, yet in the face of all this realm it appears proved. I pray to God I may die the shamefullest death that any ever died, if I may mean any such thing; and to this present hour I protest before God (who shall judge my truth, whatsoever malice shall devise), that I never practised, counselled, nor consented to anything that might be prejudicial to your person any way, or dangerous to the State by any means.

And therefore I humbly beseech Your Majesty to let me answer afore yourself, and not to suffer me to trust to your councilors – yea, and that afore I go to the Tower, if it be possible; if not, before I go further condemned. Howbeit, I trust assuredly Your Highness will give me leave to do it afore I go, that thus shamefully I may not be cried out on, as I now shall be – yea, and that without cause!

Let conscience move Your Highness to pardon this my boldness, which innocency procures me to do, together with the hope of your natural kindness, which I trust will not see me cast away without desert, which what it is I would desire no more of God but that you truly knew, but which thing I think and believe you shall never by report know, unless by yourself you hear. I have heard of many in my time cast away for want of coming to the presence of their Prince; and in late days I heard My Lord Somerset say, that if his brother[17] had been suffered to speak with him he had never suffered; but persuasions were made to him so great, that he was brought in belief that he could not live safely if the Admiral lived and that made him give consent to his death.

Though these persons are not to be compared to Your Majesty, yet I pray God the like evil persuasions persuade not one sister against the other, and all for that they have heard false report, and the truth not known.

Therefore, once again, kneeling with humbleness of heart, because I am not suffered to bow the knees of my body, I humbly crave to speak with Your Highness, which I would not be so bold as to desire if I knew not myself most clear, as I know myself most true.

And as for the traitor Wyatt,[18] he might peradventure write me a letter, but on my faith I never received any from him. And as for the copy of the letter sent to the French King,[19] I pray God confound me eternally if ever I sent him word, message, token, or letter, by any means, and to this truth I will stand till my death.

Your Highness's most faithful subject, that hath been from the beginning, and will be to the end,

Elizabeth

I humbly crave but only one word of answer from yourself.

To Philip of Spain, 1554

Elizabeth's appeal brought no response from the queen, and, without Mary's knowledge, her chancellor, Bishop Gardiner, sent a warrant to the Tower, where Elizabeth was now a prisoner, for her immediate execution. As the warrant did not bear the queen's signature, however, Mary I was informed of the proposed execution by the lieutenant of the Tower.[20] She at once had Elizabeth removed, and sent in confinement to Woodstock Manor, in Oxfordshire,[21] under the charge of Lord John Williams of Thame, and of Sir Henry Bedingfield, both staunch Roman Catholics.

Elizabeth's release from the Tower had been effected through Philip of Spain interceding on her behalf, and she was eventually to be reinstated in Mary's favour. It is supposed that Philip of Spain, realising that Mary would die childless, obtained Elizabeth's liberation as she was the sole barrier to the claim of Mary, Queen of Scots (betrothed to the Dauphin of France), to the English succession, and if this claim were not obstructed, preponderance of power would be given to Philip of Spain's old enemy, the King of France, Henry II.

It is to be wondered whether the astute Elizabeth suspected, when rendering her 'humble thanks' to his majesty, that the thread of her life had hung not on her brother-in-law's generosity, but on his lust for power.

Sire,

I have been fully informed, and am well persuaded of your generous exertions on my behalf, to liberate me from the wearisome woes of an imprisonment, so hard and so tedious, which I should have endured with more patience, if I had been accused of anything less hurtful to my feelings than that of having been wanting in fidelity to the Queen my sister.

But knowing myself as faithful and zealous in her service as I am, I cannot but feel my heart rent and torn, at the remembrance of a disgrace that could have made others believe me capable of even a sinister thought against the interests and glory of the Queen, my lady. Yea, if my heart had been capable of being stained only by the shadow of such a thought, I would pluck it out with my own hands; and this perfect consciousness of my innocence has rendered my long and painful imprisonment insupportable.

God grant, however, that I may never accuse any but myself of my misfortune, nor ever cause a shadow of reproach to the glory or the justice of the Queen, my lady. I being fully persuaded that she was moved by my unlucky star to resolve on my imprisonment, her heart being so generous and so just, that she could not devise the thought of doing wrong to the least of her subjects, and still less, to her unfortunate sister, who never has had other thought than showing her as profound obedience as does the least of her servants.

I do not think that I shall offend the equity, clemency, and august goodness of the Queen towards me, if I render very humble thanks to Your Majesty, in that you have had the goodness to espouse so generously the cause of liberty. From a king so generous and so august can proceed nothing but favour: it is this which makes me take the liberty humbly to entreat you to continue to me your protection, and to be pleased ever to consider me

Your Majesty's very humble servant and subject,
Elizabeth

When queen regnant, to Mary, Queen of Scots, 1567

Upon her accession to the throne in 1558, it was early made evident that Elizabeth I's notions of the majesty of kings were high. She was twenty-five years old when she began to reign, and she continued reigning until her seventieth year. During all this time she had no helps to lean on in her government, except such as she herself provided – no brother, uncle, or kinsman of the royal family to lighten her cares and support her authority. Further, by her own choice,[22] she had no consort to share her burden.

Elizabeth regarded Mary, Queen of Scots, as the presumptive heir to the English throne as, although Henry VIII in establishing his succession had passed over in silence the rights of his sister, Margaret Tudor, queen of James IV of Scotland, such hereditary claims descended to her granddaughter, Mary Stuart. Mary Stuart, on the death of her husband, Francis II of France, after a reign of seventeen months, returned to her own kingdom in Scotland, and married Lord Darnley. He was later found dead in mysterious circumstances, and owing to Mary's unhappy differences with him, which were common knowledge, she was suspected of having been party to Darnley's murder.

Intellectually and emotionally cold, Elizabeth – save in a crisis – would not appear to have indulged in what might be termed 'heartfelt' correspondence. She had the mind of a supreme diplomat, and there was always a clear-sighted purpose behind such letters as she wrote, more particularly after she had become queen.

In the following case, however, there is every evidence of an uncontrollable mood of anxiety, mixed with princely hauteur, in the letter the Queen Regnant of England wrote to her cousin, Mary Stuart. She was obviously dismayed at the situation in which the Scottish queen had placed herself.

Madam,

My ears have been so much shocked, my mind distressed, and my heart appalled, at hearing the horrible report of the abominable murder of your husband, my slaughtered cousin,[23] that I have scarcely as yet spirits to write about it; but although nature constrains me to lament his death so near to me in blood as he was, I must tell you boldly that I am far more concerned for you than I am for him ...

Oh, Madam! I should neither perform in office as a faithful cousin nor that of an affectionate friend, if I studied rather to please your ears than to preserve your honour; therefore I will not conceal from you that people, for the most part, say 'That you will look through your fingers at this deed instead of revenging it,' and that you have not cared to touch those who have done you this pleasure, as if the deed had not been without the murderers having had that assurance ...

For the love of God, Madam, use such sincerity and prudence in this case which touches you so nearly, that all the world may have reason to judge you innocent of so enormous a crime – a thing which, unless you do, you will be worthily blotted out from the rank of princesses and rendered not undeservedly, the opprobrium of the vulgar; rather than which fate should befall you, I should wish you an honourable sepulchre instead of a stained life.

To Mary, Queen of Scots, 1569

During a dangerous sickness when in France, Mary Stuart had, through the influence of her father-in-law, Henry II, made a will bequeathing her rights to the kingdom of Scotland, and her claims to succession to the throne of England – if she died without issue – to Henry II's heirs.

Elizabeth I became aware of the continued existence of this document, and wrote the following cautiously worded but angry letter to the Queen of Scots, which contained an obvious warning. As a result, Mary Stuart persuaded the Duke of Anjou to renounce all claims.

Elizabeth, Queen of England to the Queen of Scots.

May 25th, 1569

Madame,

To my infinite regret I have learned the great danger in which you have lately been[24] and I praise God I heard nothing of it until the worst was past, for in whatever time or place it might have been, such news could have given me little content; but if any such bad accident had befallen you in this country, I believe really I should have deemed my days prolonged too long, if, previous to death, I had received such a wound. I rely much on His goodness who has always guarded me against mal-accidents, that He will not permit me to fall into such a snare, and that He will preserve me in good report of the world till the end of my career. He has made me know, by your means, the grief I might have felt if anything ill had happened to you, and I assure you that I will offer up unto Him infinite thanksgiving.

As to the reply which you wish to receive by My Lord Boyd, regarding my satisfaction in the case touching the Duke of Anjou,[25] I neither doubt your honour nor your faith in writing to me that you never thought of such a thing, but that perhaps some relative, or rather some ambassador of yours having the general authority of your signature to order all things for the furtherance of your affairs, had adjusted this promise as if it came from you, and deemed it within the range of his commission. Such a matter would serve as a spur to a courser of high mettle; for, as we often see a little bough serve to save the life of a swimmer, so a light shadow of claim animates the combatants. I know not why they[26] consider not that the bark of your good fortune floats on a dangerous sea, where many contrary winds blow, and has need of all aid to obviate such evils, and to conduct you safely into port.

To Dr Richard Cox, 1573

Doctor Cox, Bishop of Ely, was a strong supporter of the Church of England, and had been thrown into prison in Mary I's reign. He escaped to Strasbourg, however, and on her accession Elizabeth immediately raised him to the see of Ely.

His town house, with its beautiful gardens on Holborn hill, known as Ely Place, was coveted by Sir Christopher Hatton, one of the queen's leading favourites, but the bishop obstinately refused to part with it in spite of a private request from Elizabeth.

The following stern and brief letter is a striking example of regal autocracy as practised by Elizabeth I. As a result the luckless bishop was forced to part with a large portion of the estate, reserving only for himself, and his successors, 'leave to walk at will in the gardens, and gather twenty bushels of roses therein yearly'.

Proud Prelate,
    You know what you were before I made you what you are now. If you do not immediately comply with my request, I will unfrock you, by God!
    Elizabeth

To her godson, John Harington, 1575

After she had become monarch very few personal letters were written by Elizabeth I, practically all her correspondence being concerned with matters of state. She made exceptions, however: as in the following instance, when sending a copy of her speech to Parliament to her godson, John Harington, who at the time was little more than a 'stripling.'

The youth's father, Sir John Harington, and mother, the beautiful Isabella Markham,[27] had both been committed to the Tower with Princess Elizabeth, owing to their allegiance to her.

There is a curious charm about this brief note from a great queen to a youth just out of his teens, which reflects an aspect of Elizabeth's character not often exhibited.

> Boy Jack,
>
> I have made a clerk write fair my poor words for thine use. As it cannot be such striplings have entrance into Parliament Assembly yet.
>
> Ponder them in thy hours of leisure, and play with them till they enter thine understanding; so shalt thou hereafter, perchance, find some good fruits hereof when thy godmother is out of remembrance; and I do this because thy father was ready to serve and love us in trouble and thrall.

To the Earl of Leicester, 1585

When William the Silent (great-grandfather of William III of England) was assassinated in 1584, the Dutch, eager to preserve Protestant power, sought to offer the sovereignty of the Netherlands to Elizabeth I. This she declined, but agreed to aid the states with money, and a strong force under the command of her reigning favourite, the Earl of Leicester.[28] In expectation of gratifying Elizabeth, the states honoured Leicester on his landing at Flushing with the title of Governor and Captain General of the United Provinces, gave him a special guard, and treated him as though he were a sovereign, in which glories he indulged his vanity to the full.

These proceedings, however, infuriated Elizabeth I, and she wrote in the angriest terms to her beloved favourite in consequence. A letter in much the same spirit was also sent to the representatives of the states.

How contemptuously you have carried yourself towards us you shall understand by this messenger, whom we send you for that purpose. We little thought that one, whom we had raised out of the dust, and prosecuted with such singular favour above all others would with so great contempt, have slighted and broken our commands in a matter of so great consequence, and so highly concerning us and our honour. Whereof, though you have but small regard, contrary to what you ought by your allegiance, yet think not that we are so careless of repairing it, that we can bury so great an injury in silence and oblivion.

Therefore, our express pleasure and commandment is that all delays and excuses laid apart, you do presently, upon the duty of your allegiance, obey and fulfil whatsoever the bearer hereof shall direct you to do in our name: whereof fail you not, as you will answer the contrary at your immediate peril.

To Mary, Queen of Scots, 1586

The rights and wrongs of the detention of Mary, Queen of Scots, in England, after she had been forced to fly from her Scottish kingdom, have been the subject of much controversy. It is an undoubted fact, however, that for a great number of years Elizabeth I had, as a consequence, to endure much personal anxiety and misery, haunted as she was all the time by rumours of plots, counterplots, and bloody retaliation.

At long last, the English queen permitted herself to be persuaded by her advisers that her royal cousin – in her sternly guarded 'asylum', sick, and surrounded by spies – was so dangerous a person to Elizabeth I and her Protestant subjects that it was her sovereign duty to have Mary Stuart brought to trial, on the charge of plotting against the life of the Queen of England.

The following communication was addressed by Elizabeth to Mary Stuart, without the usual superscription of 'Cousin' or 'Sister', on the Queen of Scots refusing to acknowledge the authority of the commission of peers appointed to conduct the trial.

Queen Elizabeth to Mary Queen of Scots.

You have in various ways and manners, attempted to take my life, and to bring my kingdom to destruction by bloodshed.

I have never proceeded so harshly against you, but have, on the contrary, protected and maintained you like myself. These treasons will be proved to you, and all made manifest.

Yet it is my will, that you answer the nobles and peers of the kingdom as if I were myself present. I therefore require, charge, and command that you make answer, for I have been well informed of your arrogance.

Act plainly, without reserve, and you will sooner be able to obtain favour of me.

Elizabeth

To Henry III of France, 1587

The ill feeling that had existed for some time between Elizabeth I and the Duke of Anjou, now Henry III of France, was accentuated by his attempting, ill-advisedly perhaps, to intercede on behalf of Mary Stuart. His ambassador, de Bellièvre, increased Elizabeth I's indignation by the peremptory manner in which he made his addresses to her.

As a result, Queen Elizabeth wrote the following haughty and humiliating letter to Henry III, concluding it with a sharp and pertinent reference to Henry's feeble government where his own country was concerned, of which his sister monarch was well aware. In addition, Elizabeth at first refused the unnerved ambassador a passport to France, but eventually let him depart, puzzled and discomforted.

Sir, my good Brother,

The old ground, on which I have often based my letters, appears to me so changed at present, that I am compelled to alter the style and, instead of returning thanks, to use complaints.

My God! How could you be so unreasonable as to reproach the injured party, and to compass the death of an innocent one by allowing her to become the prey of a murderess? But, without reference to my rank, which is nowise inferior to your own, nor to my friendship to you, most sincere – for I have well nigh forfeited all reputation among the princes of my own religion, by neglecting them in order to prevent disturbances in your dominions; exposed to dangers such as scarcely any prince ever was before; expecting, at least, some ostensible reasons and offers for security against the daily danger for the epilogue of this whole negotiation – you are, in spite of all this, so blinded by the words of those who I pray may not ruin you, that instead of a thousand thanks, which I have merited for such singular services, Monsieur de Bellièvre has addressed language to my ears which, in truth, I know not well how to interpret. For, that you should be angry at my saving my own life, seems to me the threat of an enemy, which, I assure you, will never put me in fear, but is the shortest way to make me dispatch the cause of so much mischief.

Let me, I pray you, understand in what sense I am to take these words; for I will not live an hour to endure that any prince whatsoever should boast that he had humbled me into drinking such a cup as that.

Monsieur de Bellievre has, indeed, somewhat softened his language, by adding that you in nowise wish any danger to accrue to me, and still less to cause me any. I, therefore, write you these few words, and if it please you to act accordingly, you shall never find a truer friend; but if otherwise, I neither am in so low a place, nor govern realms so inconsiderable, that I should, in right and honour, yield to any living prince who would injure me, and I doubt not, by the grace of God, to make my cause good for my own security.

I beseech you to think rather of the means of maintaining, than of diminishing my friendship. Your realm, my good brother, cannot abide many enemies. Give not the rein, in God's name, to wild horses, lest they should shake you from your saddle. I say this to you out of a true and upright heart, and implore the Creator to grant you long and happy life.

Elizabeth

To James VI of Scotland, *c.* 1587

While there appears to be no evidence available that Elizabeth I actually signed the Queen of Scots' death warrant, there is little question but that she was morally responsible for her cousin's death. She behaved, however, as if her sorrow were real and in the following letter to Mary Stuart's son, James VI of Scotland (who afterwards succeeded Elizabeth as James I of England), she refers to his mother's execution as a result of misinterpretation of Elizabeth's instructions.

The bearer entrusted with her letter was Robert Carey, afterwards to become Earl of Monmouth. He professed himself convinced of the genuineness of Elizabeth's grief.[29]

My dear Brother,

I would you knew (though not felt) the extreme dolour that overwhelms my mind for that miserable accident, which, far contrary to my meaning, hath befallen. I have now sent this kinsman of mine, whom, ere now, it hath pleased you to favour, to instruct you truly of that which is irksome for my pen to tell you. I beseech you, that as God and many more know how innocent I am in this case, so you will believe me that, if I had bid aught, I would have abided by it. I am not so base-minded that the fear of any living creature or prince should make me afraid to do that were just, or, when done, to deny the same.

I am not of so base a lineage, nor carry so vile a mind.

But as not to disguise fits not the mind of a king, so will I never dissemble my actions, but cause them to show even as I meant them.

Thus assuring yourself of me, that as I know this was deserved, yet, if I had meant it, I would never lay it on others' shoulders, no more will I not damnify myself that thought it not.

The circumstances it may please you to have[30] of this bearer. And for your part, think not you have in the world a more loving kinswoman nor a more dear friend than myself, nor any that will watch more carefully to preserve you and your state. And who shall otherwise persuade you, judge them more partial to others than to you. And thus, in haste, I leave to trouble you, beseeching God to send you a long reign.

Your most assured loving sister and cousin,

Elizabeth, R.

To Lady Paget, *c.* 1589

In the following letter Elizabeth I is proffering her sympathy to her old friend, Lady Paget, on hearing of the death of her daughter. The letter exhibits much good and honest feeling, and is a further example of Elizabeth's ability, in expressing deep emotions, to 'imitate the honourable Romans in brevity'.[31]

Call to mind, good Kate, how hardly we princes can brook of crossing of our commands. How ireful will the Highest Power be – may you be sure – when murmurs shall be made of His pleasing His will. Let nature, therefore, not hurt herself, but give place to the giver. Though this lesson be from a silly[32] vicar,[33] yet it is sent from a loving sovereign.

To the Lady Norris, 1597

Lady Norris, a lifelong friend and intimate of Elizabeth I, was the daughter of Lord John Williams of Thame, who with his family had befriended her, and shown her every courtesy during the critical time she underwent as a prisoner in her half-sister's reign.

The news of the death of one of Lady Norris's sons was communicated by Elizabeth I to her old friend in the following letter of sympathy, written in Elizabeth's own hand. The sobriquet 'Crow' was Elizabeth's pet name of endearment, Lady Norris having had in her youth a very dark complexion and hair black as a crow's feathers.[34]

This great monarch, who could express such philosophical and stoic sentiments, is said, when her own death was approaching not so many years later, to have found the business of dying very difficult. Doubtless the spirit was willing enough to depart, but the struggle lay with that sovereign heart and brain, that were loath to lay aside the sceptre of temporal power.

Mine own dear Crow,

Although we have deferred long to represent unto you our grieved thoughts, because we liked full ill to yield you the first reflections of our misfortunes, whom we have always sought to cherish and comfort, yet knowing now that necessity must bring it to your ears, and Nature consequently must raise many passionate workings in your heart, we have resolved no longer to smother either our care for your sorrow, or the sympathy of our grief for his death; wherein, if society in sorrowing work any diminution, we do assure you by this true messenger of our mind, that Nature can have stirred no more dolorous affection in you as a mother for a dear son, than the grateful memory of his services past hath wrought in us, his Sovereign, apprehension of the miss of so worthy a servant.

But now that Nature's common work is done, and he that was born to die hath paid his tribute, let that Christian discretion stay the flow of your immoderate grieving, which hath instructed you, both by example and knowledge, that nothing of this kind hath happened but by God's providence, and let these lines from your loving and gracious Sovereign serve to assure that there shall ever remain the lively character of you and yours that are left, in valuing rightly all their faithful and honest endeavours.

More at this time I will not write of this *unsilent* subject, but have dispatched this gentleman to visit both your lord, and to condole with you in the true sense of our love, and to pray you that the world may see, that what time cureth in weak minds, that discretion and moderation help you in this accident, where there is so opportune occasion to demonstrate true patience and moderation.

To Charles Blount, Lord Mountjoy, 1603

Elizabeth I wrote in her own hand the following note not long before her death, but it was so illegible that it had to be copied by her secretary. In her private correspondence she often indulged in fanciful literary compositions, of which this is a specimen.

Lord Mountjoy, to whom the note was written, was thirty-five years of age at the time, and Elizabeth seventy. He was her celebrated Lord Deputy of Ireland, and had written apologetically to Elizabeth, anticipating blame for some reverse that had taken place in that country.

The Queen to Lord Mountjoy.

Oh! what melancholy humour hath exhaled up into your brain from a full-fraughted heart, that should breed such doubt – bred upon no cause given by us at all, never having pronounced any syllable upon which such a work should be framed. There is no louder trump that may sound out your praise, your hazard, your care, your luck, than we have blasted in all our Court, and elsewhere indeed.

Well; I will attribute it to God's good providence for you, that (lest all these glories might elevate you too much) He hath suffered (though not made) such a scruple to keep you under His rod, who best knows we have more need of bits than spurs. Thus, *Valeant ista amara; ad Tartaros eat melancholia!*[35]

Your Sovereign.

E. R.

Endorsed (in the hand of Sir Robert Cecil, Secretary of State) 'A copy of Her Majesty's letter, lest you cannot read it.' Then, in Lord Mountjoy's hand, 'Received in January, at Arbracken.'

After a reign of forty-four years – during which time this 'weak and feeble woman with the heart and stomach of a King' established England on a level with the first nations of Europe – Elizabeth I died on 24 March 1603. She was buried in the same tomb as her half-sister Mary I, in Westminster Abbey. Her successor, James I, gave her a splendid monument, but, as a famous biographer wrote of her, 'She was one of the few whose glory required it not.'

By contrast with her predecessor, Elizabeth I would not appear to have been haunted by any religious convictions of a dogmatic kind, but rather to have regarded herself – a master mariner in command of the ship of state – as queen-under-God.[36]

The essence of her greatness lay in her love for her country and her people. The reason for the splendour of her reign may, perhaps, be attributed to the spirit in which she undertook her task as monarch – a spirit revealed in the words in which she personally instructed her judges and ministers in the execution of their duties shortly after she had ascended the throne. That spirit she maintained to the day of her death.

> Have a care over my people. You have my people: do you that which I ought to do. They are *my* people. Every man oppresseth and spoileth them without mercy. They cannot revenge their quarrel nor help themselves. See unto them, see unto them, for they are my charge. I charge you, even as God hath charged me. I care not for myself; my life is not dear to me. My care is for my people. I pray God, whoever succeedeth me, be careful as I am. They who know what cares I bear, would not think I took any great joy in wearing a crown.

In stressing that her subjects were her people, Elizabeth was wittingly expressing a dual truth. She was bone of their bone, and flesh of their flesh: in spite of the regal blood of the Plantagenets, which she derived from Elizabeth of York, her royal grandmother, Elizabeth I was British in descent, both on her father's and on her mother's side, for many generations.

With her death there died the last of the House of Tudor and the last of a line of native sovereigns of England.

10

Anne of Denmark

(*c*. 1574–1619), Queen Consort of James I

When queen consort, to George Heriot, *c*. 1595

Anne of Denmark was the second daughter of Frederick II, King of Denmark. She was married to James I when he was James VI of Scotland, and became, on his accession to the English throne on the death of Elizabeth I, first Queen Consort of England and Scotland. Anne was also the first queen consort to have a coronation since Anne Boleyn, and she and James I were the first monarchs to be crowned together since Henry VIII and Catherine of Aragon nearly a century earlier.

While having no great pretensions to beauty, Anne was a woman of considerable spirit, and possessed a lively wit. Had she chosen to plunge into the sea of politics, she might have exhibited marked abilities; but instead, she flung herself wholeheartedly into the gaiety of her English court. Her ambition was to shine as a royal 'star' in an endless succession of brilliant balls, fêtes, and masques;[1] and no expense was spared on these regal entertainments. It was a profligate and debauched court over which she and James I reigned; not only did the king himself indulge in a daily 'drunk', but Anne's ladies were often speechless from the same cause. In addition to his fondness for strong liquor, James's fondness for his favourites – his 'sweet boys' – moved Anne to fits of petulance and disgust at times, so that she treated him to open scorn and contempt. By 1606 they were living in separate establishments.[2]

Anne's letters – never dated – are unique among queenly epistles. Animated and humorous, in keeping with her temperament, they confine their meaning into such brief space that they are little more than hasty notes.

The first letter extant, apparently, of this pithy royal scribe was dashed off owing to the following happening. Her first child, Henry (who died in his teens) was born at Stirling Castle, and it was the custom in Scotland to leave the royal heir in the care of his hereditary guardian, the Earl of Mar. Finding her child handed over in this way, Anne's maternal instincts were outraged, and, all pleadings being in vain, she privately plotted to kidnap her son from his legal protector. The curious little note appended was sent by Anne of Denmark to George Heriot,[3] her jeweller and banker, with an object of raising funds for her to go to Stirling Castle and abduct the infant prince. Unfortunately for her, her scheme was discovered.

This letter is given in Anne of Denmark's original orthography, as an example of the style in which she wrote. In her letters that follow, the spelling has been corrected to serve the reader's convenience.

Ane Presept of the Queen

Geordg Heriatt, I earnestlie dissyr youe present to send me tua hundrethe pundes vith all expidition, becaus I maun hest me away presentie.

Anna, R. [*sic*]

To James I, 1603

The following letter was the first that Anne of Denmark wrote in England after James I's accession. Like all her letters, the original was written in her own hand, James I having insisted that she should not employ a secretary when writing to him. Unless she is in a bad temper, there is always to be found in Anne's 'jottings' a shade of familiar playfulness.

This note, written when she was journeying south to Windsor to join the king, shows her in a cheerful enough mood, doubtless because she was enjoying the fêtes arranged for her entertainment en route.

My Heart,

I am glad that Haddington hath told me of Your Majesty's good health, which I wish to continue. As for the blame you charge me with of lazy writing, I think it rather rests on yourself, because you are as slow in writing as myself. I can write of no mirth but of practice of tilting, of riding, of drumming, and of music, which is all, wherewith I am not a little pleased.

So wishing Your Majesty perpetual happiness, I kiss Your Majesty's hand, and rest.

Your Anna, R. [*sic*]

To James I, 1603

On arrival at Windsor, a violent dispute broke out between the English and Scottish nobles as to right of precedence. Without attempting to smooth over difficulties, Anne impetuously, as was her way, plunged headlong into the feud, and had the combatants put under guard. James sent them to the Tower as a 'corrective,' but blamed his imperious consort for her hastiness. As a result, he received the following scribbled and tempestuous letter from Anne, obviously written in fury. The bearer of the message was Sir Roger Aston. Anne's anger is not directed against him, but against the king for permitting one of the nobles who had defied her into his presence.

Sir,

What I have said to Sir Roger is true; I could not but think it strange that any about Your Majesty durst presume to bring near where Your Majesty is, one that had offered me such a public scorn, for honour goes before life, I must ever think.

So humbly kissing Your Majesty's hand, I rest ever yours,

Anna, R. [*sic*]

I refer the rest to Sir Roger.

To James I, 1603

From some dubious motive, no doubt, the king had interested himself in promoting the marriage of his beautiful nineteen-year-old cousin, Margaret Stuart, with Lord William Howard of Effingham, the ancient Armada hero, who was then well over seventy.

Anne regarded the comic alliance in which James I was such an active agent with laughter and no little scorn. Her lively note on the subject rather smacks of *Twelfth Night*. She visualises the king as Mercury and Margaret and her aged lover as Venus and Mars.

Your Majesty's letter was welcome to me. I have been as glad of the fair weather as yourself. In the last part of your letter you have guessed right that I would laugh. Who would not laugh both at the persons and the subject? But more so at so well-chosen a Mercury between Mars and Venus; and you know that women can hardly keep counsel. I humbly desire Your Majesty to tell me how I should keep this secret that have already told it and shall tell it to as many as I speak with.[4] If I were a poet, I would make a song of it, and sing it to the tune of 'Three fools well met,' So, kissing your hands, I rest

Your
Anna, R. [*sic*]

To Robert Cecil, Earl of Salisbury, 1612

The office of confidential secretary was, more often than not, held by royal favourites. Because of the beauty of his face and figure, Sir Robert Carr[5] for some time was ostensibly thus employed by James I. Being totally lacking in the necessary requirements for such an onerous post, however, he secretly obtained the help of his friend, Sir Thomas Overbury. Overbury, ambitious and arrogant in no small degree, could not resist disclosing his knowledge of state secrets, and talked publicly of the contents of some of Anne of Denmark's letters that had passed through his hands.

Anne – who had strong likes and antipathies which she made no attempt to conceal – had a great aversion to Overbury. His breach of confidence came to her knowledge, causing her no little concern, as will be gathered from the following letter regarding 'that fellow' Overbury. As a consequence of this grave indiscretion, Overbury was forced to flee the country for some time, to avoid being committed to the Tower.

> My Lord,
>
> The King hath told me that he will advise you, and some other four or five of the Council, of *that fellow*.[6] I can say no more, either to make you understand the matter or my mind, than I said the other day. Only I recommend to your care how public the matter is now, both in Court and City, and how far I have reason in that respect.
>
> I refer the rest to this bearer, and myself to your love.
>
> Anna, R. [*sic*]

To Sir George Villiers, 1614

A later favourite, and thereby confidential secretary to James I, was George Villiers, afterwards 1st Duke of Buckingham.[7]

The appointment of this youthful, elegant, and good-mannered Englishman far from met with Anne of Denmark's approval, in any event at first, but he had so wormed himself into James I's good graces, such as they were, that Anne's misgivings had no effect. She wisely put aside her personal doubts and entered into an agreement with Villiers that he should try to reform the king's manners and habits, which at times went beyond all bounds of decency. It was playfully arranged that Villiers should act as a faithful dog who lugged the sow by the ears when trespassing on forbidden ground, for as 'sow' Anne facetiously refers to James I.

The following note is in reply to a letter from Villiers in which he tells her how he has called the king to order.

> My kind Dog,
>
> I have received your letter, which is very welcome to me. You do very well lugging the sow's ear, and I thank you for it; and would have you do so still upon condition that you continue a watchful dog to him, and be always true to him.
>
> So wishing you all happiness,
>
> Anna, R. [*sic*]

To James I, 1614

In the same light spirit Anne wrote to James I, approving of Villiers's efforts. 'Steenie', to whom she refers, was the pet name given to Villiers by the king, owing to his resemblance to the beautiful head of St Stephen in an Italian masterpiece at Whitehall.

> I am glad ... that my dog Steenie does well; for I did command him that he should make your ear hang like a sow's lug, and when he comes home I will treat him better than any other dog.

To George Villiers, Duke of Buckingham, 1618

Sir Walter Raleigh, on the charge of high treason, had endured imprisonment for many years for his part in a conspiracy against the life of James I. Anne of Denmark, however, took a kindly interest in his welfare, and it was owing to her efforts that although a prisoner in the Tower, Sir Walter Raleigh retained his personal property and his income as Governor of Jersey.

When Anne herself was nearing death she interceded for his life; but notwithstanding her endeavours, Sir Walter Raleigh went to the block soon after the following letter was written by her.

After a lingering illness Anne of Denmark died at the age of forty-five in May 1619. It was reported that she 'had the happiest going out that anyone ever had' – which seems more than probable with such a blithe spirit as she possessed.

She was buried in Westminster Abbey. The hearse remained standing over her tomb during the rest of James I's reign, but was destroyed in Cromwell's time.

My kind Dog,

If I have any power or credit with you, I pray you let me have a trial of it at this time, in dealing sincerely and earnestly with the King that Sir Walter Raleigh's life may not be called in question. If you do it so that success answer my expectation, assure yourself that I will take it extraordinary kindly at your hands, and rest one that wisheth you well, and desires you to continue still (as you have been) a true servant of your master.

Anna, R. [*sic*]

11

Henrietta Maria

(1609–1669), Queen Consort of Charles I

When Princess Henrietta Maria of France, to her governess, Madame Marquise de Montglat, *c.* 1618

Henrietta Maria – loveliest of all England's queens – was the youngest child of Henry the Great of France and his second wife, Marie de Medici. Within a few months of her birth, her father was murdered in the streets of Paris by a fanatic, and this ominous opening proved to foreshadow a life destined to suffering and tragedy. In the climax of her grief, Henrietta Maria surnamed herself '*la Reine Malheureuse*', and indeed with truth.

Charles I, who succeeded his father in 1625, was madly in love with his young and fascinatingly beautiful consort, but their early married life was overshadowed with quarrels and disputes. This was in part due to the fact that a condition of the marriage had been that the king should relieve the English Roman Catholics from the operation of the penal laws. This, however, he failed to do, thereby bringing down upon himself the reproach of his consort, who though affectionate was also fiery-tempered and something of a religious bigot.

In her self-will and determination, Henrietta Maria provides the only instance of a consort refusing to be crowned or even to attend the coronation owing to her religious prejudices. This ill-advised and obstinate attitude struck a death blow to her popularity in England, and naturally caused the king himself great offence.

The relationship of the royal couple was further strained by Henrietta Maria's resentment of the influence over her husband of George Villiers, Duke of Buckingham, whose insolence at times towards herself only increased the tension. Conditions were made no more harmonious by the fact that the queen regarded her English subjects with amused contempt, and favoured her French attendants at court to such a degree that Charles I's hatred of them knew no bounds. Particularly was his ire directed against Madame de St George (daughter of Madame de Montglat), the first lady of the bedchamber, between whom and her husband Henrietta Maria was ever seeking to make peace.

Possessing not only exceptional beauty but great personal charm, Henrietta Maria was also an exquisite dancer, and had a voice which was naturally so sweet and powerful that if she had not been a queen she could have been prima donna of Europe. In addition to these individual attributes, she had a marked talent for letter writing, in which she freely indulged.

The following (undated) note of apology, for some exhibition of bad temper, is one of many little notes that Henrietta Maria wrote to her governess, Madame de Montglat. 'Mamangat'[1] would not appear to have been a very strict disciplinarian. As a result, Henrietta Maria developed, in her nursery days, the petulance and self-assertiveness that were to mar the early time of her marriage. Although these unfortunate characteristics could not fail to be subdued in the chastening school of life, Henrietta Maria never entirely conquered them.

Mamangat,

I pray you excuse me if you saw my little sulky fit which held me this morning. I cannot be right all of a sudden, but I will do all I can to content you meantime. I beg you will no longer be in wrath against me, who am and will be all my life, Mamangat,

Your affectionate friend,

Henrietta

When queen consort, to Madame de St George, 1630

Charles I finally succeeded in dismissing Henrietta Maria's colony of French attendants, including her intimate, Madame de St George. True to her loyalty of heart, however, Henrietta Maria remained faithful to her 'Mamie' through the years, and kept up a steady correspondence with her, notwithstanding the king's disapproval.

The removal of the influence of the French retinue, combined with the death of the Duke of Buckingham, who was assassinated in 1628, and Charles I's eventual relaxation of the penalties against the English Roman Catholics, brought the dissension between the king and queen to an end. The royal couple succeeded very quickly in reaching a happy relationship. In their sustained deep devotion to each other, Charles I and Henrietta Maria provide a regal romance unequalled in England's history.

The following letter was written to Mamie de St George some time after the birth of Henrietta Maria's son, Charles. In its playful naiveté it discloses that the queen is not blind to the fact that her boy is a 'fright', an unusual acknowledgment for any proud parent to make.

Mamie St. George,

The husband of the nurse of my son going to France about some business of his wife, I write you this letter by him, believing that you will be very glad to ask him news of my son of whom I think you have seen the portrait that I sent to the Queen my mother?

He is so ugly, that I am ashamed of him; but his size and fatness supply the want of beauty. I wish you could see the *gentleman*, for he has no ordinary mien; he is so serious in all that he does, that I cannot help deeming him far wiser than myself.

Send me a dozen pair of sweet chamois gloves; and also I beg you send me one of doeskin; a game *of joncheries*,[2] one of *poule*, and the rules of any species of games now in vogue.

I assure you that if I do not write to you so often as I might, it is not because I have left off loving you, but because – I must confess it – I am very idle; also I am ashamed to avow that I think I am on the increase again; nevertheless, I am not yet quite certain. Adieu! The man must have my letter.

To her son, afterwards Charles II, *c.* 1641

Her first letter to her son was written when Henrietta Maria had heard from his guardian and tutor at Richmond Palace, the Earl of Newcastle, that the Prince of Wales was a difficult little patient, and had refused to take some nauseous medicine: so she gently reproves him.

Charles,

I am sorry I must begin my first letter with chiding you, because I hear that you will not take *physic*. I hope it was only for this day, and that to-morrow you will do it; for if you will not, I must come to you and make you take it, for it is for your health.

I have given order to my Lord of Newcastle, to send me word to-night whether you will or not; therefore I hope you will not give me the pain to come.

And so I rest

Your affectionate Mother,
Henrietta Marie [*sic*]
To my dear son, the Prince.

To Charles I, 1642

While the Civil War was fast impending in England, Henrietta Maria fled to Holland to sell her own jewels, and also those of the Crown, with the object of providing Charles I with means for defence. Incidentally, she succeeded in raising nearly 2 million pounds in the king's cause. To accomplish this, however, she had to submit herself to much discourtesy and coarseness from the Dutch merchants with whom she was forced to do business. Nevertheless, her charm and feminine tact were such that, after gratifying their desire for ill behaviour in her presence to its bent, the merchants so succumbed to her attractions and regal dignity that Henrietta Maria found herself treated bountifully enough.

All the same, with what anxieties, and very human pangs, she parted with her own and with Charles's personal adornments will be gathered from the following letter, which she sent to her husband in the early stages of her negotiations with the usurers of the Netherlands.

My Dear Heart,

After much trouble, we have at last procured some money, but only a little as yet, for the fears of the merchants are not entirely passed away. It was written from London, that I had carried off my jewels secretly, and against your wish, and that if money was lent me upon them, that would be no safety for them; so that all this time, when we were ready to conclude anything, our merchants drew back. At last, it was necessary to show your power, signed under your own hand, about which I have written to you before, and immediately we concluded our business ...

I have given up your pearl buttons, and my little chain has done you good. You cannot imagine how handsome the buttons were, when they were out of the gold, and strung into a chain, and many as large as my great chain. I assure you, that I gave them up with no small regret. Nobody would take them in pledge, but only buy them. You may judge, now, when they know that we want money, how they keep their foot on our throat. I could not get for them more than half of what they are worth. I have six weeks time in which to redeem them, at the same price.

My great chain, and that cross which I had bought from the Queen my mother, is only pledged. With all these, I could not get any more money than what I send you.

I will send to-morrow to Antwerp, to pawn your ruby collar, for as to that, in Holland, they will not have it. For the largest collar, I am waiting a reply from Denmark. Every day, hopes are given me that those of Amsterdam will lend me money ...

To Madame de St George, 1642

Henrietta Maria's religious convictions, combined with her strong and active influence upon the king, caused her unpopularity in England to reach such a climax that she was virtually outlawed. While at the Hague she was at times overcome with despondency, and it was in one of these moods that she wrote to her great friend, Madame de St George, pouring out her troubled thoughts.

Mamie St. George,

This gentleman who is leaving is so fully informed of the reasons which have induced me to leave England, that when you learn them, you will be astonished that I did not do so earlier, for unless I had made up my mind to a prison, I could not remain there; but still if in this I had been the only sufferer, I am so accustomed to afflictions that that would have passed over like the rest: but their[3] design was to separate me from the King my Lord, and they have publicly declared that it was necessary to do this; and also that a Queen was only a subject, and was amenable to the laws of the country like other persons.

Moreover than that, they have publicly accused me, and by name, as having wished to overthrow the laws and religion of the Kingdom, and that it was I who had roused the Irish to revolt: they have even got witnesses to swear that this was the case, and upon that, affirmed that as long as ever I remained with the King, the

State would be in danger, and many other things too long to write; such as coming to my house, whilst I was at chapel, bursting open my doors, and threatening to kill everybody: but this I confess did not greatly frighten me; but it is true that to be under the tyranny of such persons is inexpressible misery, and during this time, unaided by anyone, judge in what a condition I was.

If it should happen that I see you, I could tell you a hundred things which cannot be written, worse than anything that I have told you. Pray to God for me, for be assured that there is not a more wretched creature in this world than I, separated far from the King my Lord, from my children, out of my country, and without hope of returning there, except at imminent peril-abandoned by all the world, unless God assist me, and the good prayers of my friends, amongst whom I number you ...

Your very good friend,

> Henrietta Marie, R. [*sic*]
> The Hague, the 28th of May.

To Charles I, 1643

After an absence of twelve months, having procured in Holland all money, stores and ammunition possible for the king's aid, Henrietta Maria sailed for England, accompanied by eleven heavily laden transports.

Her sea journeyings, however, were ill-fated. On this occasion she was destined to encounter such a terrible storm that she and her convoy, in imminent danger of death, were forced to return to the Hague, minus two ships which foundered.

Although before her terrified and seasick retinue she maintained a calm enough attitude and gay assurance – 'Comfort yourselves, *mes chères*! Queens of England are never drowned!' – from the letter which she wrote to Charles I it is obvious that Henrietta Maria was more than aware of the dangers of that grim and eventful voyage.

My Dear Heart,

As soon as I am returned to the Hague, I am anxious to let you know of it, believing you will be In trouble on my account, because of the terrible storm there has been, which by God's Grace we have escaped; after having been nine days at sea in constant danger of perishing, we were at last compelled to return to Holland, whence I hope to see out again as soon as the wind is good, although a storm of nine days is a very frightful thing: nevertheless, when your service is concerned, nothing frightens me.

I was but twenty hours distant from Newcastle when we were obliged to return. God be praised that He has still spared me to serve you, but I confess that I never expected to see you again. The only regret I felt about dying was that this accident might encourage your enemies, and discourage your friends, and this consideration I confess troubled me; for, but for your sake, life is not a thing of which I fear the loss.

I am so stupefied that I cannot easily write more for I have not slept during nine nights.

Adieu, My Dear Heart

January 27.

To Charles I, 1643

Undaunted by the alarming experience she had encountered on her first attempt to return to England, Henrietta Maria set sail once more within a few days. This time the sea passage was accomplished without outstanding event, and she landed at Burlington Bay, to witness, to her delight, a valiant escort of 1,000 Cavaliers waiting for her in sight of the hills. However, there were dangers still to be met. Parliament, in her absence, had voted her guilty of high treason for obtaining supplies of money and arms. Her life, she knew, was at forfeit.

Henrietta Maria sought refuge in a house in the little Yorkshire fishing village of Burlington, but at five o'clock the next morning the house was bombarded by the Parliamentary party's ships that had entered Burlington Bay in the night. She sent to the king the following interesting and graphic account of her adventures under fire. Characteristically she makes no mention of her recklessness in dashing back to the house to rescue her old dog, Mitte, an act which might have cost her her life.

My Dear Heart,

As soon as I landed in England, I sent Progers to you, but having learned to-day that he was taken by the enemy, I send you again this man to give you an account of my arrival, which has been very fortunate, thanks to God; for just as stormy as the sea was the first time I set sail, just so calm was it this time, till I was within fifteen hours of Newcastle, and on the coast, when the wind changed to the northwest, which forced us to make for Burlington Bay, and after two hours waiting at sea, your cavalry arrived. I landed instantly, and the next day the rest of the army came to join me.

God, who took care of me at sea, was pleased to continue His protection by land, for that night, four of the Parliament ships arrived at Burlington without our knowledge, and in the morning, about four o'clock, the alarm was given that we should send down to the harbour to secure our ammunition boats, which had not yet been able to be unloaded; but, about an hour after, these four ships began to fire so briskly, that we were all obliged to rise in haste, and leave the village to them; at least, the women, for the soldiers remained very resolutely to defend the ammunition. In case of a descent, I must act the captain, though a little low in stature, myself.

One of these ships had done me the favour to flank my house, which fronted the pier, and before I could get out of bed, the balls were whistling upon me in such style that you may easily believe I loved not such music. Everybody came to force me to go out, the balls beating so on all the houses, that, dressed just as it happened, I went on foot to some distance from the village, to the shelter of a ditch, like those at Newmarket; but before we could reach it, the balls were singing round us in fine style, and a serjeant was killed twenty paces from me.

We placed ourselves then under this shelter, during two hours that they were firing upon us, and the balls passing always over our heads, and sometimes covering us with dust.

At last, the Admiral of Holland[4] sent to tell them, that if they did not cease, he would fire upon them as enemies; that was done a little late, but he excuses himself on account of a fog which he says there was. On this they stopped, and the tide went down, so that there was not water enough for them to stay where they were.

As soon as they were retired, I returned to my house, not choosing that they should have the vanity to say that they had made me quit the village. At noon, I set out again to come to the town of Burlington, as I had previously resolved. All to-day, they have unloaded our ammunition in face of the enemy. I am told that one of the captains of the Parliament ships had been beforehand to reconnoitre where my lodging was, and I assure you that it was well marked, for they always shot upon it.

I may truly say, that by sea and by land, I have been in some danger, but God by His favour has saved me, and I have such confidence in His goodness as to believe that He will not leave me in other things, since in this He has protected me; and I protest to you, that in this confidence, I should dare to go to the very cannon's mouth, only that we should not tempt Him.

This bearer is witness to all that has passed. Nevertheless, I would not refrain from giving you this relation. It is very exact, and after this, I am going to eat a little, having taken nothing to-day but three eggs, and slept very little.

Adieu, My Dear Heart
Burlington, February.

To Sir Theodore Mayerne, 1644

In due course the royal lovers, once more united, established their court at Oxford, and – most unpropitiously, in view of the pressure of circumstances – in the passage of time Henrietta Maria found herself expecting another and eighth child. For her safety, it was considered wise that she should go to Exeter for her confinement and, racked with a fever and distraught in mind, Henrietta parted with the king at Abingdon. They were never to meet again.

The equally distracted and devoted Charles I, prosecuting his hopeless war against Parliament, yet found time to write to his household physician, Theodore Mayerne,[5] though only a note of one line: 'Mayerne, for the love of me, go to my wife!' At the same time, Henrietta Maria also wrote to the physician, although she well knew that he had no affection for her, Mayerne deeming her religious views to be one of the principal causes of the unsettled state of the country. Despite this he at once obeyed the plea in the pathetic note she sent him.

Exeter, this third of May.

Monsieur de Mayerne,

My indisposition does not permit me to write much to entreat you to come to me, if your health will suffer you; but my malady will, I trust, sooner bring you here than many lines. For this cause, I say no more but that, retaining always in my memory the care you have ever taken for me in my utmost need, it makes me believe that, if you can, you will come, and that I am, and shall be ever,

Your very good mistress and friend,
Henrietta Marie (R.) [*sic*]

To Charles I, 1644

On arrival at Exeter for the expected confinement Henrietta Maria became so ill that she believed herself to be dying. This view, too, was held by Mayerne, the physician. In this belief, she wrote to Charles I a letter which is in the nature of a final communication from a loving wife to her husband. Such fears were ill grounded, however, and she gave birth to a daughter shortly after she had written the letter.

Within two weeks of the birth of her baby, under the threat of being taken as a prisoner to London by Parliament's orders, Henrietta Maria – still a very sick woman – was forced to fly from Exeter, managing to elude the besieging army of Roundheads (on which faction, incidentally, Henrietta Maria had wittily conferred their title on account of their shaven heads) which was approaching the city. The ship that she boarded for Brest was chased by a Parliamentary cruiser and fired on, but the queen urged the captain to continue his course. If escape was impossible, he was to fire the powder magazine, rather than let her fall into the hands of the king's enemies. In the heat of the chase she was rescued by a fleet of vessels from Dieppe, and safely landed at Brest.

My Dear Heart,

I have so few opportunities of writing, that I will not lose this, which will I believe, be the last before I am brought to bed (since I am now more than fifteen days in my ninth month), and perhaps it will be the last letter you will ever receive from me. The weak state in which I am, caused by the cruel pains I have suffered since I left you, which have been too severe to be experienced or understood by any but those who have suffered them, makes me believe that it is time for me to think of another world. If it be so the Will of God be done! He has already done so much for us, and has assisted us so visibly in all our affairs, that certainly whatever way He may be pleased to dispose of me will be for your good and mine. I should have many things to say to you, but the roads are so little sure, that I should not dare to trust this letter, only I beg you to believe what *Lord Jermyn* and *Father Philip*[6] will say to you from me.

If that should happen to me, it is a great comfort to me to have written this letter to you. Let it not trouble you, I beg. You know well that from my last confinement, I have reason to fear, and also to hope. By preparing for the worst, we are never taken by surprise, and good fortune appears so much the greater. Adieu, my dear heart. I hope before I leave you, to see you once again in the position in which you ought to be. God grant it. I confess that I earnestly desire this, and also that I may be able yet to render you some service.

Exeter, this 18th June.

To Charles I, 1645

Anne of Austria, Queen Regent of France and Henrietta Maria's sister-in-law, showed every kindness and generosity to the exiled Queen of England, and gave her possession of apartments at the Louvre. This establishment proved the rallying point for the loyal emigrants from England: they fled there for shelter when the various plans devised for the restoration of Charles I fell to atoms.

In deepening depression Henrietta Maria spent much of her time while at the Louvre writing to her husband, who, as he said himself, 'loved her above all earthly things', and whose devotion she as ardently returned.

The following letter was in answer to one from Charles I, in which he wrote explaining his reason for accepting the proposal that he should go to London to treat with the rebel commissioners, and promising his wife great caution in such a step. He added that 'no danger of death or misery (which I think much worse) shall make me do anything unworthy of thy love'.

The fears Henrietta Maria expresses were all too well founded, but even if her husband had followed her advice, his tragic fate may not have been any different:

My Dear Heart,

Tom Elliot, two days since, hath brought me much joy and sorrow; the first, to know the good estate you are in; the other, the fear I have that you go to London. I cannot conceive where the wit was of those that gave you this counsel, unless it be to hazard your person to save theirs. But, thanks be to God, to-day I received one of yours by the Ambassador of Portugal, dated in January, which comforted me much to see that the treaty shall be at Uxbridge. For the honour of God, trust not yourself in the hands of those people. If ever you go to London before the Parliament be ended, or without a good army, you are lost. I understand that the propositions for peace must begin by disbanding your army. If you consent to this, you are lost; they having the whole power of the militia, they have and will do whatsoever they will.

I received yesterday letters from the Duke of Lorraine[7] who sends me word, that if his services be agreeable, he will bring you 10,000 men. Dr Goffe, whom I have sent into Holland, shall treat with him in his passage upon this business, and I hope very speedily to send you good news of this, as also of the money. Assure yourself I shall be wanting in nothing you can desire, and that I will hazard my life that is, I will die with famine rather than not send it to you. Send me word, always, by whom you receive my letters, for I write both by the Ambassador of Portugal and the resident of France. Above all, have a care not to abandon those who have served you, as well the Bishops as the poor Catholics. Adieu.

Paris, January.

To Charles I, 1645

Exiled, and desperate in her enforced separation from Charles I, Henrietta Maria's mental stress at time was such that she was unable even to decipher his letters to her.

The following poignant message was written by the overwrought queen in reply to one she had received from her husband, inferring that Henrietta Maria had shown his letters to people other than Lord Jermyn and Cowley,[8] who were the only two entrusted with the royal code.

My Dear Heart,

There is one thing in your letter which troubles me much where you would have me 'keep to myself your despatches' as if you believe that I should be capable to show them to any, only to Lord Jermyn to uncipher them, my head not suffering me to do it myself; but If It please you, I will do it, and none in the world shall see them. Be kind to me, or you will kill me.

I have already affliction enough to bear, which, without your love I could not do, but your service surmounts all. Farewell, dear heart! Behold the mark which you desire to have, to know when I desire anything in earnest.

Paris.

To Monsieur de Grignan, 1649

While in retreat at the Louvre Henrietta Maria endured poverty and brought herself to the point of starvation in order to send to Charles I all the material resources at her command. As the long and wearisome Civil War dragged on, rendering the king's cause ever more hopeless, Henrietta Maria's anxiety for her husband's personal safety took the place of all other feelings. In the depths of her misery and destitution she received the heartbreaking news that Charles I was to be brought before a tribunal for sentence. She at once wrote the following letter to M. de Grignan, French ambassador in London, entreating permission to return to England and share the king's fate. The English Commons refused her request.

Monsieur de Grignan,

The state to which the King my Lord finds himself reduced will not let me expect to see him by the means he heretofore hoped. It is this that has brought me to the resolution of demanding of the two Chambers[9] and the General of their Army, passports to go to see him in England.

You will receive orders from M. le Cardinal[10] to do all that I entreat you for this expedition, which will be to deliver the letters that I, send you herewith, according to their address. I have specified nothing to the Parliaments and to the General but to give me the liberty to go to see the King my Lord, and I refer them to you, to tell them all I would say more particularly. You must know then that you are to ask passports for me to go there, to stay as long as they will permit me, and to be at liberty all the time I may be there, and likewise all my people; in regard to whom it will be necessary to say, that I will send a list of those that I wish shall attend me, in order that if there are any in the number of them that may be suspected or obnoxious, they may be left behind. There are letters for the *Speakers* of both Houses, and for the General.[11] You will see all these persons, and let me know in what manner they receive the matter, and how you find them disposed to satisfy this wish. I dare not promise myself that they will accord me the liberty of going; I wish it too much to assure myself of it at a time when so little of what I desire succeeds; but if, by your negotiation, these passports can be obtained, I shall deem myself obliged to you all my life, as I shall (whatever may happen) for all the care you have taken, of which make no doubt. I shall add no more, except to assure you that I am, Monsieur de Grignan, most truly,

Your very good friend,
Henrietta Marie, R. [*sic*]
From the Louvre
This 6th of January, 1649.

In exile, to Madame de Motteville, 1658

Henrietta Maria received no news regarding the king's trial, and was not even informed of his execution until a month or more had elapsed after his death. Then, for a time, her reason went and her life was despaired of by those around her. At long last, with supreme courage of which she had abundance, Henrietta Maria took up the remaining threads of her worldly interests once more.

The death of Oliver Cromwell, the Protector, raised no hopes at first in the mind of the widowed queen that her son Charles would be restored to the English throne. This will be seen from the letter she wrote to Madame de Motteville,[12] her lifelong confidante, in reply to the latter's congratulations to Henrietta Maria on the removal of the persecuting Cromwell.

You might accuse me with reason of showing little sensibility to The kindness of my friends, if I did not inform you that I only received your letter this morning, though dated on Sunday. I thought you would hear with joy the news of the death of that *Scélérat*,[13] but I own to you, whether it be that my heart is so wrapped in melancholy that it is incapable of it, or that I really see not, as yet, any great advantages that will accrue to us, but I feel no very great satisfaction; the most I have is, seeing the hopes of all my friends. I beg you will thank Madame du Plessis and Mademoiselle de Belnave very warmly. I should be indeed rejoiced to make the fourth in your company. I would dwell long on the tried friendship of all of you for me, but in truth there is more in my heart than can be expressed, and my actions shall make you see it on all occasions.

I entreat you to believe, or you will wrong me, that I am, from the depth of my soul,

Your friend,
Henrietta Marie, R. [*sic*]

To her son, Charles II, 1660

In spite of her misgivings, Henrietta Maria was destined to witness the Restoration of the English monarchy, and to share with her son and the Royalists in the general rejoicings that broke out when Charles II ascended the throne.

In the following short letter to her son, in which Henrietta Maria refers to her intention to 'hear the Te Deum sung,' and 'have bonfires lighted,' she bravely makes no mention of the late king's tragic end, or of her own long years of suffering and hardship. In due course, she returned for a time to England, and continued to live an active and interesting life, as dowager queen, for several years.

This lovely, indomitable, and ill-fated queen died in 1669, at the age of sixty, 'in a sweet sleep' – it was rumoured from an overdose of a narcotic ignorantly prescribed by her doctor. She was buried in the abbey at St Denis, near Paris, where her royal ancestors lay. Her heart was placed in a silver urn, inscribed in Latin: 'Henrietta Maria, Queen of England, France, Scotland and Ireland; daughter of the French king, Henry IV, the Victorious; wife of Charles I, the Martyr; and mother of the restored king, Charles the Second.' The heart encased in the silver urn was royal indeed.

Progers arrived on Monday evening; you may judge of my joy and if you are torn to pieces in England with 'kindness,' I have my share of it also in France. I am going this instant to Chaillot[14] to hear the *Te Deum* sung, and from thence to Paris, to have bonfires lighted. We made them yesterday – I think I shall have all Paris. In fact, you cannot imagine the joy that prevails here.

We must amidst all this, praise God; all this is from His hand; you can see that it is. I will not trouble you more. God bless you.

Colombe, 5 o'clock in the morning.
June 9, 1660.

12

Catherine of Braganza

(1638–1705), Queen Consort of Charles II

When queen consort, to the Duke of Ormond, 1679

Catherine of Braganza, the not unhandsome consort of Charles II, was a daughter of John, Duke of Braganza.

It was her lot, as queen of the so-styled 'Merry Monarch', to witness those most exciting and interesting periods in England's history – the joys of the Restoration, the appalling Plague, the Great Fire, and the rebuilding of London. It was also her fate, as wife of that same 'Merry Monarch', to be personally subjected to insults and degradations (owing to the king's blatant infidelities) almost without comparison. In fact, never had any Queen of England, except Anne of Cleves, been treated so contemptuously by the king, his ministers, and his mistresses, and been so powerless to find means of defending herself.

Brought up in a convent, of simple tastes and retiring manners,[1] Catherine of Braganza was no match for the beautiful courtesans – in particular, the infamous Lady Castlemaine and Nell Gwynne, 'a bold, merry slut', as Pepys termed her – who fawned upon the dissolute monarch. Perhaps the least of the queen's troubles was the threat of divorce because she had not produced an heir. Far more disturbing must have been the endless intrigues with which she found herself surrounded at court, victimised, as she was, like her mother-in-law, Henrietta

Maria, because of her 'Popish' upbringing. In this connection an iniquitous attempt was made to charge her with plotting to poison the king.

Even after Charles II's death she was unable to free herself from the machinations and enmity of the powers behind or on the throne, but she managed to disentangle herself at last, and in 1692 Catherine of Braganza fled back gladly to her native Portugal.

It is of interest to note that this much-persecuted and abused queen, who was the subject of cheap lampoons, and generally regarded as a dumb simpleton, should – once restored to her home soil – have disclosed such outstanding abilities and talents that she was to find herself constituted Queen Regent of Portugal. It is worth remarking too that, despised and rejected for over twenty years, she exhibited her latent high qualities and force of character to the full in the last lap of her life. These last years, indeed, were to prove the best and brightest Catherine of Braganza had known. Suddenly, at the age of sixty-seven, on the last day of the year 1705, she died, in all her well-earned honours, and was most sincerely mourned.

Unfortunately for posterity, Catherine of Braganza appears to have been no 'intimate' letter writer while in this country, having an established rule – possibly a wise one, which certain later queens of England would have done well to emulate – of never putting pen to paper except on matters of necessity. On one occasion, in any event, she departed from this set principle. The death of the Duke of Ormond's son, her lord chamberlain, when she was queen consort, was much regretted by Catherine, and she wrote in her own hand the following gentle letter to his bereaved father.

My Lord Duke of Ormond,

I do not think anything I can say will lessen your trouble for the death of my lord Ossory, who is so great a loss to the King and the public, as well as to my own particular service, that I know not how to express it; but every day will teach me, by showing me the want I shall find of so true a friend. But I must have so much pity upon you as to say little on so sad a subject, conjuring you to believe that I am,

My Lord Duke of Ormond,

Your very affectionate friend,

Catherine, Regina

13

Mary Beatrice of Modena

(1658–1718), Queen Consort of James II

When queen consort, to the Pope, 1688

Mary Beatrice of Modena, the graceful Italian consort of the last of the Stuart kings – James II – was the daughter of Alphonso d'Este, Duke of Modena.

Inclined to emotional attachments, and of strong religious leanings, she had hoped to become a nun, but destiny – or perhaps more accurately, Mary Beatrice's mother, that stern disciplinarian, the Duchess of Modena – decreed otherwise. Protesting in vain, the fifteen-year-old Mary Beatrice was married to James as his second wife, when he was Duke of York and in his forties. He had previously married the Lady Anne Hyde, daughter of the 1st Earl of Clarendon, by whom he had two surviving children: Mary, who in due course was married to William, Prince of Orange, and Anne, who married Prince George of Denmark. Both in turn became queens-regnant of England.

Mary Beatrice primarily commands interest as the much maligned mother of James Stuart – known later as 'The Old Pretender', whose legitimacy was the subject of so much strife and contention at the time, but today is accepted by all leading historians for a fact. Prior to the boy's birth, Mary Beatrice of Modena had had four children by James II, the legitimacy of at least one of which had been called into question. None of these children had survived long, however, and, some years having elapsed since the death of the last infant in 1681, the birth in 1688 of a son – who would, of course, be brought up in the Roman Catholic faith – caused the Protestant faction in England to start a whispering campaign. It was fast rumoured abroad that he was not a child of the queen consort, but had been smuggled into the palace in a warming pan, a scandal which Anne did much to foster.

On the birth of the Prince of Wales, the queen consort was much gratified to receive a letter from the Pope in which he assured her that the great blessing had been conferred upon her owing to his fervent prayers and supplications on her behalf. Mary Beatrice was so polite and tactful as meekly to accept his assertion, as appears from the following answer she made to the head of her Church.

As great as my joy has been for the much-sighed-for birth of a son, it is signally increased by the benign part which your Holiness has taken in it, shown to me with such tender marks of affection in your much prized brief, which has rejoiced me more than aught beside, seeing that he is the fruit of those pious vows and prayers which have obtained from Heaven this unexpected blessing; whence there springs within me a well-founded hope, that the same fervent prayers of Your Holiness that have procured me this precious gift, will be still powerful to preserve him, to the glory of God and for the exaltation of His Holy Church. For this purpose, relying on the benignity of Your Holiness to grant the same to me, I prostrate myself, with my royal babe, at your holy feet, entreating that Your Holiness's apostolical benediction may be bestowed on both of us.

> Your most obedient daughter,
> Maria, R. [*sic*]
> At London, the 3rd of August, 1688.

To Mary, Princess of Orange, 1688

The libellous and far-spread rumours that broke out on the birth of the Prince of Wales were, if not mainly perpetrated, certainly ably sustained by Princess Anne. In her hatred of her stepmother, Mary Beatrice, she took infinite pains to encourage her sister Mary, Princess of Orange, in her suspicions that there was a plot afoot to deprive the sisters of their rights in the succession by the imposition of a pretended heir to the throne. In fact, the title of 'Pretender' is said to have been coined by Anne herself.

In the early days, being of similar age, Mary Beatrice and James II's eldest daughter had been intimate friends. Owing to her temperament and blood, the affections of Mary Beatrice were of an ardent character, and she was naturally greatly upset when she realised that Mary showed no interest in her stepbrother's birth and only mentioned him with reluctance. Finally, Mary Beatrice felt forced to make gentle remonstrance at the attitude of her one-time friend.

In answer to the following note from the queen, the Princess of Orange tersely and cryptically replied, 'All the king's children shall ever find as much affection and kindness from me as can be expected from children of the same father.' This answer could have done little to reassure Mary Beatrice, and shows how well Princess Anne was succeeding in poisoning her sister's mind against the queen consort.

Windsor, August 17.

Even in this last letter, by the way you speak of my son, and the informal name you call him by, I am confirmed in the thoughts I had before, that you have for him the last indifference. The King has often told me, with a great deal of trouble, that as often as he has mentioned his son in his letters to you, you never once answered anything concerning him.

To Mary, Princess of Orange, 1688

James II's attempt to overthrow the Protestant Church resulted in the leaders of the Protestant faction in England turning hopefully to William of Orange to come to the rescue of the country.

For some time; even after the birth of the Prince of Wales, Princess Mary had maintained a friendly relationship with her father, whatever her private views may have been as to his son's legitimacy. It seems evident, however, from the following letter that the queen consort was entertaining some doubts as to the nature of the Princess of Orange's attitude to the king, who, although far from an ideal parent, admired and loved his elder daughter.

> I am much troubled what to say, at a time when nothing is talked of but the Prince of Orange coming over with an army; this has been said for a long time, and believed by a great many, but I do protest to you that I never did believe till now, very lately, that I have no possibility of doubting it. The second part of the news I will never believe, which is, that you are to come over with him, for I know you to be too good. I do not believe you could have such a thought against the worst of fathers, much less to perform it against the best, who has always been so kind to you, and I do believe, has loved you better than any of his children.

To Louis XIV of France, 1688

James II was quickly to learn that in his determined efforts to re-establish Roman Catholicism in England he had played hopelessly into the hands of his enemies, and had to face the prospect of the usurpation of his throne as a consequence.

The landing of the Prince of Orange plunged the king into despair, which was almost paralytic. He soon found himself deserted by his generals – including his own son-in-law, Prince George of Denmark, and Lord Churchill, who went over to the triumphant invader. In his dire distress James II's one thought was for the safety of his son and his consort.

Mary Beatrice was persuaded to abscond to France, with her six-month-old baby, and it was while a fugitive in Calais that she wrote a pathetic appeal for protection to her old friend and her husband's cousin, Louis XIV. As a result, she and James II, who after many trials had escaped from England to join her, were permitted to set up court at St Germains. There whole families – not only Catholics – went into exile with them rather than own allegiance to William and Mary.

The agitation and confusion of mind in which she wrote to the French king is clearly evidenced in Mary Beatrice's letter, which commences in the third person to describe her desolate state, and concludes, in somewhat obscure terms, in the first person.

Sire,

A poor fugitive Queen, bathed in tears, has exposed herself to the utmost perils of the sea in her distress, to seek for consolation and an asylum from the greatest monarch in the world. Her evil fortune procures her a happiness of which the greatest nations in the world are ambitious. Her need of it diminishes not that feeling, since she makes it her choice, and it is as a mark of the greatness of her esteem that she wishes to confide to him that which is the most precious to her, the person of the Prince of Wales, her son. He is as yet too young to unite with her in the grateful acknowledgments that fill her heart. I feel, with peculiar pleasure, in the midst of my griefs, that I am now under your protection.

In great affliction, I am, sir,
Your very affectionate servant and sister,
The Queen of England

In exile, to Angelique Priolo, Abbess of Chaillot Convent, 1692

James II's plan to recover his kingdom by counter invasion met with signal failure, and in due course the exiled king was to witness the utter defeat of his fleet at La Hogue and the consequent annihilation of all his high hopes.

Back at St Germains Mary Beatrice was hourly expecting another child, and sent anxious messages to her husband, imploring him to return. In addition to her personal fears as to her confinement, there was the anxiety that the king's inexplicable absence from her side at such a time would offer confirmation of the imputations that had been made regarding the birth of their son. Nothing, however, could rouse James II from the mental and physical stupor into which he had temporarily fallen.

Unable to understand her husband's conduct, Mary Beatrice poured out her agitation of mind to her great friend Angelique Priolo, abbess of the convent at Chaillot, where the exiled queen spent so much of her spare time. To this same retreat her mother-in-law, Henrietta Maria, had often fled in bygone days.

June 14th, 1692

What shall I say to you, my beloved mother, or rather, what would not you say to me, if we could be one little quarter of an hour in each other's arms? I believe, however, that time would be entirely passed in tears and sighs, and that my eyes and my sobs would tell much more than my mouth; for, in truth, what is there after all that can be said by friendship in the state in which I am? ... Oh, but the ways of God are far from our ways, and His thoughts are different from our thoughts. We perceive this clearly in our last calamity,[1] and by the unforseen and almost supernatural mischances by which God has overthrown all our designs, and has appeared to declare Himself so clearly against us for our overwhelming ...

What then can we say to this, my beloved mother? Or rather, is it not better that we should say nothing; but, shutting the mouth, and bowing the head, to adore and to approve, *if we can*, all that God does, for He is the Master of the universe, and it is very meet and right that all should be submitted to Him. It is the Lord; He has done what was good in *His* eyes.

This, my dearest mother, is what I wish to say and do; and to this I believe you have yourself encouraged me by your words, as you do by your letters, which are always so precious to me; but I say it, and I do it with so bad a grace, and so much against my will, that I have no reason to hope that it can be agreeable to God. Aid me to do it better by your prayers, and encourage me constantly by your letters, till we have the happiness of embracing each other again.

I suffered much, both in body and mind, some days ago, but now I am better in both. I linger on still, in continued expectation of the hour of my accouchement. It will come when God wills it. I tremble with the dread of it; but I wish much that it were over, so that I might cease to harass myself and everyone else any longer with this suspense.

When I began this letter yesterday, I was in uncertainty what the King would do, and of the time when I might have the happiness of seeing him; for he has not yet chosen to retire from La Hogue, though he has nothing to keep him there, and the state In which I am speaks for itself to make him come to me. In the meantime, he would not resolve on anything; but he will find all well done, although it has cost me much to have it so without his orders, which my lord Melfort[2] came to bring us this morning. It seems that, for the present, the King has nothing to do but return hither, till they can take other measures ...

Behold, my dear mother, a little statement of what has passed, and is passing in my poor heart; you know and can comprehend It better than I do myself. I pray you to embrace all our dear Sisters, and to take leave of them for me before my lying-in, not knowing what may occur ...[3]

To Princess Anne, 1701

On the death in 1701 of the dethroned king, Mary Beatrice had the unpleasant task of passing on a message he had left for his daughter, Princess Anne, whose attitude and aspersions regarding the young prince had caused James II and Mary Beatrice so much distress.[4]

In the circumstances, the letter is restrained and dignified. While not stooping to reproaches, the widowed consort clearly indicates that Princess Anne stands in need of forgiveness for the wrong she has done to her own father. The letter had no effect however, except perhaps to increase Princess Anne's hatred of her stepbrother who dares to suggest that Anne is in need of Mary Beatrice's prayers.

> I think myself indispensably obliged to defer no longer the acquainting you with a message, which the best of men as well as the best of fathers, has left with me for you. Some few days before his death he bid me find means to let you know that he forgave you from the bottom of his heart, and prayed God to do so too; that he gave you his last blessing, and prayed to God to convert your heart, and confirm you in the resolution of repairing to his son the wrongs done to himself; to which I shall only add, that I join my prayers to his herein, with all my heart, and that I shall make it my business to inspire into the young man who is left to my care the sentiments of his father, for better no man can have.
>
> Sept. 27.

To Angelique Priolo, Abbess of Chaillot Convent, 1712

The death of her daughter, Princess Louisa, from smallpox at the age of twenty dealt a disastrous blow not only to Mary Beatrice, but to the cause of the House of Stuart, of which

Princess Louisa was heiress-presumptive. With no shadow over her birth, much more would have been ventured by the Jacobites for her sake than for her brother. Regret for the loss of the young princess, and general sympathy for her bereaved mother, were even felt and expressed by persons in the court of Queen Anne, who had ever been enemies of Princess Louisa's family, and also, it is said, by Anne herself.

In her grief Mary Beatrice turned once again to her old friend, Angelique Priolo. Bitter as was her loss, she shows unfailing courage and resignation, ever sustained by her faith.

May 19th.

But what shall I say to you, my dear mother, of that beloved daughter whom God gave me, and hath now taken away? Nothing beyond this, that, since it is He who hath done it, it becomes me to be silent, and not to open my mouth unless to bless His holy Name. He is the Master, both of the mother and the children; He has taken the one, and left the other,[5] and I ought not to doubt that He has done the best for both, and for me also, if I knew how to profit by it. Behold the point, for, alas! I neither do as I say, nor as God requires of me, in regard to His dealings with me. Entreat of Him, my dear mother, to give me grace to enable me to begin to do it. I cannot thank you sufficiently for your prayers, both for the living and for the dead. I believe the latter are in a state to acknowledge them before God, for in the disposition He put into my dear girl at the commencement of her malady to prepare herself for death, I have every reason to hope that she enjoys, or soon will enjoy, His blessedness with our sainted King; and that they will obtain for me His Grace, that so I may prepare to join them when, and where, and how it shall please the Master of all things in His love to appoint …

I shall never forget, in all my life, the services which Marie Henrietta[6] has rendered to my dear daughter, nor the good that she has done her soul, although the whole of our dear community have contributed to that which would oblige me, if it were possible, to redouble my friendship for them all ... M. R.

To Angelique Priolo, Abbess of Chaillot Convent, *c.* 1717

Never did any queen of England in the reigns under review die so poor in worldly goods as Mary Beatrice of Modena, but she was rich in her faith in providence, as the following excerpt from an undated letter to Angelique Priolo makes evident. It was written when the cause of her son, as rightful heir to the throne, was regarded, even by herself, as hopeless.

After thirty years in exile Mary Beatrice died in 1718, at the age of sixty, from an incurable complaint which she had endured for many years. She was buried at Chaillot, in the habit of the nuns of the monastery, in which community, had her early ambition been realised, she would have taken the veil. Arrangements were made for her body to be transported to England should the Stuart cause eventually prevail, but the queen had decreed that her heart and part of her entrails should rest in perpetuity with the nuns of the convent at Chaillot.

... Truth to tell, there remains to us at present neither hope nor human resource from which we can derive comfort of any kind whatsoever; so that, according to the world, our condition may be pronounced desperate, but, according to God, we ought to believe ourselves happy, and bless and praise Him for having driven us to the wholesome necessity of putting our whole trust in Him alone so that we might be able to say, *Et nuncque est expectatio mea! Nonni, Dominus!*[7] Oh, blessed reliance! Oh, resource infallible!

14

Mary II

(1662–1694)

When Princess of Orange, to Sarah, Lady Churchill, 1686

James II, when Duke of York, had made a love match with the Lady Anne Hyde, a maid-of-honour and daughter of the Lord Chancellor, Clarendon. Her father had wished Mary – his beloved firstborn daughter – to make a love match as he had done himself, but by authorisation of her uncle, Charles II, she was married to her stolid cousin William, Prince of Orange,[1] 'The Dutch Monster', as he was dubbed by the ladies of the English court, who objected to his bearing and behaviour. The marriage did not at first promise much domestic happiness because it had been brought about chiefly by political considerations.

In his *History of England from the Reign of James the Second* Macaulay writes that it did not seem likely 'that any strong affection would grow up between a handsome girl of sixteen, well disposed indeed, and naturally intelligent, but ignorant and simple, and, a bridegroom who, though he had not completed his twenty-eighth year, was in constitution older than her father, whose manner was chilling, and whose head was constantly occupied by public business or by field sports. For a time he was a negligent husband. He was indeed drawn away from his wife by other women, particularly by one of her ladies, Elizabeth Villiers, who, though destitute of personal attractions, and disfigured by a hideous squint, possessed talents which well fitted her to partake of his cares. He was indeed ashamed of his errors, and spared no pains to conceal them; but, in spite of all his precautions, Mary well knew that he was not strictly faithful to her.'

Mary bore these wrongs, however, with such patience that she gained William's esteem and gratitude, and her generous affection and love, disclosed in so many of the letters she wrote to her husband, eventually won his heart.

Apart from the domestic and personal angle, William III had probably the most statesmanlike brain of any man of his day, and this Mary could not have failed to recognise and respect.

As certain of the correspondence between Mary and her sister Anne is concerned with Sarah, Duchess of Marlborough, this is perhaps the best place to insert mention of that exceptional woman's powerful influence, not only on affairs of state but on the life and fate of Princess Anne, who had formed for her a strong and an uncontrollable affection.

Sarah Jennings, born in 1660, self-reputed as the granddaughter of an impoverished baronet, was attached to the court of James II when he was Duke of York, and after her marriage to Colonel John Churchill, she and her husband served together at this court. Churchill was created a peer by Charles II in 1682, and the following year Princess Anne married Prince George of Denmark. At Anne's urgent request Sarah was appointed a lady of her household, and quickly secured the post of first lady of the princess's bedchamber.

The Princess of Orange had never liked her sister's avowed favourite, and had on occasion ventured to mention to Anne her distrust of Sarah's character, and her suspicion as to Lady Churchill's Protestant beliefs, if indeed she had any religious beliefs at all. Anne's strong protest, undoubtedly dictated by the favourite herself, caused Mary to try to retrieve her blunder, for she realised – or perhaps was made to realise – that there might be political repercussions should the Churchills not ally themselves to the Prince of Orange in schemes already afoot to depose her father.

Mary therefore wrote the following letter to Lady Churchill in an attempt to soothe the feelings of the woman whose spell over Anne was in time to cause an open breach between the royal sisters – a breach destined never to close.

> Loo, September 30th
>
> Dr Stanley's[2] going to England is too good an opportunity for me to lose of assuring Lady Churchill she cannot give me greater satisfaction than in letting me know the firm resolution both Lord Churchill and you have taken never to be wanting in what you owe to your religion. Such a generous resolution, I am sure, must make you deserve the esteem of all good people, and my sister's in particular. I need say nothing of mine: you have it upon a double account as my sister's friend, besides what I have said already, and you may be assured that I shall always be glad of an occasion to show it both to your lord and you.
>
> I have nothing more to add; for your friendship makes my sister as dear to you as to me, and I am persuaded we shall ever agree in our care of her, as I believe she and I should in our kindness for you, were we near enough to renew our acquaintance.
>
> Marie [*sic*]

To Lady Bellasyse, *c.* 1688

In furtherance of the plan to dethrone James II, Princess Mary, somewhat inexplicably, carried on a secret correspondence with the traitors in her father's court.

Under instruction, she learned to write with her left hand, so that had the king chanced on her letters, he would not have known they were written by his own daughter. Mary's instructor in this cunning art was Lady Bellasyse, for whom, after the death of their mother, the Duchess of York, when Mary and Anne were still small children, James had conceived an infatuation. A widow, whose husband had been killed in a drunken duel, was regarded as an even less suitable wife for the heir presumptive than had been the Lady Anne Hyde, and Charles II forced James to break off his engagement to Susanna Armine Bellasyse. However, when James succeeded to the throne, he arranged – as was the wont of incontinent monarchs, among whom James can be classed as a confirmed libertine – for Lady Bellasyse to be one of Mary of Modena's household.

The opportunity to revenge herself for a past injury, possibly more deeply seated than James suspected, was not to be missed by the jilted Susanna Armine. This spy in the queen consort's bedchamber, deftly writing with her malicious left hand herself, earnestly advised the king's daughter to imitate her example.

The following note from Princess Mary shows that she was obediently attempting to become an 'ambidextress'.

Hounslardyke, June 24.

I pity you very much now Mr. Fortrey[3] is at Ostend; but the comfortable peace will quickly send him home again to you. You might very well have expected a letter from me before now in answer to your letter of your left hand; but because I could not answer it in the same manner, I did resolve to stay till I was perfect in it; but though I am not yet, I would not stay longer, but send you word that I had done as you desired, as you shall always find me your very affectionate friend,

Marie [*sic*]

To her father, James III, 1688

There is no reason why Princess Mary should not have been persuaded in the prevailing belief at the time that Mary

Beatrice's son was not a legitimate offspring of her royal father, especially as she was so dependent on hearsay. It was obviously in the interests of the enemies of James II that this rumour should be believed, particularly by the Protestant Princess Mary herself, as the next in the line of succession.

As will have been gathered from Mary Beatrice's letter, James II had been much distressed at Princess Mary's studied indifference and coldness where the young Prince of Wales was concerned. It came to the king's knowledge that in her English chapel at the Hague prayers for the prince had sometimes been offered, but more often had been omitted. James II therefore wrote a letter of remonstrance, in which he asked his daughter, 'What offence had been given?

Macaulay aptly remarks that Mary's letters 'were so well expressed that they deserved to be well spelt'. This comment will be appreciated from the following letter to her father, and from the further example given, however, her correspondence discloses no small literary skill, despite at times her faulty orthography.

Sir,

Being to go to Loo next Thursday, if please God, I am come to this place[4] to go bake at night. Last Thursday I received Your Majesty's of the 31st July, by which I see that you had heard that the Prince of Wales was no more prayed for in my chapel: but long before this, you will know, that it had onely bin something forgot. M. d'Albeville can assure you I never told him it was forbid, so that they were only conjectures made upon its being something neglected: but he can tell, as I find Your Majesty already knows, that he[5] was prayed for heer long before it was done in England.

This excessive hot wether continues longer than I ever knew it, which I shall find sufficiently in my journey; I have nothing more to add at present, than only to beg Your majesty to believe, wherever I am, I shall still be Your Majesty's most obedient daughter and servant,

Marie [*sic*]

When queen regnant, to William III, 1690

In 1689, having succeeded in depriving James II of his throne, William and Mary became joint sovereigns of the kingdom. Resolutely refusing to rule by 'apron strings', William (who might be deemed to have forced himself upon the country as self-elected king) departed for Ireland, in his continued campaign against James II.

Left to participate alone in the sovereignty, Mary wrote daily to her husband on all occurrences, domestic and political.

The following letter is moving in its devotion and loyalty, exhibiting as it does a wife's concern for the wellbeing of her husband. At the same time one wonders what thoughts must have passed through Mary's mind in regard to her father's personal welfare as she penned this letter.

Whitehall, June 29, 1690

You will be weary of seeing every day a letter from me, it may be; yet being apt to flatter myself, I will hope you will be as willing to read as I to write. And indeed it is the only comfort I have in this world, besides that of trust in God. I have nothing to say to you at present that is worth writing, and I think it unreasonable to trouble you with my grief, which I must continue while you are absent, though I trust every post to hear some good news or other from you; therefore I shall make this very short, and only tell you I have got a swelled face, though not quite so bad yet, as it was in Holland five years ago. I believe it came by standing too much at the window, when I took the waters. I cannot enough thank God for your being so well past the dangers of the sea; I beseech Him in His mercy still to preserve you so, and send us once more a happy meeting upon earth. I long to hear again from you how the air of Ireland agrees with you, for I must own I am not without my fears for that, loving you so entirely as I do, and shall till death.

To William III, 1690

In her *Conduct* the Duchess of Marlborough expresses the view that Mary II 'wanted bowels'. This opinion is open to challenge. Had Mary permitted herself full rein she might have disclosed no small ability as queen regnant. There were times, however, when she seemed to handle her responsibilities at a level below her understanding and capacity. How much this was due to diffidence on her part, and how much to the regard she had for her husband, can only be a matter for surmise.

In the following instance, she had ordered a prayer to be said in all places of Church of England worship for the success of William III's campaign against her father in Ireland. Lord Feversham, chamberlain to the Catholic queen dowager, Catherine of Braganza, stopped the prayer being said at the Savoy chapel, where the Protestant members of the dowager queen's household worshipped, because it was under the jurisdiction of the dower-palace of Somerset House, Catherine of Braganza's province.

Queen Mary was intensely indignant at this considered grave offence, and wrongfully attributed the blame to the queen dowager, as will be seen from the letter she wrote at that time to her husband.

I was *extreme* angry, which the Privy Council saw, but I shall not trouble you with it. I told them, that I thought there was no more measures to be kept with the Queen-Dowager herself after this: that is, if it were her order, which no doubt it is. When Lord Nottingham[6] told him all I said, Feversham seemed much concerned, and desired to come and throw himself at my feet, and own all the matter as a very great fault in him, but done out of no ill design. To be short, he came yesterday to my bedchamber, at the hour when there was a great deal of company, (I mean just before dinner); he looked as pale as death and spoke in great disorder. He said 'that he must own it was a very great fault, since I took it so; but he begged me to believe that it was done not out of any ill intention, nor by agreement with anybody.' He assured me 'the Queen-Dowager knew nothing of it; that it was a fault, a folly, an indiscretion, or anything I would call it.' I told him 'that after doing a thing of that nature, the best way was not to go about excusing it, for *that* was impossible, since, to call it by the most gentle name I could give it, 'twas an unpardonable folly, which I did not expect after the protestations he had made.' Upon which he said an abundance of words: I doubt whether he himself knew what he meant by them. At last he spoke plain enough. He said 'God pardoned sinners when they repented, and so he hoped I would.' I told him, 'God saw hearts, and whether their repentance was sincere, which, since I could not do, he must not find it strange if I trusted only to actions' and so I left him. I pity the poor man for being obliged thus to take the Queen-Dowager's faults upon him, yet I could not bring myself to forgive him. I remember I did say more, 'that if it had been myself, I could have pardoned him; but when it immediately concerned your person, I would not, nor could not.'

The Queen-Dowager sent me a compliment yesterday on a swelled face. I do not know whether I have writ you word of it. Yesterday I had leeches set behind my ears, which has done but little good, so that it mends but slowly; and one of my eyes being again sore, I am fain to write this at so many times, that I fear you will make but ill sense of it. Queen-Dowager will come to-day to see me, but desired an hour when there was least company, so I imagine she will speak something of herself; and that which inclines me the more to this opinion is, that she has sent for Lord Halifax, and was shut up in her chamber about business with him and others the whole morning. I shall give you an account of this before I seal up my letter.

The Queen-Dowager has been, but did not stay a moment, or speak two words.

Since she went, I have been in the garden, and find my face pretty well; but it is now candle-light, therefore I dare say no more. I have still the same complaint to make that I have not time to cry, which would a little ease my heart, but I hope in God I shall have such news from you as will give me no reason; yet your absence is enough, but since It pleases God, I must have patience.

Do but continue to love me, and I can bear all things with ease.

To William III, 1690

The long-expected battle in Ireland having at last taken place, news of the victory over James II at Boyne Water caused Mary II to write the following emotional and congratulatory epistle to her husband. Her joy, however, is not so unrestrained that she fails to remember her father – to whom she refers as the 'late king' – towards the end of her letter. The knowledge that he was safe must have come as a great relief to the queen. Had ill befallen James II personally, both she and William III would have had to face the censure of their enemies, and had a fatality occurred, Mary personally could not have failed to suffer remorse.

Whitehall, July, 1690

How to begin this letter I don't know, or however to render to God thanks enough for His mercies, – indeed, they are too great if we look on our deserts; but, as you say, 'tis His own cause,' and since 'tis for the glory of His great name, we have no reason to fear but He will protect what He has begun. For myself in particular my heart is so full of joy and acknowledgment to that great God who has preserved you, and given you such a victory, that I am unable to explain it. I beseech Him to give me grace to be ever sensible as I ought, and that I and all may live suitable to such a mercy as this is ... I was yesterday out of my senses with trouble. I am now almost so with joy, so that I can't really as yet tell what I have to say to you by this bearer, who is impatient to return. I hope in God, by the afternoon, to be in a condition of sense enough to say much more, but for the present I am not.

When I writ the foregoing part of this, it was in the morning, soon after I had received yours, and 'tis now four in the afternoon; but I am not yet come to myself, and fear I shall lose this opportunity of writing all my mind, for I am still in such a confusion of thought that I scarce know what to say, but I hope in God you will more readily consent to what Lord President wrote last, for methinks you have nothing more for you to do. I will hasten Kensington as much as it's possible, and I will also get ready for you here, for I will hope you may come before that is done. I must put you in mind of one thing, believing it now the season; which is, that you would take care of the Church in Ireland. Every body agrees 't is the worst in Christendom. There are now bishoprics vacant, and other things; I beg you will take time to think who you will fill them with. You will forgive me that I trouble you with this now, but I hope you will take care of these things, which are of so great consequence as to religion, which I am sure will be more your care every day, now it has pleased God still to bless you with success.

I am very uneasy in one thing, which is, want of somebody to speak my mind freely to, for 't is a great restraint to think and be silent, and there is so much matter, that I am one of King Solomon's fools, who am ready to burst ...

This morning, when I heard the joyful news ... I was in pain to know what was become of the late King, but durst not ask but when Lord Nottingham came, I did venture to do it, and had the satisfaction to hear he was safe. I know I need not beg you to let him be taken care of, for I am confident you will for your own sake; yet add that to all your kindness, and, for my sake, let people know you would have no hurt come to his person. Forgive me this.

To William III, 1690

While the queen was ably striving to hold the reins of government, a menacing French fleet – in support of James II's cause and now threatening invasion – had appeared off the coast, and was riding victorious in the English and Irish Channels.

Mary was full of fears that William would be intercepted on his return journey from Ireland, as she indicates in the appended letter.

Incidentally, the property to which she refers consisted of private estates inherited by her father. Doubtless Mary guessed instinctively that her husband meant to present this property to Elizabeth Villiers, his mistress, who caused Mary bitter unhappiness throughout her married life. She voices the pious hope that William will convert the property to a 'virtuous' use. Her request, however, was unavailing, and the estates went to Elizabeth Villiers.

All my fears is [*sic*] the French ships, which are going to St George's Channel, and are already at Kinsale. If those should hinder you, what will become of me? I think the fright would take away my reason. But I hope the express, which goes this evening to Sir Cloudesley Shovel,[7] will come time enough to prevent any surprise. I am the most impatient creature in the world for an answer about your coming, which I do hope may be a good one, and that I shall see you, and endeavour myself to let you see, if it be possible, that my heart is more yours than my own.

I have been desired to beg you not to be too quick in parting with the confiscated estates, but consider whether you will not keep some for public schools, to instruct the poor Irish. For my part, I must needs say that I think you would do very well, if you would consider what care can be taken of the poor souls there; and, indeed, if you would give me leave, I must tell you

I think the wonderful deliverance and success you have had, should oblige you to think upon doing what you can for the advancement of true religion and promoting the Gospel.

To William III, 1690

Whether from personal preference for Mary II, as a native-born monarch, or with the object of creating open contention between the jointly reigning sovereigns from some motives of their own, a strong party had arisen in William III's absence eager to persuade Mary to acts of independent royalty.

She, however, through her deep attachment to her husband, combined, possibly, with no desire for regal preferment, resisted every temptation for her separate aggrandisement. In fact, the schemers might well have saved their energies for while such plans were rife, and very evident to the queen, she was writing in the following loving strain to her husband.

Whitehall, August, 1690

Last night I received your letter with so much joy, that it was seen by my face, by those who knew the secret of it, that you were coming. I will not take more of your time by endeavouring to tell you what is impossible to be expressed; but you know how much I love you, and therefore you will not doubt of my delight to think I shall soon see you. But I will not, at this time, tell you anything that can be writ by others.

One thing more I must desire to know positively, which is about Kensington, whether you will go there though my chamber is not ready. Your own apartment, Lord Portland's, Mr. Overkirk's, and Lady Derby's[8] are done; but mine impossible to be used, and nobody else's lodgings ready. The air there is now free from smoke, but your closet as yet smells of paint, for which I will ask pardon when I see you. This is the true state of your two houses, but if you will go only to lie at Kensington, for I suppose your business will keep you here[9] all day, pray let me know. You may be sure I shall be willing to suffer any inconvenience for the sake of your dear company, and I wish I could suffer it all; for I deserve it, being something in fault, though I have excuses which are not lies ... I hope this long letter may meet you so near, that you may bring your own answer. If not; if you love me, either write me a particular answer yourself, or let Lord Portland do it for you. You see the necessity of it for the public; do a little also for my private satisfaction, who love you much more than my own life.

To William III, 1690

Some measure of amusement may be derived from certain of Mary II's letters to her husband, particularly so in the case of the following epistle, which is devoted to the personal and private arrangements of the royal couple.

In this letter the queen exhibits herself as an overanxious housewife, making hurried preparations for her husband's unexpected return, and displaying homely worries over scaffoldings and sleeping accommodation.

As may, perhaps, be read between the lines, William had written a reproof to his loving wife on the subject of Kensington Palace not being ready for his reception, and she – in spite of the heavy pressure of duties of state – is full of 'a million of fears' in consequence.

Whitehall, August.

Last night I received yours ... I have been this evening at Kensington, for though I did believe you would not be willing to stay at Whitehall, yet what you write me word makes me in a million of fears, especially since I must needs confess my fault, that I have not been pressing enough till it was too late.

The outside of the house[10] is the fiddling work, which takes up more time than one can imagine; and while the schafolds are up, the windows must be boarded up. But as soon as that is done, your own appartments may be furnished; and though mine cannot possibly be ready yet awhile, I have found out a way, if you please, which is, that I may make use of Lord Portland's, and he ly in some other rooms; we[11] may ly in your chamber, and I go throw the Council-Room down, or els dress me there. And as I suppose your business will bring you often to town, so I must take such time to see company here; and that part of the family[12] which can't come there must stay here for 'tis no matter what inconveniencys any els suffers for your dear sake. I think this way the only one yourself will have will be my lying in your chamber, which you know I can make as easy to you as may be. I hope this letter will not come to your hands, but that you will be on your way hither before this. My greatest fear is for your closets here; but if you consider how much sooner you come back than any one durst have hoped, you will forgive me, and I can't but be extreme glad to be so deceived. God in His mercy send us a happy meeting, and a quick one, for which I am more impatient than I can possibly express.

To William III, 1690

Mary's standard of literary skill is evidenced to the full in the following letter which she wrote to her sole confidant, her husband, still delayed in Ireland. In its simplicity and sincerity it would be difficult for any professional pen to equal this royal one in expressing the emotions of an overwrought mind and heart.

Mary had no intimate friends. She was weighed down with affairs of state. In her loneliness and troubled condition, she pours out her grief to her absent consort.

Sadly enough, only a few years later, at the early age of thirty-two, Mary II was to sit throughout one tragic night, alone except for the companionship of awaiting death, destroying

– to posterity's loss – all papers and documents that might throw any light of certainty on her personal history. Only her letters provide a slight clue of all that she chose to bury from curious and prying eyes.

Whitehall, September.

... I never do anything now without thinking, it may be, you are in the greatest dangers, and yet I must see company upon my set days. I must play twice a-week – nay, I must laugh and talk, though never so much against my will. I believe I dissemble very ill to those who know me, – at least, 'tis a good constraint to myself, yet I must endure it. All my motions are so watched, and all I do so observed, that if I eat less, or speak less, or look more grave, all is lost in the opinion of the world. So that I have this misery added to that of your absence and my fears for your dear person, that I must grin when my heart is ready to break, and talk when it is so oppressed I can scarce breathe. I don't know what I should do, were it not for the Grace of God, which supports me. I am sure I have great reason to praise the Lord while I live, for His great mercy that I don't sink under this affliction, nay, that I keep my health, for I can neither sleep nor eat. I go to Kensington as often as I can for air, but then I can never be quite alone; neither can I complain, – that would be some ease; but I have nobody whose humour and circumstances agree with mine enough to speak my mind freely. Besides, I must hear of business, which, being a thing I am so new in, and so unfit for, does but break my brains the more, and not ease my heart. I see I have insensibly made my letter too long upon my own self, but I am confident you love enough to bear it for once. I don't remember I have been guilty of the like fault before, since you went, and that is now three months; for which time of almost perpetual fear and trouble this is but a short account, and so I hope may pass.

'Tis some ease to me to write my pain, and 't is some satisfaction to believe you will pity me. It will be yet more when I hear it from yourself in a letter, as I am sure you must, if it be but out of common good-nature; how much more, then, out of kindness, if you love me as well as you make me believe, and as I endeavour to deserve a little by that sincere and lasting kindness I have for you. But, by making excuses, I do but take up more of your time, and therefore I must tell you that this morning Lord Marlborough went away. As little reason as I have to care for his wife, yet I must pity her condition, having lain-in but eight days; and I have great compassion for wives, when their husbands go to fight.

I have almost forgot to tell you, that in the *Utrecht Courant* they have printed a letter of yours to the States of Holland, in which you promise to be soon with them. I can't tell you how many ill hours I have had about that, in the midst of my joy when I thought you were coming home, for it troubled me to think you would go over and fight again there.

To her sister, Princess Anne, 1692

Mary II's distrust of Sarah Churchill (now Lady Marlborough, an honour conferred by William III on her husband for his treacherous desertion of James II) culminated in the queen demanding that Princess Anne should dismiss her confidante from her household. Mary was forced to this decision, not only on account of Lady Marlborough's subversive influence over her sister, but because the Marlborough's had become unmasked enemies, and were now intriguing with the Jacobites for the return of James II.

Moreover, William and Mary were aware that, abetted by the Marlboroughs, Anne had already written to her father asking for his forgiveness. As a result of this knowledge, Lord Marlborough had received a curt message from William III to the effect that he had no further use for his services, and commanding Marlborough to sell or dispose of all his employments under the Crown. Further, he must forthwith absent himself from the presence of the king and queen.

The none-too-popular William dared not openly accuse the Marlboroughs of influencing Princess Anne in a reconciliation with the exiled king, for such a course might, he knew, have led to a third of his subjects following Anne's example.

Yet, despite the disgrace that had befallen her husband, Lady Marlborough had been bold enough, a few days later, to accompany Princess Anne to a court reception.

In view of the circumstances, the queen's letter – although somewhat long-winded – seems far from unreasonable.

> Kensington,
> February 5th

Having something to say to you, which I know will not be very pleasing, I choose rather to write it first, being unwilling to surprise you; though I think what I am going to tell you should not, if you give yourself the time to think that never anybody was suffered to live at Court in my lord Marlborough's circumstances. I need not repeat the cause he has given the King to do what he has done, nor his unwillingness at all times to come to such extremities, though people do deserve it.

I hope you do me the justice to believe it is as much against my will that I now tell you that after this it is very unfit Lady Marlborough should stay with you, since that gives her husband so just a pretence of being where he ought not.

I think I might have expected you should have spoke to me of it. And the King and I both believing it, made us stay thus long. But seeing you was so far from it, that you brought Lady Marlborough hither last night, makes us resolve to put it off no longer, but tell you she must not stay, and that I have all the reason imaginable to look upon your bringing her as the strangest thing that ever was done. Nor could all my kindness for you, which is ever ready to turn all you do the best way at any other time, have hindered me showing you that moment, but I considered your condition,[13] and that made me master myself so far as not to take notice of it then.

But now I must tell you, it was very unkind in a sister, would have been very uncivil in an equal, and I need not say I have more to claim, which though my kindness would make me never exact, yet when I see the use you would make of it, I must tell you I know what is due to me and expect to have it from you. 'Tis upon that account I tell you plainly Lady Marlborough must not continue with you in the circumstances her lord is.

I know this will be uneasy to you, and I am sorry for it; and it is very much so to me to say all this to you, for I have all the real kindness imaginable for you, and as I ever have, so will always do my part to live with you as sisters ought. That is, not only like so near relations but like friends. And as such I did think to write to you. For I would have made myself believe your kindness for her made you at first forget that you should have for the King and me, and resolved to put you in mind of it myself, neither of us being willing to come to harsher ways ...

But the sight of Lady Marlborough having changed my thoughts does naturally alter my style. And since by that I see how little you seem to consider what even in common civility you owe us, I have told it you plainly, but withal assure you that let me have never so much reason to take anything ill of you, my kindness is so great that I can pass most things and live with you as becomes me. And I desire to do so merely from that motive. For I do love you as my sister, and nothing but yourself can make me do otherwise. And that is the reason I choose to write this, rather than tell it you, that you may overcome your first thoughts; and when you have well considered, you will find that although the thing be hard, which I again assure you I am sorry for, yet it is not unreasonable, but what has ever been practised, and what you yourself would do were you in my place.

I will end this with once more desiring you to consider the matter impartially and take time for it. I do not desire an answer presently, because I would not have you give a rash one. I shall come to your drawing room to-morrow before you play, because you know why I cannot make one.[14] At some time we shall reason the business calmly, which I will willingly do. Or anything else that may show it shall never be my fault if we do not live kindly together. Nor will I ever be other by choice, but your truly loving and affectionate sister.

M. R.

To Princess Anne, 1692

In reply to Anne's protest that she should not be expected to endure the 'mortification and misery' of dismissing Lady Marlborough, Mary, in the letter that follows, makes it clear that only by obedient response to her command can Anne prove her goodwill towards the queen. Princess Anne, however, stubbornly refused to part with her first lady and, rightly anticipating that Mary would debar her from court for as long as Lady Marlborough remained one of the princess's household, salved her conscience by spreading abroad the rumour that she had made all possible advances to the queen. The bad feeling, long festering, which Lady Marlborough had created between the two royal sisters now came to a head, and was never dispelled.

Within a short period of time Mary II was afflicted with smallpox. The blow was so severe to her husband that he was carried away in fits from her deathbed, for over the years a strong friendship and entire confidence had been established between himself and Mary. On his own death it was found that he wore on a piece of black ribbon next to his skin a gold ring and a lock of his wife's hair.

After a troubled reign, this self-isolated queen regnant – childless, and at enmity with all her relations – died on 28 December 1694, 'between night and morning'. All her life she might be said to have lived in a psychological twilight, and in the half-light she was destined to die. For six years Mary had virtually ruled the country alone, and with her passed away perhaps the most able, but certainly the most admirable, of the Stuart monarchs. She was buried in Westminster Abbey.

I have received yours by the Bishop of Worcester, and have little to say to it, since you cannot but know that as I never use compliments, so now they cannot serve. 'Tis none of my fault that we live at this distance, and I have endeavoured to show my willingness to do otherwise; and I will do no more. Don't give yourself unnecessary trouble,[15] for be assured 't is riot words can make us live together as we ought.

You know what I required of you; and now I tell you, if you doubted it before, that I cannot change my mind, but expect to be complied with, or you must not wonder that I doubt of your kindness. You can give me no other marks that will satisfy me, nor can I put any other construction upon your actions than what all the world must do that sees them.

These things do not hinder me from being very glad to hear that you are well, and wishing that you may continue so, and that you may yet, while it is in your power, oblige me to be your affectionate sister,

Marie, R. [*sic*]

15

Anne

(1665–1714)

When Princess Anne of Denmark, to her sister, Mary, Princess of Orange, 1686

William III reigned alone for eight years after Mary II's death, and was succeeded by Princess Anne in 1702. She had married the kind, self-indulgent and lazy Prince George of Denmark, when she was the Lady Anne Hyde, on St Anne's Day, 1683. Unlike the private wedding in her own bedchamber of her wretched sister Mary, Anne's marriage took place at ten o'clock at night, with public ceremonials, at St James's Chapel.

George of Denmark, having no particular interest in, or pecuniary benefits from, his own country, was more than content to take up residence with Anne at the English court. Thus Anne's married life started with advantages such as her sister never knew. She was not torn from her family and country. On the contrary, Charles II had presented her with The Cockpit,[1] an establishment adjoining Whitehall Palace, and, by an Act of Parliament, had settled on his niece the sum of £20,000 per annum, which sum was later increased to £50,000.

While Mary had been childless, Anne was more than fruitful, if unluckily so. She and her husband were almost yearly 'blessed' with offspring, but none of their children survived for any length of time. On one occasion, the unfortunate parents were to experience the loss of two of their children on the same day and within a few hours of each other.

A born gossip, and an indefatigable correspondent, many of the letters of this destined queen regnant expose all too clearly her limited mentality. In their lack of restraint and total absence of style, they would have horrified that scholarly mistress-of-the-pen, Elizabeth I. The fact was that Anne, unlike her sister, had never had any interest in learning or literature, and so grew up virtually illiterate. This lack of knowledge was to prove a stumbling block for her when she finally came to the throne. She was, however, most proficient at the card table, and excelled at other tables as a gourmand, becoming crippled with dropsy and gout before middle age. So infirm did she become that she had to be carried in an open-chair to her coronation, although she was only thirty-seven years old at the time.

From early days, but particularly from the time of her marriage, Anne came under the domination of Sarah, Lady Churchill. In truth, the attachment was so marked and uninhibited that scandal could not fail eventually to become busy with their names. The Duchess of Marlborough herself, in her *Conduct*, confesses to the 'unrestrained intimacy of friendship in which we for many years lived together,' and to enjoying 'so high a place in her [Anne's] favour as perhaps no person ever arrived at a higher with Queen or Princess'. Anne, for her part, constantly assures Sarah, 'I will live and die entirely yours.' Such an extravagant avowal, however, may have been little more than a maudlin expression of sentimentality on the part of an emotional woman.

At the same time, Anne's sister, Mary, undoubtedly had a strong hold over Anne's mind. It would appear that Mary and the duchess, who had no love for each other, exercised something of a 'pull devil, pull baker' influence over the easily swayed, yet stubborn, Anne.

In reply to Princess Mary's expressions of distrust of Anne's first lady, Anne sent the following indignant letter.

Unquestionably the hand guiding the princess's pen was the hand of Sarah Churchill.

> The Cockpit, March.
>
> ... Sorry people have taken such pains to give you so ill a character of [Lady] Churchill: I believe there is nobody in the world has better notions of religion than she has. It is true she is not so strict as some are, nor does not keep such a bustle with religion; which I confess I think is never the worse, for one sees so many saints mere devils, that if one be a good Christian, the less show one makes it is the better, in my opinion. Then, as for moral principles, 'tis impossible to have better; and without that, all the lifting up of hands and eyes, and going often to church, will prove a very lame devotion.
>
> One thing more I must say for her, which is that she has a true sense of the doctrine of our Church, and abhors all the principles of the Church of Rome; so as to this particular, I assure you she will never change.
>
> The same thing I will venture, now that I am on this subject, to say for her Lord; for though he is a very faithful servant to King James, and that the King is very kind to him, and, I believe, he will always obey the King in all things that are consistent with religion, yet rather than change that, I dare say, he will lose all his places that he has ...

To the Princess of Orange, 1687

The Princess Anne, busily engaged in her unworthy intrigues, exerted all her craft as a gossip writer to poison the mind of her sister against their father. However, she obviously feared the possibility of a personal meeting between Mary and James II. Had such an interview occurred, the fate of the unfortunate king might perhaps have been averted, as direct human contact without intermediary can dispel many abstract and false suspicions. From the following letter, it is clear that Anne was overanxious to prevent such meeting, so much so that she does not hesitate to draw the line against including homicidal tendencies among their much-maligned parent's shortcomings.

The reason that this treasonable letter was not burnt, as Anne requests, was probably due to the fact that William of Orange preserved his sister-in-law's letters as proof, if necessary, that the seeds of sedition against James II were planted in England, and did not originate in Holland.

The Cockpit, March 13th.

... You may remember I have once before ventured to tell you that I thought Lord Sunderland[2] a very ill man, and I am more confirmed every day in this opinion. Everybody knows how often this man turned backwards and forward in the late King's[3] time; and now, to complete all his virtues, he is working with all his might to bring in Popery. He is perpetually with the priests and stirs up the King to do things further than I believe he would of himself ...

This worthy Lord does not go publicly to Mass, but hears it privately at a priest's chamber, and never lets anybody be there but a servant of his. So that there is nobody but a priest can say they have seen him at Mass, for to be sure his servant will turn at any time as he does. Thus he thinks he carries his matters swimming, and hopes you will hear none of these things that he may always be as great as he is now.

His Lady,[4] too, is as extraordinary in her kind, for she is a flattering, dissembling, false woman; but she has so fawning and endearing a way that she will deceive anybody at first and it is not possible to find out all her ways in a little time. She cares not at what rate she lives, but never pays anybody. She will cheat, though it be for a little. Then she has had her gallants, though it may be not so many as some other ladies have; and with all these good qualities she is a constant Church woman; so that to outward appearance one would think her a saint, and to hear her talk you would think she was a very good Protestant; but she is as much one as the other, for it is certain that Lord does nothing without her.

There is one thing about yourself which I can't help giving my opinion in, which is, that if King James should desire you and the Prince of Orange to come over to make him a visit I think it would be better (if you can make any handsome excuse) not to do it; for though I dare swear the King could have no thought against either of you, yet since people can say one thing and do another, one cannot help being afraid. If either of you should come, I should be very glad to see you; but really, if you or the Prince should come I should be frightened out of my wits for fear any harm should happen to either of you.

Pray don't let anybody see this, nor don't speak of it; pray let me desire you not to take notice of what I have said to anybody except the Prince of Orange, for it is all treason that I have spoke ... Therefore as soon as you have read this, pray burn it; for I would not that anybody but the Prince of Orange and yourself should know what I have said.

When I have another opportunity it is possible that I may have more to say, but for this time having written so much already I hope you will forgive me for saying no more now, but that no tongue can ever express how much my heart is yours.

To the Princess of Orange, 1688

In the following letter to her sister, Princess Anne advances the theory that her stepmother, Mary Beatrice of Modena, is none too ingeniously 'padding' herself, in an attempt to deceive observers as to her professed pregnancy. In this duplicity the queen consort would appear to have had the approval of the Pope!

If the Roman Catholics would 'stick at nothing' to promote their own interests, is one being uncharitable to Anne in concluding from her letter that she had unwittingly tarred herself with the same brush?

The Cockpit, March 14.

I have now very little to say, however would not miss writing by this bearer by whom you told me I might say anything; and therefore knowing nothing else of any consequence I must tell you I can't help thinking Mansell's[5] wife's great belly is a little suspicious. It is true indeed she is very big, but she looks better than she ever did, which is not usual: for people when they are so far gone, for the most part look very ill. Besides, it is very odd that the Bath, that all the best doctors thought would do her a great deal of harm, should have had so very good effect so soon, as that she should prove with child from the first minute she and Mansell met, after her coming from thence.

Her being so positive it will be a son, and the principles of that religion being such that they will stick at nothing, be it never so wicked, if it will promote their interest, give some cause to fear that there may be foul play intended. I will do all I can to find it out, if it be so: and if I should make any discovery, you shall be sure to have an account of it ...

To the Princess of Orange, 1688

When it became certain that Mary Beatrice of Modena was pregnant, the tone of Anne's letters changed to open vindictiveness. Whether this was due to her fear of losing her chances of ascending the throne, or genuine dread of the continuance of Roman Catholicism and its protracted tyrannies, it is impossible to judge. One thing, however, is clear; in her revilings of her stepmother, Anne herself shows up in a poor light indeed.

It may be that her libellous pen, in her early days, owed some of its venom to the guidance of Lady Churchill. But in any event, slanderous thoughts seem to have flowed easily enough and imprinted themselves on her letters, without any specific outside agency being responsible.

In this respect the following letter speaks for itself.

> The Cockpit, March 20th.
>
> I hope you will instruct Bentley what you would have your friends do if any alteration should come, as it is to be feared there will, especially if Mansell has a son, which I conclude he will, there being so much reason to believe it is a false belly. For methinks, if it were not there having been so many stories and jests made about it, she should; to convince the world, make either me, or some of my friends feel her belly; but quite contrary, whenever one talks of her being with child she looks as if she were afraid one should touch her. And whenever I happen to be in the room as she has been undressing, she has always gone into the next room to put on her smock. These things give me so much just cause for suspicion that I believe when she is brought to bed, nobody will be convinced it is her child, except it prove a daughter. For my part, I declare I shall not, except I see the child and she parted ...

To the Princess of Orange, 1688

During this revealing correspondence with her sister, Anne was suddenly taken ill, to the alarm of her father. Unaware of the slanderous letters that were going over to Holland by almost every post, James II hurried to Anne's beside. In due course he took her to his palace at Richmond to recuperate.

Anne had developed an ever-increasing hatred of her stepmother after Mary Beatrice had become queen, although there is evidence that the queen consort showed great kindness to both her stepdaughters. At the same time, Anne was fostering a dislike, which she wished to instil into Princess Mary's mind, of Lady Sunderland, wife of the president of the council. Unknown to Anne, however, Lady Sunderland was a secret agent on behalf of William of Orange ...

It was while convalescing at Richmond that Anne wrote the following letter to Princess Mary, in which any sense of loyalty or gratitude is conspicuously absent.

Richmond, May 9.

The Queen, you must know, is of a very proud and haughty humour, and though she pretends to hate all form and ceremony, one sees that those who make their court that way are very well thought of. She declares, always, that she loves sincerity and hates flattery; but when the grossest flattery in the world is said to her face, she seems exceedingly well pleased with it. It really is enough to turn one's stomach to hear what things are said to her of that kind, and to see how mightily she is satisfied with it. All these things Lady Sunderland has in perfection, to make her court to her; she is now much oftener with the Queen than she used to be.

It is sad, and a very uneasy thing, to be forced to live civilly, and as it were freely, with a woman that everyone knows hates one, and does all she can to undo everybody; which she[6] certainly does.

One thing I must say of the Queen, which is, that she is the most hated in the world of all sorts of people; for everybody believes that she presses the King to be more violent than he would be himself, which is not unlikely, for she is a very great bigot in her way. All ladies of quality say she is so proud, that they don't care to come oftener than they needs must, just out of mere duty; and, indeed, she has not so great Court as she used to have. She pretends to have a great deal of kindness for me; but I doubt it is not real, for I never see proofs of it, but rather the contrary.

To the Princess of Orange, 1688

James II's consort gave birth to a son on 10 June 1688, to the consternation of Anne, who must have seen her chances as heir presumptive considerably reduced by the unwelcome advent of a brother. She had gone to Bath on the pretext of her own pregnancy, but one is left wondering if she had not deliberately planned to be absent from the birth chamber. In this way, not having seen, she need never believe.

Anne duly announced the event to the Princess of Orange on her return from Bath to The Cockpit. Her indecision between conscience and self-interest is clear in the following letter. The 'very comfortable thing' for everyone to believe, to which Anne refers, is that her father is imposing on himself, his family, and his country, a spurious Prince of Wales.

Judging from her letters at this time to Princess Mary, Anne obviously wishes to appear in a good light with her sister. This suggests that the latter was receiving Anne's reports with some caution.

The Cockpit, June 18.

My dear sister can't imagine the concern and vexation I have been in, that I should be so unfortunate to be out of town when the Queen was brought to bed, for I shall never now be satisfied whether the child be true or false. It may be it is our brother, but God only knows, for she never took care to satisfy the world, or give people any demonstration of it. It is wonderful, if she had really been with child, that nobody was suffered to feel [it] but Madam Mazarin[7] and Lady Sunderland, who are people that nobody will give credit to. If out of her pride she would not have let me touch her, methinks it would have been very natural for her sometimes, when she has been undressing, to have let Mrs Robarts,[8] as it were by chance, have seen her belly; but instead of endeavouring to give one any satisfaction, she has always been very shy both to her and to me. The great bustle that was made about her lying in at Windsor, and then resolving all of a sudden to go to St. James's, which is much the properest place to act such a cheat in; and Mr[s] Turine's lying in the bedchamber that night she fell in labour, and none of the family besides being removed from Whitehall, are things that give one great cause to be suspicious.

But that which to me seems the plainest thing in the world, is her being brought to bed two days after she heard of my coming to town,[9] and saying that the child was come at the full time, when everybody knows by her own reckoning, that she should have gone a month longer.

After all this, 't is possible it may be her child; but where one believes it, a thousand do not. For my part, except they do give very plain demonstrations, which is almost impossible now, I shall ever be of the number of unbelievers. I don't find that people are at all disheartened, but seem all of a mind, which is a very comfortable thing at such a time as this ...

To the Princess of Orange, 1688

The Princess of Orange, clearly indicating doubts as to Anne's being a reliable scribe in matters relating to the birth of Mary Beatrice of Modena's son, sent a list of categorical questions which she required answered.[10]

Anne's reply shows her at least as a conscientious investigator in procuring information of interest on the subject, even if defamatory to her father and stepmother. She mentions the queen's distress at so many being present in the birth chamber: in all, there were reputed to be sixty-seven people in attendance. Anne herself gave her sister the names of over forty-four male and female spectators, apart from 'pages of the back stairs and priests'.

The remark about being 'very ill at invention' must surely have been written by Anne with her tongue in her cheek. There is little in her private correspondence to indicate that she lacked a lively imagination.

The Cockpit, July 24.

I received yesterday yours of the 19th, by which I find that you are not satisfied with the account I have given you in my last letter; but I hope you will forgive me for being no more particular, when you consider that not being upon the place, all I could know must be from others; and having then been but a few days in town, I had not time to inquire so narrowly into things, as I have since; but, before I say any more, I can't help telling you I am very sorry you should think I would be negligent in letting you know things of any consequence. For though I am generally lazy, and it is true, indeed, when I write by post, for, the most part I make those letters very short, not daring to tell you any news by it, and being very ill at invention, yet I hope you will forgive my being lazy when I write such letters, since I have never missed any opportunity of giving you all the intelligence I am able; and pray be not so unjust to believe I can think the doing anything you can desire, any trouble; for, certainly, I would do a great deal more for you, if it lay in my power, than the answering your questions, which I shall now do exactly as you desire.

I never heard anybody say they felt the child stir; but I am told Lady Sunderland and Madam Mazarin say they felt it at the beginning. Mrs Dawson[11] tells me she has seen it stir but never felt it.

I never saw any milk; but Mrs Dawson says she has seen it upon her smock, and that it began to run at the same time it used to do of her other children.

For what they call restringing draughts, I saw her drink two of them; and I don't doubt but that she drank them frequently and publicly before going to the Bath. Dr Waldgrave was very earnest with Sir Charles Scarbrough[12] to be for her going thither; but he was so fierce against it, that there was another consultation of doctors called, Sir Charles Scarbrough, Dr Waldgrave, Wetherby, Brady, and Brown. After that there was only Sir Charles Scarbrough and Dr Waldgrave (and for the first I believe he knew but little), excepting once when she was to be let blood, and when she was to have gone to Windsor. Then some of the others were called in to give their opinions.

All I can say in this article is, that once in discourse, Mrs Bromley[13] told Mrs Robarts, one day Roger's daughter came into the room, when Mrs Mansell was putting off her clouts, and she was very angry at it, because she did not care to be seen when she was shifting.

She fell in labour about eight o'clock.

She sent for the King at that time, who had been up a quarter of an hour, having lain with her that night, and was then dressing.

As soon as the King came he sent for the Queen-Dowager and all the Council. After that, it was known all over St. James's.

Most of the other men, I suppose, that were there, was at the King's rising.

They came into the room presently after the Queen-Dowager came, which is about half-an-hour before she was brought to bed.

There was no screen. She was brought to bed in the bed she lay in all night, and in the great bedchamber, as she was of her last child.

The feet curtains of the bed were drawn, and the two sides were open. When she was in great pain, the King called in haste for my Lord Chancellor, who came up to the bedside to show he was there; upon which the rest of the Privy Councillors did the same thing. Then the Queen desired the King to hide her face with his head and periwig, which he did, for she said she could not be brought to bed and have so many men look on her; for all the Council stood close at the bed's feet, and Lord Chancellor upon the step.

As soon as the child was born, the midwife cut the navel-string because the after-burthen did not follow quickly; and then she gave it to Mrs Labaudie,[14] who, as she was going by the bedside [a]cross the step, to carry it into the little bedchamber, the King stopped her, and said to the Privy Councillors, that they were witnesses there was a child born, and bid them follow it into the next room, and see what it was, which they all did; for till after they came out again, it was not declared what it was; but the midwife had only given a sign that it was a son, which is what had been done before ...

Her labour never used to be so long.

I never heard what you say of the child's limbs. As for seeing it dressed or undressed, they avoid it as much as they can. By all I have seen and heard, sometimes they refuse almost everybody to see it; that is, when they say it is not well; and methinks there is always a mystery in it, for one does not know whether it be really sick, and they fear one should know it, or whether it is well, and they would have one think that it is sick, as the other children used to be. In short, it is not very clear anything they do; and for the servants, from the highest to the lowest, they are all Papists.

The Queen forbid Lady Powis[15] to bring the child to her before any company; but that, they say, she used to do to her other children. I dined there the other day, when it was said it had been very ill of a looseness, and it really looked so; yet when she came from prayers she went to dinner without seeing it, and after that played at comet, and did not go to it till she was put out of the pool.

I believe none of the bedchamber women have any credit with the Queen but Mrs Turine; but they say Mrs Bromley has an interest with the King.

I am going to Tunbridge; but if I was to stay here I could not watch the child, for it is to be at Richmond. Lady Churchill does not go with me at first, and as long as she stays here I am sure she will do all in her power to give you and I an account if anything happens that is worth knowing.

I have done my endeavour to inform myself of everything, for I have spoke with Mrs Dawson,[16] and asked her all the questions I could think of: for not being in the room when the Queen was brought to bed, one must enquire of somebody that was there; and I thought she could tell me as much as anybody, and would be less likely to speak of it; and I took all the care I could when I spoke to her, to do it in such a manner that I might know everything; and in case she should betray me, that the King and Queen might not be angry with me ...

All she says seems very clear; but one does not know what to think; for methinks it is wonderful if it is no cheat, that they never took no pains to convince me of it.

I hope I have answered your letter as fully as you desire; if there be anything else you would know, pray tell me by the first safe hand, and you shall always find me very diligent in obeying you, and showing by my actions how real and sincere my kindness is ...

To the Prince of Orange, 1688

Supported by the power-seeking Churchills, the invasion of England by William of Orange had been carefully fostered by Anne. In secret communication with William, she advised him of the intention of her husband, Prince George of Denmark, to desert James II, and join forces with the invading William.

It should be noted that the letter which follows was written by Anne eight days prior to the one she 'left about' at The Cockpit for Mary Beatrice of Modena to discover, or not, after Anne had made her well-planned flight – by way of a back staircase, oddly enough! – to ally herself with the revolutionary party.

This, and the succeeding letter, provide all the evidence necessary as to Anne's guileful bent at this stage of her history.

The Cockpit, Nov. 18.

Having on all occasions given you and my sister all imaginable assurances of the real friendship and kindness I have for you both, I hope it is not necessary for me to repeat anything of that kind; and on the subject you have now wrote to me, I shall not trouble you with many compliments, only, in short, to assure you that you have my wishes for your good success in this so just undertaking; and I hope the Prince[17] will soon be with you, to let you see his readiness to join with you, who, I am sure, will do you all the service that lies in his power. He went yesterday with the King towards Salisbury, intending to go from thence to you as soon as his friends thought proper. I am not yet certain if I shall continue here, or remove into the city. That shall depend upon the advice of my friends; but wherever I am I shall be ready to show you how much I am

Your humble servant,

Anne

To the queen consort, Mary Beatrice, 1688

Anne's character is all too patently exposed by her correspondence, in which she unwittingly displays the weaknesses of her disposition.

A letter ostensibly 'left' for Mary Beatrice – but which neither she nor the king apparently received – was published in the *Gazette* by the partisans of Anne, the day after her hurried flight from The Cockpit.

In the meantime rumour spread like a flame in the wind that the absconding princess had been made a prisoner by the queen consort. As a consequence, Mary Beatrice was rudely abused by her own household, and her life endangered by a threatening mob that gathered outside Whitehall Palace demanding the release of Princess Anne.

Appeasement only came with the publication of the letter which follows. If this is read in conjunction with the one Anne wrote over a week previously to William of Orange, no doubt will be cast on Anne's studied deceitfulness. Neither of these letters, however, is in Anne's usual phrasing, but even if Lady Churchill inspired them, which she denied, they were penned by Anne herself.

(Found at The Cockpit, Nov. 26, 1688)

Madam,

I beg your pardon if I am so deeply affected with the surprising news of the Prince's[18] being gone as not to be able to see you, but I leave this paper to express my humble duty to the King and yourself, and to let you know that I am gone to absent myself to avoid the King's displeasure, which I am not able to bear, either against the Prince or myself; and I shall stay at so great a distance, as not to return till I hear the happy news of a reconcilement. And as I am confident the Prince did not leave the King with any other design than to use all possible means for his preservation, so I hope you will do me the justice to believe that I am incapable of following him for any other end. Never was anyone in such an unhappy condition, so divided between duty to a father and a husband; and therefore I know not what I must do, but to follow one to preserve the other.

I see the general falling-off of the nobility and gentry, who avow to have no other end than to prevail with the King to secure their religion, which they saw so much in danger from the violent councils of the priests, who, to promote their own religion, did not care to what dangers they exposed the King. I am fully persuaded that the Prince of Orange designs the King's safety and preservation, and hope all things may be composed without blood-shed, by the calling of a Parliament.

God grant an happy end to these troubles, and that the King's[19] reign may be prosperous, and that I may shortly meet you in perfect peace and safety; till when, let me beg of you to continue the same favourable opinion that you have hitherto had of

Your most obedient daughter and servant,

Anne

To her father, James II, 1691

How greatly Princess Anne was influenced by the Marlboroughs in their hard pursuit of political power may be gathered from the letter which she was persuaded by them to write to her father, the exiled King James.

The discovery of their treachery resulted, as the reader will recall, in the Marlboroughs' total fall from grace with William and Mary.

Whatever friendly message Anne may have sent verbally by the bearer of her letter, Captain Davy Lloyd (one of James II's old sea-commanders), was more than likely never delivered to Mary Beatrice of Modena. That bluff and honest fellow held both Anne and Mary II in the greatest contempt for their treatment of their father, and at times never scrupled to express his feelings very strongly.

December 1691.

I have been very desirous of some safe opportunity to make you a sincere and humble offer of my duty and submission, and to beg that you will be assured that I am both truly concerned for the misfortune of your condition, and sensible, as I ought to be, of my own unhappiness. As to what you may think I have contributed to it, if wishes could recall what is past, I had long since redeemed my fault. I am sensible it would have been a great relief to me if I could have found means to have acquainted you earlier with my repentant thoughts, but I hope they may find the advantage of coming late – of being less suspected of insincerity than perhaps they would have been at any time before. It will be a great addition to the ease I propose to my mind by this plain confession, if I am so happy as to find that it brings any real satisfaction to yours, and that you are as indulgent and as easy to receive my humble submissions as I am to make them, in a free, disinterested acknowledgment of my fault, for no other end but to deserve and receive your pardon.

I have had a great mind to beg you to make one compliment for me; but fearing the expressions which would be properest for me to make use of might be, perhaps, the least convenient for a letter, I must content myself, at present, with hoping the bearer will make a compliment for me to the Queen.[20]

To her sister, Queen Mary II, 1692

As a result of the disgrace that had befallen the Marlboroughs in their insatiable ambitions, the dissension between Mary II and Princess Anne in regard to Lady Marlborough developed into open warfare between the two sisters which continued until Mary's death.

Anne's reply to Mary's letter shows her double-minded attitude, but does not disguise her fixed determination not to be severed from her much-loved Sarah.

The Cockpit, February 6, 1692.

Your Majesty was in the right to think your letter would be very surprising to me. For you must needs be sensible enough of the kindness I have for my Lady Marlborough to know that a command from you to part with her must be the greatest mortification in the world to me, and indeed of such a nature as I might well have hoped your kindness to me would have always prevented. And it would be extremely to her advantage if I could here repeat every word that ever she said to me of you in her whole life. I confess it is no small addition to my trouble to find the want of Your Majesty's kindness to me upon this occasion, since I am sure I have always endeavoured to deserve it by all the actions of my life.

Your care of my present condition[21] is extremely obliging. And if you would be pleased to add to it so far as upon my account to recall your severe command (as I must beg leave to call it so in a matter so tender to me and so little reasonable, as I think, to be imposed upon me, that you would scarce require it from the meanest of your subjects) I should ever acknowledge it as an agreeable mark of your kindness to me. And I must freely own that as I think this proceeding can be for no other intent than to give me a very sensible mortification, so there is no misery that I cannot readily resolve to suffer rather than the thoughts of parting with her. If after all this that I have said, I must still find myself so unhappy as to be farther pressed in this matter, yet Your Majesty may be assured that as my past actions have given the greatest testimony of my respect both for the King and you, so it shall always be my endeavour, wherever I am, to preserve it carefully for the time to come, as becomes

Your Majesty's very affectionate sister and servant.

To Queen Mary II, 1692

The only answer received from Mary II in reply to the foregoing letter from Princess Anne was a message delivered by the lord chamberlain, forbidding Lady Marlborough's presence any longer at The Cockpit.

As a final gesture of defiance, Anne immediately decided to burn her boats where her sister was concerned, and leave The Cockpit – all too aptly named! – rather than remain there without Lady Marlborough at her side. She shortly removed herself to Sion House.[22]

Mary II retorted by ordering the court not to pay her sister the royal respects to which the princess had been entitled, removed Anne's guards, and let it be publicly known that Princess Anne was under the queen's displeasure.

In the following letter Anne is 'warning' Mary of her intentions.

From The Cockpit,
February 6th.

I am very sorry to find that all I have said myself, and my Lord Rochester[23] for me, has not had effect enough to keep Your Majesty from persisting in a resolution, which you are satisfied must be so great a mortification to me, as, to avoid it, I shall be obliged to retire and deprive myself of the satisfaction of living where I might have frequent opportunities of assuring you of that duty and respect, which I always have been and shall be desirous to pay you upon all occasions.

My only consolation in this extremity is that, not having done anything in all my life to deserve your unkindness, I hope I shall not be long under the necessity of absenting myself from you, the thought of which is so uneasy to me, that I find myself too much indisposed to give Your Majesty any further trouble at this time.

To the Lady Marlborough, 1692

Anne's unbalanced devotion to her arrogant high favourite caused her often to write to that lady three or four times a day. This fact she was in later years to regret, as Lady Marlborough retained chest-loads of Anne's tender and indiscreet epistles which, when she fell out of favour with Queen Anne, she threatened to publish.

In the following letter Princess Anne sympathises with her beloved intimate in the loss of Lady Marlborough's eldest son. She then goes on to expose her plan to make it as public as possible that Mary II had refused to see her, despite the fact that

Anne well knew that the only reason for Mary's attitude was Anne's obstinate refusal to dismiss her 'Dear Mrs Freeman'.

In the early days of their intimacy Anne – who had a passion for nicknames – had decided on the informal titles of 'Mrs Freeman' and 'Mrs Morley' for Sarah and herself respectively so that they could communicate as equals by affection.

May 22nd, Sion House.

I am very sensibly touched with the misfortune that my dear Mrs Freeman has in losing her son, knowing very well what it is to lose a child; but she knowing my heart so well, and how great a share I bear in all her concerns, I will not say any more on this subject, for fear of renewing her passion too much.

Being now at liberty to go where I please, by the Queen's refusing to see me, I am mightily inclined to go to-morrow, after dinner, to The Cockpit, and from thence, privately, in a chair to see you …

The Bishop[24] brought me the Queen's letter early this morning, and by that letter, he said he did not seem so well-satisfied with her as he was yesterday. He has promised to bear me witness that I have made all the advances that were reasonable: and, I confess, I think the more it is told about that I would have waited on the Queen, but that she refused seeing me, is the better; and therefore I will not scruple saying it to anybody when it comes in my way.

There were some in the family[25] as soon as the news came this morning of our fleet beating the French,[26] that advised the Prince[27] to go in the afternoon to compliment the Queen; and another[28] asked me 'if I would not send her one?' But we neither of us thought there was any necessity of it then, and much less since I received this arbitrary letter. I don't send you the original, for fear an accident may happen to the bearer, for I love to keep such letters by me for my justification. Sure never anybody was so used by a sister! But I thank God I have nothing to reproach myself withal in this business; but the more I think of all that has passed, the better I am satisfied. And if I had done otherwise, I should have deserved to have been the scorn of the world, and to be trampled upon as much as my enemies would Rave me.

Dear Mrs Freeman, farewell! I hope in Christ you will never think more of leaving me, for I would be sacrificed to do you the least service, and nothing but death can ever make me part with you. For, if it be possible, I am every day more and more yours.

To the Lady Marlborough, 1692

Whenever her wishes were crossed, or she desired to weaken Princess Anne's resistance, the tyrannical Sarah intimidated her loving mistress with the proposal that she should take her leave of her.

The following ranting and sentimental letter – only one of many – was written by the royal matron because the queen had now threatened to halve Princess Anne's income, much of which, Mary II suspected, was passing into the Marlborough coffers.

The letter is without date, but as there is some inference of Marlborough being in the Tower (where the queen had had him sent under the shadow of sedition), the lengthened absence of Lady Marlborough from Anne's presence was doubtless due to her being in attendance on her husband.

I really long to know how my dear Mrs Freeman got home; and now I have this opportunity of writing, she must give me leave to tell her, that if she should ever be so cruel as to leave her faithful Mrs Morley, she will rob her of all the joy and quiet of her life; for if that day should come, I could never enjoy a happy minute, and I swear to you I would shut myself up, and never see a creature.

You may see all this would have come upon me if you had not been, if you do but remember what the Queen said to me the night before your Lord was turned out of all, when she began to pick quarrels. And if they[29] should take off twenty or thirty thousand pounds [per annum], have I not lived on as little before? When I was first married we had but twenty (it is true, the King[30] was so kind as to pay my debts); and if it should come to that again, what retrenchment is there in my family[31] I would not willingly make, and be glad of that pretence to do it? Never fancy, dear Mrs Freeman, if what you fear should happen, that you are the occasion; no, I am very well satisfied, and so is the Prince,[32] too, it would have been so, for Caliban[33] is capable of doing nothing but injustice, therefore rest satisfied that you are no ways the cause. And let me beg once more, for God's sake, that you would never mention parting more – no, nor so much as think of it; and if you should ever leave me, be assured it would break your faithful Mrs Morley's heart.

P.S. I hope my dear Mrs Freeman will come as soon as she can this afternoon, that we may have as much time together as we can. I doubt you will think me very unreasonable, but I really long to see you again, as if I had not been so happy this month.

When queen regnant, to the Duchess of Marlborough, 1708

After the death of Mary II, which, in spite of the bad relationship between them, was a genuine shock to Princess Anne, she was to know the loss, a few years later, of her only surviving child, the Duke of Gloucester, at eleven years of age.

Anne and William III had for long entertained a strong aversion to each other, which the former attempted to break through when she knew that William was dying. He, however, flatly refused to see her on his deathbed. The king's death in 1702 could have been no sorrow to Anne, in consequence, especially as it brought her to the throne she coveted.

Anne's actions in earlier years, as an uneducated and a self-indulgent woman, are thrown into marked contrast by the undeniable improvement in her character when she took over the heavy responsibilities of a reigning sovereign: it was when she succeeded to the throne that a subtle change almost at once took place in her attitude towards Sarah – who had now become Duchess of Marlborough. Although Anne outwardly behaved towards her quondam favourite with the meekness of old, she was clever in disguising her deepest feelings, and it was some time before the Duchess realised, to her intense chagrin, that her power over Anne was on the wane.

While this change in their relationship was slowly taking place, Anne's genial and unassuming husband died, and Anne found herself very much alone. She was surrounded by intrigue and party strife, and although she had been bullied to her limits by her once-beloved Sarah, it was to her that she turned in her immediate sorrow.

The following pathetic note is the only record left by Queen Anne of her pain at the loss of her husband, to whom she had been married for twenty years.

> St. James's, October 28th, 1708.
>
> I scratched[34] twice at dear Mrs Freeman's door, as soon as Lord Treasurer went from me, in hopes to have spoke one more word to him before he was gone; but nobody hearing me, I wrote this, not caring to send what I had to say by word of mouth: which was, to desire him, that when he send his orders to Kensington, he would give directions that there may be a great many yeomen of the guards to carry the Prince's dear body, that it may not be let fall, the great stairs being very steep and slippery.

To the Duke of Marlborough, 1709

In the following sensible letter to the Duke of Marlborough it is clear that Anne has freed herself at last from the domination of 'Dear Mrs Freeman'.

Maybe the long and intense friendship had exhausted itself. On the other hand, the advent of a female rival, in the person of Abigail Hill, played no small part in alienating Anne's affections. In this connection the Duchess of Marlborough, in her *Conduct*, refers bitterly to Anne's loss of dignity towards the end of her reign, 'when a very brutal woman got into her favour.' The duchess must have been doubly incensed by this happening, because Abigail Hill was a poor relation of her own, whom she had introduced into the queen's household. All the same, in spite of the duchess's inferences, Abigail – known to history as Lady Masham – does not appear to have suffered from the lust for power, but to have exercised her influence over the queen with reasonable discretion.

As queen regnant, Anne did much permanent good, and little harm. She was genuinely concerned with the welfare of her subjects. When this queen – the last of the Stuart monarchs – died in 1714, there died with her, in the English people, that blind, unconditional homage to a sovereign which was destined never to be reinstated.

Queen Anne was buried in Westminster Abbey.

Windsor, October 25.

I saw very plainly your uneasiness at my refusing the mark of favour you desired,[35] and believed from another letter I had from you on that subject, you fancied that advice came from [Lady] Masham; but I do assure you, you wrong her most extremely, for upon my word she knows nothing of it, as I told you in another letter; what I said was my own thoughts, not thinking it for your service or mine to do a thing of that nature; however, if when you come home you still continue in the same mind I will comply with your desires.

You seem to be dissatisfied with my behaviour to the Duchess of Marlborough. I do not love complaining, but it is impossible to help saying on this occasion I believe nobody was ever So used by a friend as I have been by her ever since coming to the

Crown. I desire nothing but that she would leave off teasing
and tormenting me, and behave herself with the decency she
ought both to her friend and Queen, and this I hope you will
make her do.

By an Act of Settlement passed in 1701, the successors of
James II, and all other Catholic claimants, were excluded
from the throne of England. There being no issue of Mary II,
or surviving issue of Queen Anne, the Crown became thus
entailed on the Electress of Hanover, Sophia (twelfth child of
Elizabeth Stuart, Queen of Bohemia, daughter of James I), as
the nearest Protestant heir to the throne.

The electress, mother of George I, was a woman of extreme
good sense and talent. Although towards the end of her days
she expressed the hope that 'Queen of England' would be
inscribed on her coffin, she was, nevertheless, far from anxious
that her own son should become King of England. In fact, she
made the suggestion that James Stuart, 'The Old Pretender',
would do well to become a Protestant, and thus have a chance
of reigning as James III. In her view, her own son, George, was
unfitted by training and temperament to inherit the English
throne. However, she finally accepted her right to the throne,
and came very near to having her wish for the inscription
'Queen of England' to appear on her coffin fulfilled, for she
died – at the grand age of eighty-four – not very long before
Queen Anne herself departed.

Her son had married, at the age of twenty-two, Princess
Sophia Dorothea of Zell (1666–1726), who was herself sixteen
at the time. During all her wedded life, Sophia Dorothea had
to endure neglect, contempt, and afterwards cruelty from her
profligate husband, with his strong bent for ugly women.
Romantically enough, love was offered to the discarded Sophia
by Philip Christo Königsmark, a Swedish soldier of fortune,
and she did not repel it. As a result, her lover came to his
death by special order – one version has it, by the very hand

– of George himself, the elector, and owner of two notorious mistresses.[36] The unhappy wife was banished to the castle of Ahlden, on the River Aller, where she remained in melancholy captivity for thirty-two years.

It is supposed that one reason for George I's hatred of his son was because of the latter's sympathy for his mother's sufferings. He had on more than one occasion tried unsuccessfully to visit her in her prison. On her death, a story was current that she left all her worldly possessions to the Prince of Wales, but the will was given to George I, and he composedly destroyed it. In his own will, the king himself left large legacies to the Duchess of Kendal and other ladies of his fancy, and it is said that on the Archbishop of Canterbury handing the will to George II, he put it in his pocket and it was never seen again. It is to be hoped that this story is true, if only for the sake of poetic justice.

As Sophia Dorothea of Zell was never a queen consort of England officially, her letters do not come into this collection.

16

Caroline of Brandenburg-Anspach

(1683–1737), Queen Consort of George II

When princess of Brandenburg-Anspach, to Gottfried Wilhelm Leibnitz, 1704

Caroline of Anspach was the only daughter of John Frederick Margrave of Brandenburg-Anspach, by his second wife, Eleanor, daughter of the Duke of Saxe-Eisenach.

After her father's death, when she was nine years of age, her mother married again, and Caroline's education was sadly neglected. Yet so intense was the child's desire for knowledge that she sturdily determined to teach herself, and struggled unaided to make her pen obey her wishes, and to wrest sense from the printed page. Her spidery handwriting and indifferent orthography proved something of a setback in later life,[1] but despite this initial handicap Caroline developed into a cultured woman and one of the most remarkable of her day.

Fortunately for her, on her mother's death, when Caroline was still in her early teens, she was taken under the guardianship of Frederick, Elector III of Brandenburg (afterwards Frederick I of Prussia). His wife, Sophia Charlotte, was the talented and intellectual daughter of the equally gifted Sophia, Electress of Hanover, heiress by the Act of Settlement to the throne of England. The affection and understanding of these two women caused them to have strong ascendancy over Caroline, and their influence laid the foundation of her sterling character.

During her guardianship the Queen of Prussia – who, owing to her generous sympathies, love of art and letters, and ability to raise the intellectual life of those around her, caused the best brains in Europe to throng to her salons – never denied Caroline, 'in spite of her youth, a part in the famous receptions at her château of Lützenburg'. It was there that Caroline met Gottfried Wilhelm Leibnitz. This great scholar, one of the most learned of his time as a theologian, mathematician, and a man of affairs, became Caroline's guide, philosopher and friend, and his influence upon her was second only to that of the Queen of Prussia.

He appears to have had much to do with Caroline's decision not to marry the Archduke Charles, titular King of Spain, by which alliance she would have had to become a Roman Catholic. Believing in the freedom of conscience, and having an open mind on all forms of religion, Caroline shrank from embracing a faith that was 'positive'. The persuasive arguments of the Jesuit Father Urban, who sought to convert her, left Caroline in tears, but adamant in her opinions. As a result of declining the marriage, she came under the disapproval of her guardian, the King of Prussia, and thought it wise to leave Berlin and go to stay with her brother, now Margrave, at Anspach. It was from there that she wrote the following letter to her mentor and friend Leibnitz.

Anspach, 28th December.

I received your letter with the greatest pleasure, and am glad to think that I still retain your friendship and your remembrance. I much desire to show my gratitude for all the kindness you paid me at Lützenburg. I am delighted to hear from you that the Queen and the Court regret my departure, but I am sad not to have the happiness of paying my *devoirs* to our incomparable Queen. I pray you on the next occasion assure her of my deep respect. I do not think the King of Spain is troubling himself any more about me. On the contrary, they are incensed at my disinclination to follow the advice of Father Urban. Every post brings me letters from that kind priest. I really think his persuasions contributed materially to the uncertainty I felt during those three months, from which I am now quite recovered. The Electress[2] does me too much honour in remembering me; she has no more devoted servant than myself, and I understand her pleasure in having the Crown Prince[3] at Hanover.

To Gottfried Wilhelm Leibnitz, 1705

In departing from Berlin Caroline was not to know that she had said her last farewell to her beloved 'foster-mother', who died, at the age of thirty-seven, a few months later. Her health was never strong, and it is probable that the parting with Caroline and with her own son – Frederick William, who had been sent on a tour of foreign travel – preyed upon the Queen of Prussia's mind. Her death was one of the great sorrows of Caroline's life; a splendid light had gone out for many, but particularly for Caroline.

In a letter of grief and sympathy which he wrote to Caroline on this occasion, Leibnitz profoundly remarks, 'If we had the power now to realize the marvellous beauty and harmony of things, we should reduce happiness to a science, and live in a state of perpetual blessedness. But since this beauty is hidden from our eyes, and we see around us a thousand sights that shock us, and cause temptation to the weak and ignorant, our love of God and our trust in His goodness are founded on faith, not yet lost in Sight or verified by the senses ... I have often discussed these broad principles with the late queen. She understood them well, and her wonderful insight enabled her to realize much that I was unable to explain.'[4]

From the answer that Caroline sent to him she reveals in her grief that she has not yet arrived at the heights of Leibnitz's philosophy.

April 2nd.

Heaven, jealous of our happiness, has taken away from us our adored and adorable Queen. The calamity has overwhelmed me with grief and sickness, and it is only the hope that I may soon follow her that consoles me. I pity you from the bottom of my heart, for her loss to you is irreparable. I pray the good God to add to die Electress Sophia's life the years that the Queen might have lived, and I beseech you to express my devotion to her.

When Electoral Princess of Hanover, to Gottfried Wilhelm Leibnitz, 1713

That same year, Caroline married George, Electoral Prince of Hanover (who was to become George II), and 5 February 1707 saw the advent of her firstborn, Frederick, afterwards Prince of Wales. The birth of this prince was to cause no little stir in the English court, as it had direct bearing on the English succession.

For some time Queen Anne had displayed misgivings as to the Hanoverian rights to her crown. It is more than probable that, in her heart of hearts, she believed that the so-termed 'Pretender' was in fact her lawful brother. In addition, the serious situation that had arisen recently in England regarding international policy (with which we are not here concerned) culminated in creating bad blood between Anne and the Elector of Hanover, Caroline's father-in-law, and the old electress Sophia. Popular enthusiasm began to look ominous for the Hanoverian hopes, and all pointed to the possibility of the Act of Settlement of 1701 being repealed any day.

The vacillating Anne, in poor health and nearing her end, found herself encompassed by the machinations of her ministers, whose objectives were to safeguard their own interests at all costs, whichever claimant should succeed the dying Queen of England. Among those who watched the tide of events with keen, personal interest was Caroline herself, as the following letter does not disguise. It was written in reply to one she had received from Leibnitz, in the course of which he says, 'I pray that you may one day enjoy the title of Queen of England so well worn by Queen Elizabeth, which you so highly merit. Consequently I wish the same good things to His Highness, your consort, since you can only occupy the throne of that great Queen with him.'

In comparing her to Elizabeth I, Leibnitz pays Caroline too high a compliment. All the same, Caroline was to prove the greatest of the queens-consort of England, and is not known to history as 'Caroline The Illustrious' – as she was termed by her contemporaries – without just cause.

Hanover, December 27th.

I assure you that of all the letters which this season has brought me yours has been the most welcome. You do well to send me your good wishes for the throne of England, which are sorely needed just now, for in spite of all the favourable rumours you mention, affairs there seem to be going from bad to worse. For my part (and I am a woman and like to delude myself) I cling to the hope that, however bad things may be now, they will ultimately turn to the advantage of our House.

I accept the comparison which you draw, though all too flattering, between me and Queen Elizabeth as a good omen. Like Elizabeth, the Electress's rights are denied her by a jealous sister[5] with a bad temper, and she will never be sure of the English Crown until her accession to the throne. God be praised that our Princess of Wales[6] is better than ever, and by her good health confounds all the machinations of her enemies.

When Princess of Wales, to Mrs Clayton, *c.* 1720

Of obscure origin, Mrs Clayton was a friend of the Duchess of Marlborough, and through the latter's agency had been appointed a bedchamber woman to Caroline when she became Princess of Wales. She is said to have exercised more power over Caroline than anyone, with the exception of the Prime Minister, Sir Robert Walpole, who hated Mrs Clayton, and with whom the latter was for ever at variance.[7]

In the following cautious and cryptically worded letter, Caroline is apparently referring, by 'that ugly scheme', to the South Sea Company, from which emanated that enormous fabric of national delusion known as 'The South Sea Bubble'.

There are times when man's nature seems to yearn for financial seduction. This was one such time.

Briefly, the object of this scheme was to wipe out the national debt, which on Queen Anne's death had reached £52 million. All it mainly succeeded in doing, however, was to plunge thousands throughout the country into ruin and despair. Truly, in their mad rush for material gain, high and low had 'eaten the insane root that takes the reason prisoner', and in the resultant panic when the 'Bubble' burst, suicides became common. Many, on the other hand – especially those in 'honourable' places – reaped fortunes before the fabulous 'Bubble' exploded and what had seemed so corporal melted like a breath into the wind. Among these was the Prince of Wales himself, who netted a profit of £40,000. Walpole, too, by adroitly selling out at the right time, at 1,000 per cent, confessed himself as 'fully satisfied'. It must, however, be acknowledged that this first-class financier statesman had never had any trust in the scheme, and had openly said so.

I just received your letter, my dear friend, with extreme joy. Your friend may depend entirely upon the Prince and me, and you shall not have the less of our friendship. I can assure you, upon my honour, that Walpole is sincere, and has not entered into that ugly scheme. I'll take care to spur him up. He is furious in the affair, and violent against all those who have bought. We will do all we can. I hope everything with the assistance of our friend.

Caroline

To Mrs Clayton, *c.* 1726

Doctor Steighertahl, referred to by Caroline in the letter that follows, was a native of Hanover, and physician-in-ordinary to George I. He had been one of the doctors in attendance at the birth, in 1717, of her second son, who had died within twelve months. The despotic treatment by George I of Caroline and her husband at that time created an open rupture between the Prince of Wales and his father, and was, in a measure, the cause of the child's death. The king's cruel conduct in denying the parents the care of their three daughters, and then the newborn son, could not fail to engender a deep bitterness. It is supposed that the child pined away through lack of mother care.

Caroline's attitude, disclosed in this letter to Mrs Clayton, doubtless had its roots in that tragic happening.

Caroline had eight children by George II. Her second daughter, Amelia (usually known as Emily), to whom she is referring here, had contracted a severe catarrhal infection with complications. Obviously Caroline has no faith in her father-in-law's physician, preferring the unknown doctor 'friend' recommended by Mrs Clayton.

Incidentally, Amelia was the destined bride of the Crown Prince of Prussia, but the marriage scheme falling through, she remained single – although not indifferent to male admiration – all her life. Of pleasing temperament when young, and a fine horsewoman, she developed into a hard, mean, and inquisitive character, whose sole loves seem to have been cards and scandal.

> I come from a great dispute with that knave Steighertahl. I would not let her[8] take that mountebank prescription. She is well, but I fear the return. If God restores her to me, it is certainly to your friend that the Prince and I owe the obligation. As I find her so well, I cannot be a hindrance to the poor people

from having the benefit of his salutary advice, but I earnestly beg that he will return soon. Sincerely all my confidence is in him. I am afraid for your health, my dear friend. Take good care, for the love of

Caroline.

When queen consort, to the Duchess of Kendal, 1727

The sudden death of George I while on a visit to his beloved Hanover brought Caroline, Princess of Wales, to the throne as the first Hanoverian queen consort.

The only person in the world who genuinely mourned the loss of the late king was the Duchess of Kendal – one of his two permanent mistresses. She had been with him on his last journey, and was so overcome by his death that, as we learn, 'she beat her breast, tore her hair, and rent the air with her cries'.

Caroline had never harboured any ill will against the duchess, who, unlike the Countess of Darlington – the late king's other unofficial wife – was no mischief-maker. She had, in fact, earned Caroline's gratitude for her attempt – albeit abortive – to persuade George I to restore Caroline's children to their parents.

Caroline wrote the following letter to the bereaved duchess immediately upon hearing the news of her father-in-law's death. Her expressions of affection, and of love for the departed monarch, while doing Caroline credit, were doubtless dictated as much by her sense of propriety as by sympathy.

On her return to England, the duchess retired to Kendal House, Twickenham, wearing the deepest weeds (which she continued to wear until her death at the age of eighty-five) and tending, in a golden cage, a raven which she believed to be the reincarnation of her dead lover, George I.

Kensington, June 25th.

My first thought, my dear Duchess, has been of you in the misfortune that has befallen us; I know well your devotion and love for the late King, and I fear for your health; only the resignation which you have always shown to the Divine Will can sustain you under such a loss. I wish I could convey to you how much I feel for you, and how anxious I am about your health, but it is impossible for me to do so adequately. I cannot tell you how greatly this trouble has affected me. I had the honour of knowing the late King. You know that to know him was sufficient to make one love him also. I know that you always tried to render good service to the King;[9] he knows it, too, and will remember it himself to you by letter. I hope you realize that I am your friend. It is my pleasure and my duty to remind you of the fact, and to tell you that I and the King will always be glad to do all we can to help you. Write to me, I pray you, and give me an opportunity to show how much I love you.

Caroline

To Augusta, Princess of Wales, 1737

Frederick Louis, eldest son and heir of George II, had been left behind at Hanover, on the instructions of the late king, when the Prince and Princess of Wales had accompanied George I to England. The separation from his parents lasted thirteen years, and during that time Frederick developed into a self-willed, irresponsible and arrogant character. Once he had been created Prince of Wales after his father's accession, he formed an opposition party to the king and queen, and did all he could to set their authority at defiance.

In 1736 he married Princess Augusta, daughter of the Duke of Saxe-Gotha, in consideration of his father agreeing to allow him £50,000 a year, which sum, promptly following his marriage, he wished increased to £100,000. This the king refused, as he likewise refused to make his son regent, in his own absences in Hanover, in place of Caroline – an office which the queen consort upheld with great distinction.

The growing antipathy between the son and his parents was fast reaching a climax, and came to a head on the birth of Augusta's first child the following year. When the confinement was expected, Frederick rushed his wife from Hampton Court Palace – where they were in residence with the king and queen – to St James's, not desiring, apparently, that his parents should be present at the birth. This extraordinary and reckless conduct nearly cost the lives of the Princess of Wales and her infant – 'a little rat of a girl', as the unfortunate child was described. As a result of the prince's high-handedness, not only was doubt cast upon the infant's legitimacy, but the king banished him from the palace. He and his wife went to Kew, and it was while they were there that Caroline wrote the following letter to Augusta. As a result of his behaviour, Caroline's antipathy towards her eldest son turned to physical repulsion – so much so, that she refused to see him in her last hours.

The death of the queen consort, on Sunday evening, 20 November of that same year, was regarded as a national calamity. Aided by her chosen minister, Walpole, Caroline can be said to have ruled England for ten years, and by her death the people knew themselves to be bereaved of their true sovereign.

One fated most to mourn her was the king himself, who, despite his ridiculous amours, had loved and respected his consort. She had dealt with his infidelities with patience and wisdom, and, without letting George II realise it, had really been the monarch on the throne.[10] As Carlyle so rightly said, 'There is something stoically tragic in the history of Caroline with her flighty, vapouring little king: Seldom had foolish husband so wise a wife.'

Caroline was buried in Westminster Abbey, and by his special request on the king's death many years later, one side of his coffin and of Caroline's were opened, 'so that their bodies should mingle and in death be not divided'.

Hampton Court.

I am delighted, my dear Princess, to know that you are completely recovered after your confinement. Rest assured, as you have never offended either the King or me, that I shall not fail to show you the marks of my respect and affection.

I think it would be unfitting to both of us if I entered into a discussion with you about the unhappy differences between the King and my son. When you have become fully acquainted with the various declarations on the subject of your journeys from Hampton Court, and by whom and to whom, you will be convinced that your husband's conduct has not been set at all in a false light. I hope that time, and a mature consideration, will bring my son to a just sense of his duty towards his father. That is the only means of attaining that happy change which you cannot wish for more sincerely than I.

Caroline.

17

Charlotte Sophia of Mecklenburg-Strelitz

(1744–1818), Queen Consort of George III

When queen consort, to her son, George, Prince of Wales, 1770

George II reigned for nearly a quarter of a century after the death of his consort, Caroline of Anspach, and was succeeded in 1760 by his grandson, whose father, Frederick, had died nine years previously. Within twelve months of his accession George III married Charlotte Sophia, second sister of the Duke of Mecklenburg-Strelitz. The royal groom was twenty-three, and his bride seventeen years of age.

Charlotte Sophia was undoubtedly plain, but it was, as Northcote the painter said, 'an elegant, not a vulgar plainness'. The populace, however, were frankly exasperated on discovering that their young queen was not handsome. As always they demanded that a female sovereign should have physical beauty before all else, and were indifferent to the more desirable attributes which Charlotte Sophia possessed: a good, kindly, sensible nature. In addition, general opinion considered that the king should have sought a more illustrious consort than a daughter from so humble and poor a German house. However, the king himself proved satisfied with his choice, and Charlotte Sophia was particularly fortunate in her husband. In private and domestic virtues, George III far excelled any other king of England.[1]

A woman of no outstanding ability, in no way interested in affairs of state, content to be merely a puppet figure on ceremonial occasions: such was contemporary opinion of the queen consort. Charlotte Sophia's concern, however, was for the king and her family, and in maintaining a high standard of court life.[2] It is said that to no other woman, probably, had good morals in England ever owed so great an obligation: no mean praise, as those who have interested themselves in the manners and morals of the eighteenth century will appreciate. It was Charlotte Sophia's earnest desire, too, to inculcate into her children the same principles which she upheld at her court. This is exemplified in the appended letter which, as a young mother, she wrote to her son, George Augustus Frederick.

In its sound ethics, sympathy of understanding, and unquestionable sincerity, the letter provides a memorable contribution to this collection of the queen's intimate correspondence.

My dear Son,

The demand of a pocket-book[3] furnishes me with an opportunity of stating you my wishes concerning your future conduct in life. Time draws near when you will be put into the hands of Governors; under whose care you will study more manly learning than what you have done hitherto. My advice will be short, but sincere; and therefore I flatter myself, not less serviceable to you.

Above all things I recommend unto you, to fear God; a duty that must lead to all the rest with ease; as His assistance, being properly implored, will be your guide through every action of life. Abhor all vice, in private as well as in public, and look upon yourself as obliged to set good examples. Disdain all flattery; it will corrupt your manners, and render you contemptible before the world. Do justice unto everybody, and avoid partiality. The first will acquire to you happiness in this world, as well as hereafter; the latter will make you unhappy, because it leaves after it an unhappy conscience; a situation which seems to me the most wretched in life, as it deprives us of the greatest enjoyment of life; that is, peace of mind. Love and esteem those that are about you. Confide in, and act with sincerity towards, them; as that alone will be productive of a lasting friendship. Treat nobody with contempt, for that will deprive you of it. Be charitable to everybody; not forgetting your meaner servants. Don't use them with indifference; rather pity them that they are obliged to serve, and do unto them as you would be done by. I mean by that, you should not think yourself above doing good unto them. The contrary will make you appear vain; and vanity is the root of all vice and a sure proof of ignorance. For what is man to man? We are all equal, and become only of consequence by setting good examples to others; and these must be given, with a view of doing our duty, but not with the idea of superiority: for then the action loses its merits.

Lastly, I recommend unto you the highest love, affection, and duty towards the King. Look upon him as a friend: Nay, as the greatest, the best, and the most deserving of all friends you can possibly find. Try to imitate his virtues, and look upon everything that is in opposition to that duty, as destructive to yourself. After this, I am sure you can't be unacquainted with what belongs to me, as I am the next to the King. Keep in love and friendship with your brothers and sisters; for I am sure they will deserve and require it of you: and as you ought to seek your happiness in that of others, I am sure you will contribute to that of your own family. I, for my part, can safely say, You will contribute greatly towards mine, in following the advice of

Your most affectionate Mother,
12 August, 1770. Charlotte

To Lady Harcourt, 1784

Charlotte Sophia's skill in writing intimate and diverting letters is one of the outstanding features of her correspondence.

During a friendship which extended over some forty years, she wrote hundreds of letters to Lady Harcourt, who was one of the ladies of her bedchamber. Lady Harcourt's father-in-law had been delegated to bring the young queen consort elect from Mecklenburg, for her marriage to George III, and he and his family remained confidential friends of the royal couple for the rest of their days.

The tone of Charlotte Sophia's letters to her confidante is mainly gay and good-humoured, of which the following are faithful specimens.

Madam,

I am particularly happy, by the King's commands, of acquainting you that we propose storming your castle[4] on Saturday, the 18th, if perfectly convenient to you and Lord Harcourt; and though we shall be a large party, pray don't be alarmed, for we are all *good friends* and *well-wishers* to the owners of the castle, but none more sincerely so than my dear Lady Harcourt's very affectionate friend,

Charlotte.

(*c.* 1795)

I have of late seen several ladies just returned from Paris, some very much improved in looks, and others far otherwise. Mrs Goldburn is quite formidable by three immense feathers, which so directly ran into my eyes when she was presented, I was under the necessity of drawing myself back in order to avoid mischief; and I rejoiced a little in Lady Claremont's distress who presented her ...

Now let us *compare notes*. You talk of Loquacity as an Evil. I, on the contrary of *Taciturnity* as drudgery; for the words of *Yes and No* is what I experience daily; and if it goes a little further, I have the History and Distress of the Bellies, Harries, etc. etc. etc., of the Families. Some people attribute it to shyness; and poor me attributes it to S——ss,[5] and think myself quite a Philosopher to hear it with patience: but as Necessity has no law, I do not look upon this as a particular merit; for I am *Philosophe Malgré, moi*. And you may apply our style of life to this:

'They ate, they drank, they slept, what then?

They slept, they ate, they drank again!'

Yet after I have said this, though we are not *la Bande joyeuse*, we are *la Bande Contente, et c'est beaucoup dire en peu de mots*.

Charlotte.

To George, Prince of Wales, 1795

Despite their own virtuous qualities, not many of their fifteen children could be termed 'blessings' to George III and Charlotte Sophia. Some, indeed, were a source of deep anxiety and sorrow, particularly the Prince of Wales. Certain allowance should in fairness be made for the prince's sowing his wild oats, in view of the severity of his early surroundings and his dull and restrained upbringing. All the same, as a royal personage he would not have been subjected to the unenviable vituperation poured out upon him in prose and verse by writers of his day,[6] and have been styled the most ungentlemanly first gentleman of Europe, merely for reasons of individual antipathy.

His disastrous marriage added nothing to his popularity, especially with the populace at large, and was probably brought upon him as a natural sequence of his unprincipled and intolerant outlook.

The queen consort had hoped that her eldest son would marry Princess Louise of Mecklenburg – afterwards to become the deeply loved Queen of Prussia. As a consequence, she never liked Caroline of Brunswick, whom the Prince of Wales eventually married at the age of thirty-three.

In the same month of her son's wedding the disappointed Charlotte Sophia wrote the following charming and characteristic letter to the royal bridegroom.

Friday Morning, April, 1795.

Oh! Huffen Puffen indeed to-day, for it is even warmer than it was yesterday. I hope you are not fatigued, and that the Princess is well. I send a Fan, which is a present to the Princess of Mr. Bolton, at Birmingham, which I am ashamed of having kept till now. The sticks are not wood, but *papier machi*, and therefore curious; and I think its curiosity is its real beauty.

We are now preparing to leave town, and provided we do not melt upon our journey, I hope to see you to-morrow morning, when I shall have the pleasure *de vous assuré de bouche combine vous ete amié de*

Votre très affectionée Mère,
Charlotte

To Lady Harcourt, 1796

Some five years after he came to the throne the young George III – harassed by affairs of state and beset by dictating and insolent ministers – had had a mental breakdown. This was followed, some twenty years later, by one of a much more serious nature, and although the king made some recovery the mental disorder continued intermittently.

From 1788 the care of his person and the disposal of his household was placed exclusively in the hands of Charlotte Sophia; and she was to cope, spiritedly, with this appalling situation until her death.

The following restrained letter to her great friend was written by the sorely tried queen consort during this time.

How many unpleasant things have passed since we saw one another. To know them, and not to have the power of assisting and soothing the sufferer is real martyrdom. I hear all sides, and know so many things which must not be revealed, that I am most truly wore down with it; and my dislike to the world in general gets quite the better of me; for those who do know one, and those who do not, all talk *à tort* and *à travers*, and say indeed most cutting things.

Our ball looked gay. Whether it was truly so I do not ask, my feelings were far other ways; but we did go through it tolerably well. The best part of the day was the end of it.

Charlotte

To Lord Harcourt, 1803

In her vividly written memoirs, Fanny Burney[7] – who was for some time assistant keeper of the robes to the queen consort – has left many glimpses of the life at Charlotte Sophia's court. In spite of the kindliness of both the king and queen, and the very human side that they displayed, strict attention to etiquette and discipline was much in force.

All the same, one has the feeling, in reading the following 'tippling letter' – as the queen consort herself describes it – regarding a misdemeanour of her footman, Oby, that Charlotte Sophia penned her complaint with something of a twinkle in her eye, for she had a pleasing sense of the ridiculous, as many of her personal letters testify.

My Lord,

I want you to exert your authority in dismissing my footman, Oby, the service as soon as possible, as his unquenchable thirst is now become so over-powering, that neither our absence nor presence can subdue it any more.

Some messages of consequence being sent by him to the apothecary's, were found in his pockets when lying dead drunk in the street a few days ago, luckily enough by the Duke of Cumberland,[8] who, knowing they were for the family, sent them to Brandi. I do not want him to starve, but I will not have him do any more duty. This, I hope, will be an example to the others; but as I write a tippling letter, I think it not amiss to mention that Stephenson has appeared twice a little boosey, the consequence of which was a fall from his horse yesterday, by which he was very much bruised: and the surgeon who came to bleed him at the Duke of Cambridge's[9] house, who very humanely took him in, declared him to be at least over dry, if not drunk. A reprimand to him will be necessary; for should it happen again, he must go.

Charlotte
Kew, 8th July.

To her son, the Prince Regent, afterwards George IV, 1812

In 1810 the afflicted king and his unhappy consort were to suffer the death of their youngest daughter, Amelia (her father's favourite), at the age of twenty-seven years.[10] As a result of this unexpected shock, George III became permanently insane. He had, in addition, to endure being both deaf and blind.

Her daughters had rallied round their mother during these calamitous years, and showed reluctance to leave her side, at any rate for some long time. Eventually, however, they were to find the tragic home conditions unbearable, and they either hastened into marriage or had themselves set up in separate establishments. Their devotion to their mother remained otherwise unaffected.

On his father's final relapse the Prince of Wales had become regent, and the breach that had existed between Charlotte Sophia and her eldest son, caused by the latter's open anxiety to take over the rule of the country, was more or less healed.

In the following letter the worn-out old queen is protesting at her daughters' want of seemliness of behaviour, in view of their stricken father's condition. Charlotte, to whom the queen consort refers, was the only child of the Prince of Wales by Caroline of Brunswick. She had been placed in the care of Charlotte Sophia after the prince became regent.

Frogmore, December 2nd, 1812.

My dearest Son,

I want words to express my obligations to you for the letter I have just received and although I am desirous to return to the castle as soon as possible, I am anxious to profit by the opportunity afforded me to be explicit upon so painful a subject as that of your sisters.

I never did oppose their going to town at any time, and did tell them so one and all, but I did, and do now this moment, object to their going to London when I feel it more decent that, in their situation as personal witnesses of the distressing situation of their Father, they should, upon particular occasions decline appearing in public.

This was the case on Saturday, when the Duke of York brought your message, and upon Augusta informing me of it, I immediately gave to her, as well as Elizabeth, my reason against it, which I am convinced, if you reflect one moment, can by no means injure me in the world.

You will allow that your appearance in the House, which was your duty to do, is in reality more melancholy than the King's death.[11]

Can there be, I appeal to your feelings, a more painful, a more horrible situation than the one your Father labours under? And was it not my duty to state to your sisters, that they, having no personal duty which calls upon their presence at the House of Lords, it would show more attention to female delicacy to decline it, but left it to their option to do as they pleased.

For your own daughter[12] there could be no doubt about her going; she could not have those feelings that the aunts ought to have; and which as they did so, appears to me a full declaration to the world that the King can never recover, and which, you will know, not even any of the physicians have ever ventured to declare.

I come now to the other part of your letter about the Princesses appearing with Charlotte. To that I did agree as far as sometimes, but not every week; as you must be sensible that with the small society I have here, I should by that be left almost alone ... As to the representation your sisters have made of what did pass on Sunday night before they left Windsor, I am ignorant of; but I will not deny (though I do not mean to justify my own conduct) that the answer I received from Mary, when I found fault with her for not even telling me she intended to go, provoked me to the quick; for she assured me she could no longer lead the life she had led, and that Sir H. Halford[13] was of the same opinion, and when Elizabeth, by defending her own conduct, struck upon a book, saying she had done all in her power to please, it provoked me; in short, this last journey of theirs has given a blow which cannot easily be effaced; for the coming to ask my advice, and hearing my objections, and not following them, is treating me like a fool.

The telling me that living with me in my distress is disagreeable, and to repeat to anybody that which concerns the interior of a family, is more than imprudent.

You have now my whole confession. I have not spared myself, consequently, it must be sincere; and having made you my father confessor, I do desire that no brothers or sisters nor any minister may say more upon this subject ...

I promise you I will keep peace. I am conscious I have often made it when it was least expected; but I do not always meet with it again, why, I feel, you can easily imagine – to forget it is out of my power, but I will do what I can, for it is so hard a blow that only I can feel. I am truly grieved to learn that there should have occurred further unpleasant circumstances from another quarter.[14]

That you may never feel what I feel now is the sincere wish of, my dearest son,

> Your ever most affectionate mother,
> Charlotte

To her son, the Prince Regent, 1817

Yet another, and final sorrow, was in store for Charlotte Sophia.

Her granddaughter, Princess Charlotte – a very popular princess, of determined character, and lovable qualities – had married Prince Leopold of Saxe-Coburg[15] in May 1816, when she was twenty years of age. Devoted to her indiscreet mother, Caroline of Brunswick, the young princess had known restraints, and some unhappiness, during the guardianship of her grandmother. From this, doubtless, her marriage provided a happy release. With her father she was not on the best of terms. The prince regent appears, in some curious way, to have been jealous of his daughter's popularity, as one direct in the line of succession. She had hoped to be queen some day, and the whole country shared in that hope. The young princess, however, was destined to die in childbirth in November 1817.

The following letter was written by the saddened Charlotte Sophia to her son on hearing the ill news, while she was at Bath and herself in a low state of health. The shock weakened her, and Charlotte Sophia died, in the same month as her granddaughter, the following year.

She was buried in St George's Chapel, Windsor.

Bath, November 7th, 1817.

How painful it is to me to take up my pen at this moment, when I had flattered myself to make use of it by giving you joy, which it has pleased the Almighty to change into grief and mourning for us all. I need not, I am sure, tell you that as I always share in your prosperity most sincerely, so do I most deeply feel your present loss and misery upon this melancholy event; and pray most anxiously to the Almighty that your health may not suffer from it.

You must allow me to add to this, that I rejoice in the comfort you must find of having had it in your power to make your child completely happy by granting her to marry the man she liked and wished to be united to, and who made her happy; as also upon the bestowing upon her a place[16] she did enjoy with every possible gratitude, and in which she spent to the very last almost complete felicity.

These reflexions I do hope will alleviate your grief in some respects, as much as they give me real comfort upon your account.

18

Caroline of Brunswick

(1768–1821), Queen Consort of George IV

When Princess of Wales, to her husband,
George, Prince of Wales, 1796

Caroline of Brunswick was the second daughter of Charles William Ferdinand, Duke of Brunswick-Wolfenbüttel, and Augusta, sister of George III.

Her marriage with her cousin, the Prince of Wales, in 1795, was a union of convenience only. By his reckless extravagance the heir apparent had contracted debts to the amount of £650,000 and, as a condition of agreeing for his son to be got out of his pressing difficulties, George III insisted on his alliance with Princess Caroline.

It was a curious situation, for the Prince of Wales was already married to the beautiful Mrs Fitzherbert – a twice-widowed Roman Catholic some six years his senior. However, it was considered that the Royal Marriage Act[1] rendered this alliance nugatory, and so the royal wedding took place without impediment. The marriage, however, was virtually doomed to failure from the first meeting between the couple. On this occasion the Prince of Wales, having saluted his bride-to-be, retired to a distant part of the compartment and said to Lord Malmesbury, who had brought the princess over from Brunswick, 'Harris, I am not well; pray get me a glass of brandy.'

In extenuation of the prince's attitude where his wife was concerned, it must be acknowledged that there are well-authenticated stories relating to Caroline of Brunswick's innate vulgarity, coarse habits, and indefensible conduct at times, which would seem to justify him, in some measure.

After the birth of their daughter, the Princess Charlotte, the Prince of Wales removed himself from their residence at Carlton House to Windsor, declining any more to live with Caroline on the grounds that (as he says in a letter he wrote to her at the time) 'nature has not made us suitable to each other'. In this parting letter he frankly states, in conclusion, 'that even in the event of any accident happening to my daughter, which I trust Providence in his mercy will avert, I shall not infringe the terms of the restriction by proposing, at any period, a connexion of a more particular nature'.

In the following reply which Caroline of Brunswick made, her threat to appeal to the king was of no avail. George III was the only member of the royal family who had any sympathy for the deserted princess, and he did all in his power to help his niece.

The avowal of your conversation with Lord Cholmondley neither surprises nor offends me: it merely confirmed what you have tacitly insinuated for this twelve month. But after this, it would be a want of delicacy, or rather an unworthy meanness in me, were I to complain of those conditions which you impose upon yourself.

I should have returned no answer to your letter, if it had not been conceived in terms to make it doubtful whether this arrangement proceeds from you, or from me; and you are aware that the dishonour of it belongs to you alone.

The letter which you announce to me as the last, obliges me to communicate with the King, as to my Sovereign and my father, both your avowal and my answer. You will find enclosed the copy of my letter to the King. I apprize you of it, that it may not incur the slightest reproach of duplicity from you. As I have at this moment no protector but His Majesty, I refer myself solely to him upon the subject: and if my conduct meet his approbation, I shall be in some degree at least, consoled.

I retain every sentiment of gratitude for the situation in which I find myself, as Princess of Wales, enabled by your means, to indulge in the free exercise of a virtue dear to my heart – I mean, Charity.

It will be my duty, likewise, to act upon another motive – that of giving an example of patience, and resignation, under every trial.

Do me the justice to believe, that I shall never cease to pray for your happiness, and to be

Your most devoted,

Caroline

To the queen consort, Charlotte Sophia, 1814

Not long after the separation of the royal couple, the Princess of Wales retired to the village of Charlton, near Blackheath, where she continued to live for some years. While there, her rashness of behaviour, choice of associates, and imprudence in adopting the son of a dock labourer gave rise to injurious suspicions. In defence of her nonchalant conduct, it should be recollected that Caroline of Brunswick had come from one of the gayest courts in Germany, and she must have been distracted at times by the staidness of the court of Charlotte Sophia.

Her indiscretions culminated in the appointment of a royal commission in 1806, at the instigation of the prince, to investigate the conduct generally of the Princess of Wales. He must have been sorely frustrated on the commissioners finding no more serious charges to bring against his wife than those of 'carelessness to appearances' and 'levity'. In consequence of these findings, George III redoubled his kindnesses towards his daughter-in-law, gave her apartments at Kensington Palace, and directed that at court she should receive marked attention. Her invidious position, however, as a discarded wife could not fail to be a source of constant embarrassment, not only to herself, but to the royal family and visiting imperial guests. Such mortifications were to reach a serious crisis when preparations were afoot for the reception in London of the allied sovereigns to celebrate the abdication of Napoleon.

The queen, who was about to hold drawing rooms and give other entertainments, had no technical excuse for refusing to receive her daughter-in-law; on the other hand, the prince regent resolutely declined to have his wife recognised. This placed Charlotte Sophia in a painful difficulty. On her son's instructions, however, she wrote informing the Princess of Wales that the regent considered his own presence at the queen's court indispensable, and that he desired the Princess of Wales to be made distinctly aware, 'for reasons of which he alone can be judge, of his fixed and unalterable determination not to meet the Princess of Wales upon any occasion, either in public or private'.

The following letter is the reply that the queen consort received from the thus insulted Princess of Wales, in which she states her intention to make public the cause of her absence from court. As a result, the correspondence between herself and the queen appeared in the press. It must have caused no little astonishment to the public, already scandalised at the prince regent's behaviour, not only towards his wife, but in his own mode of living.

Connaught House,
May 24th, 1814

Madam,

I have received the letter which Your Majesty has done me the honour to address to me, prohibiting my appearance at the public drawing-rooms which will be held by Your Majesty in the ensuing month, with great surprise and regret.

I will not presume to discuss with Your Majesty, topics which must be as painful to Your Majesty as to myself.

Your Majesty is well acquainted with the affectionate regard with which the King was so kind as to honour me, up to the period of his Majesty's indisposition, which no one of his Majesty's subjects has so much cause to lament as myself: and that his Majesty was graciously pleased to bestow upon me the most unequivocal and gratifying proof of his attachment and approbation, by his public reception of me at his Court, at a season of severe and unmerited affliction, when his protection was most necessary to me. There I have since uninterruptedly paid my respects to your Majesty. I am now without appeal or protector. But I cannot so far forget my duty to the King and to myself, as to surrender my right to appear at any public drawing-room to be held by your Majesty.

That I may not, however, add to the difficulty and uneasiness of your Majesty's situation, I yield in the present instance to the will of his Royal Highness the Prince Regent, announced to me by your Majesty, and shall not present myself at the drawing-rooms of the next month.

It would be presumptuous in me to attempt to inquire of your Majesty the reasons of his Royal Highness, the Prince Regent, for his harsh proceeding, of which his Royal Highness can alone be the judge. I am unconscious of offence; and in that reflection, I must endeavour to find consolation for all the mortifications I experience: even for this, the last, the most unexpected, and the most severe; the prohibition given to me alone, to appear before your Majesty, to offer my congratulations upon the happy termination of those calamities with which Europe has been so long afflicted, in the presence of the illustrious personages who will, in all probability, be assembled at your Majesty's court, with whom I am so closely connected by birth and marriage.

I beseech your Majesty to do me an act of justice, to which, in the present circumstances, your Majesty is the only person competent, by acquainting those illustrious strangers with the motives of personal consideration towards your Majesty, which alone induce me to abstain from the exercise of my right to appear before your Majesty: and that I do now, as I have done at all times, defy the malice of my enemies to fix upon me the shadow of any one imputation which could render me unworthy of their society or regard.

Your Majesty will, I am sure, not be displeased that I should relieve myself from a suspicion of disrespect towards your Majesty, by making public the cause of my absence from Court at a time when the duties of my station would otherwise peculiarly demand my attendance.

> I have the honour to be
> Your Majesty's most obedient
> Daughter-in-law and servant,
> Caroline, P.

To a Friend, *c.* 1814

The following (undated) letter is an example of Caroline of Brunswick's literary style.[2] She never bothered to master the English tongue, preferring French, in which language she usually wrote and spoke.

In this letter she certainly exhibits herself as a tactless gossip, with a decidedly irresponsible attitude of mind. All the same she succeeded in gathering around her, while in England, men and women of intellect.

The dramatist Sheridan, to whom she refers, was at one time welcomed to Carlton House by the Prince of Wales on account of the brilliance and wit by which he entertained the prince's assemblies, but with the failure of his health and spirits Sheridan found the doors of Carlton House closed to him. He died in poverty in 1816.

Sheridan, I hear, is gone abroad, dying. I never knew much of him; for he also was one of the Great Mahomed's favourites, to whom by-the-way, the latter has not behaved with the most royal bounty, or steady friendship.

As to myself, I have nothing agreeable to tell you dear. I hear plenty of ill-natured stories put about by dat old witch de queen; but I say to dose who tell them, you do me no good by repeating these reports. You do not gain favour with me either by so doing, I assure you. When I answered Lady Oxford in this fashion, de oder day, she did look quite *ebahie*, and ashamed of herself. 'T is true, my dear —,'pon honour, I never wish to be told these things. I know them to be said. I know quite enough, God knows, and wish never to know more, if I can help it.

I did much regret your absence from my little party last night, for we were all very merry. The Gell,[3] Berry, Sidney Smith,[4] Lewis,[5] Lady Oxford (de Miscellany Harleyan, as all de world does call her now), and Milord Byron, did make it very pleasant; and we all laugh till we cry. Lewis did play the part of Cupidon, which amuse us, as you will suppose. He is grown so embonpoint, he is more droll than ever in dat character; but he tink himself charming, and look so happy when he make *les yeux doux* to the pretty ladies, dat it is cruel to tell him: 'You are in de paradise of de fools,' so we let him sigh on to my lady Oxford, which do torment Lord Byron, who wanted to talk wid her, and never could contrive it. Lady Anne[6] is en *petite santé*, just now she is truly interesting; yet, as your song says, 'Nobody's coming to marry her,' nor I fear never will; so I and Joan shall live and die together, like two turtle doves, or rather like dem two foolish women, Lady Eleanor Butler and Mlle. Ponsonby, who must be mad, I should tink, to choose to leave the world, and set up in a hermitage in Wales – *mais chacun a son goût* – it would not be mine. My dear —, I do dread being married to a lady friend. Men are tyrants, *mais* de women – Heaven help us! Dey are *vrais neros* over those they rule. No, no – give me my sweet Prince, rather than a female governess.

A Princess, and no Princess, a married woman, and no husband, or worse than none! – Never was there a poor devil in such a plight as I am. Lady Euphemia Stewart, that old *commere*, talked to me till I thought my ears never would be able to hear again. She thought I listened. Well, no matter. What think you I did? I dare say they all said I was mad. I sent them all away, ordered the carriages and set off wid a chosen few to the Play. The first one made me cry; and, strange to tell you, I felt a satisfaction in being able to weep. And den de second piece was a farce, and it made me laugh; so dat amusement compensated for the dullification of the first part of the night. Little Lewis came into the box: he affected to be sentimental, dat is always laughable in him, and I quizzed him, I do not think he enjoyed the fun.

To the Lady Charlotte Campbell, *c.* 1814

Fundamentally generous and good-natured, Caroline of Brunswick was capable of displaying great magnanimity of character when she chose.

On the occasion that the following note was written, the prince regent had invited all her ladies-in-waiting to a fête – probably during the celebrations arranged for the allied sovereigns in London – from which he had excluded the Princess of Wales. Yet, in spite of this appalling slight, Caroline of Brunswick presented each of her ladies with a dress for the ball, and the note which follows is a copy of that which accompanied each handsome gift.

Dear —,

Pray do me the favor to accept and wear de accompanying gown, and when you are In de ball at Carlton House tink of me, and wish me well.

For ever your affectionate,

C. P.

To her daughter, Princess Charlotte, 1815

For a number of years Caroline of Brunswick was permitted free access to her daughter. When, however, the Princess Charlotte was approaching womanhood, the prince regent withdrew her totally from her mother's influence. This added contention between the parents, raging over the head of their luckless child, quickly became public property and created deep commiseration for the aggrieved heiress to the throne of England.

Princess Charlotte herself was acutely aware of the failings of both of her parents, as the historic remark she made in later days indicates;[7] but she took the side of her mother, who had always shown her warmth of affection. This separation between mother and daughter, however, was fated to prove final. The prince regent's behaviour in this separation is reminiscent of that of Henry VIII's treatment of Catherine of Aragon and her daughter, Mary.

In that same year (1814) of national festivities and celebrations, Caroline of Brunswick – thwarted, mortified, and irked by her intolerable position – fled to the Continent, where she remained for the next six years. Unfortunately, her indiscretions and erratic mode of life while abroad were to have serious repercussions when later she wished to demand her rights as a Queen of England.

The following are literal translations of two letters that Caroline of Brunswick wrote in French to her daughter, Princess Charlotte, while on her restless travels.

Geneva, 13 May.

My dear daughter I have just received your charming letter – still at Geneva finding me indeed at a Ball – which the good Genevians have given me. Lady Barbara Ponsonby was there and she was very glad to know that you are in perfect health and fairly content with your present circumstances; I have ordered two of the most beautiful views of Naples by an Artist who is at present the most celebrated in Germany – and they will be sent to you on the first Ship that returns to England addressed to Lord Liverpool[8] – I leave tomorrow Morning for Milan to be present at the fête which is being given during the sojourn of the Archduke Jan[9] who arrives there today to receive homage in the name of the Emperor his brother. Have the kindness to write to me addressed to Monsieur Marriatti[10] who is my Good Father [Bonpère] because I plan to stay all summer on Lake Como – which is only two hours from Milan – Lady Charlotte Campbell and all her family is with me and are enjoying themselves very much. She asks me to remember her to You – as for Lady Charlotte Lindsey She will soon be able to tell you verbally all that interests You about my present life and believe me always and at all times Your very

Faithful and most affectionate Friend
and Mother.

Lake Como, 12 August, (1815)

Your letter, my dear Daughter, was most salutary balm after the smarting chagrin of having lost the being most dear to my heart a brother[11] who had been at all times and places my most faithful friend; I have for so long been deprived' of the *happiness* of receiving your letters my dear daughter that this consolation has been a very sweet moment for me – and I have flattered myself that in the future I shall much more often enjoy the happiness of having news of You for in my absence it is absolutely my only felicity to learn from You yourself that you are in good health happy content and that You still think sometimes of the mother who adores You and who has only the most fervent desires for your happiness – present and future – and it is with these same undoubted feelings and the most inviolable attachments that I flatter myself oil being for the test of my sad life my dear Daughter your affectionate and Faithful

Mother

I flatter myself that [by] this time the two Pictures of Naples have safely arrived with You – They are addressed to Lord Liverpool it Contains two very beautiful views of Naples and the Painter Benvenuti has executed them solely for You!

When queen consort, to her husband, George IV, 1820

On the death of his forlorn and anguished father, the new sovereign, George IV, made it his first business of state, which he prosecuted with the utmost zeal, to secure a divorce from his consort. Determined to claim her rights as Queen, Caroline of Brunswick returned to England, only to find herself faced with a trial, now famous in history,[12] at the House of Lords, on the grounds of her adultery with her courier in Italy, one Bartolomeo Pergami.

The sympathies of the populace were, from the beginning, with the queen, and the sensational and prolonged trial caused such heated controversy and spirited political reaction throughout the country, that the king's ministry was threatened with imminent downfall. In consequence, after much washing of dirty royal linen in public, the charge against Caroline of Brunswick was dropped, and the king failed to obtain his divorce.

On the other hand, the queen's claim to a coronation, being viewed as a ceremony dependent only upon the will and favour of the king, was rejected by the privy council by a large majority, and on the day of the coronation Caroline of Brunswick found the doors of Westminster Abbey barred against her. This final humiliation, coupled with the long strain she had undergone during the trial, broke the queen's spirit and she died a few weeks later.

The strong feeling that had swept the country in the queen's favour was violently revived by her death. On the day that the funeral cortège passed through London, on its way to Harwich, for the burial in the queen's native Brunswick, riots broke out, accompanied by bloodshed and death.

One of Caroline of Brunswick's last requests was that her coffin should bear the simple inscription 'Here lies Caroline of Brunswick; The Injured Queen of England.' This request was not permitted. All the same, there is something about the choice of the appellation 'injured' that has a ring of truth, especially when one remembers the treatment she had received from the moment of her landing on English soil. In spite of her great imprudence of conduct, and her many short-comings, may not Caroline of Brunswick, after all, have been the victim of premeditated injury?

In a long letter that she wrote to George IV, and which was made public during her trial, her case is ably set out. It was undoubtedly drafted by Brougham, her advocate, who put up such a magnificent defence at the trial. In the following excerpts, although at times the phraseology descends to melodrama, facts are recounted relative to her husband's treatment of her which are indisputable.

Brandenburg House,
August 7th.

Sir,

... A sense of what is due to my character and sex forbids me to refer minutely to the real causes of our domestic separation, or to the numerous unmerited insults offered me previous to that period; but leaving to your Majesty to reconcile with the marriage vow the act of driving, by such means, a wife from beneath your roof, with an infant in her arms, your Majesty will permit me to remind you, that that act was entirely your own; that the separation, so far from being sought for by me, was a sentence pronounced upon me, without any cause assigned, other than that of your own inclinations, which as your Majesty was pleased to allege, were not under your own control.

Not to have felt, with regard to myself, chagrin at this decision of your Majesty, would have argued great insensibility to the obligations of decorum; not to have dropped a tear in the face of that beloved child, whose future sorrows were then but too easy to foresee, would have marked me as unworthy of the name of mother; but, not to have submitted to it without repining would have indicated a consciousness of demerit, or a want of those feelings which belong to affronted and insulted female honour ...

From the very threshold of your Majesty's mansion the mother of your child was pursued by spies, conspirators, and traitors, employed, encouraged, and rewarded to lay snares for the feet, and to plot against the reputation and life of her whom your Majesty had so recently and solemnly vowed to honour, to love, and to cherish ...

While that great and good father and Sovereign remained in the exercise of his royal functions, his unoffending daughter-in-law had nothing to fear. As long as the protecting hand of your late ever-beloved and ever-lamented father was held over me, I was safe. But the melancholy event which deprived the nation of the active exertions of its virtuous King bereft me of friend and protector, and of all hope of future tranquillity and safety...

To enumerate all the various privations and mortifications which I had to endure – all the insults that were wantonly heaped upon me, from the day of your elevation to the Regency to that of my departure for the Continent – would be to describe every species of personal offence that can be offered to, and every pain short of bodily violence that can be inflicted on, any human being. Bereft of parent,[13] brother, and father-in-law, and my husband for my deadliest foe; seeing those who have promised me support bought by rewards to be amongst my enemies; restrained from accusing my foes in the face of the world, out of regard for the character of the father of my child, and from a desire to prevent her happiness from being disturbed; shunned from motives of selfishness by those who were my natural associates; living in obscurity while I ought to have been the centre of all that was splendid; thus humbled, I had one consolation left – the love of my dear and only child. To permit me to enjoy this was too great an indulgence. To see my daughter; to fold her in my arms, to mingle my tears with hers, to receive her cheering caresses, and to hear from her lips assurances of never-ceasing love; thus to be comforted, consoled, upheld, and blessed, was too much to be allowed me. Even on the slave mart, the cries of 'Oh! my mother, my mother! Oh! my child, my child!' have prevented a separation of the victims of avarice. But your advisers, more inhuman than the slave-dealers, remorselessly tore the mother from the child.[14]

Thus bereft of the society of my child, or reduced to the necessity of embittering her life by struggles to preserve that society, I resolved on a temporary absence, in the hope that time might restore me to her in happier days. Those days, alas! were never to come. To mothers – and those mothers who have been suddenly bereft of the best and most affectionate and only daughters – it belongs to estimate my sufferings and my wrongs. Such mothers will judge of my affliction on hearing of the death of my child, and upon my calling to recollection the last look, the last words, and all the affecting circumstances of our separation. Such mothers will see the depths of my sorrows. Every being with a heart of humanity in its bosom will drop a tear in sympathy with me. And will not the world then learn with indignation that this event, calculated to soften the hardest heart was the signal for new conspiracies and indefatigable efforts for the destruction of this afflicted mother? Your Majesty had torn my child from me; you had deprived me of the power of being at hand to succour her; you had taken from me the possibility of hearing her last prayers for her mother; you saw me bereft, forlorn, and broken-hearted; and this was the moment you chose for redoubling your persecutions ...

I have now frankly laid before your Majesty a statement of my wrongs, and a declaration of my views and intentions. You have cast upon me every slur to which the female character is liable. Instead of loving, honouring, and cherishing me, agreeable to your solemn vow, you have pursued me with hatred and scorn, and with all the means of destruction. You wrested from me my child, and with her my only comfort and consolation. You sent me sorrowing through the world, and even in my sorrows pursued me with unrelenting persecution. Having left me nothing but my innocence, you would now, by a mockery of justice, deprive me even of the reputation of possessing that. The poisoned bow and the poniard are means more manly than perjured witnesses and partial tribunals; and they are less cruel, inasmuch as life is less valuable than honour. If my life would have satisfied your Majesty, you should have had it on the sole condition of giving me a place in the same tomb with my child: but since you would send me dishonored to the grave, I will resist the attempt with all the means that it shall please God to give me.

Caroline R.

19

Adelaide of Saxe-Meiningen

(1792–1849), Queen Consort of William IV

When Duchess of Clarence, to her niece, Princess Victoria, afterwards Queen Regnant of England, 1822

Princess (Amelia) Adelaide, eldest daughter of George, duke of the miniature German duchy of Saxe-Meiningen, married William IV, in 1818, when he was Duke of Clarence. Their wedding was one of several that hurriedly took place among the elderly offspring of George III after the unexpected death of the Princess Charlotte, the heiress apparent. The tragedy created a rush in the royal family to provide a legitimate heir in the interests of the Hanoverian succession to England's throne.

When, at the age of twenty-six, Adelaide married William, that unattractive royal duke of fifty-three had already been rejected by two princesses and three ladies of title. He was, furthermore, up to his eyes in debt in his efforts to support ten illegitimate children. For over twenty years he had been openly living, in contented domesticity, with the renowned actress Mrs Dorothea Jordan,[1] and had thus become the father of these ten – known as the Fitzclarence family – of that productive lady's fifteen children.

On the death of George IV in 1830 (William's elder brother, Frederick, Duke of York, having died three years previously without lawful issue) the Duke of Clarence succeeded to the throne, and the retiring and gentle Adelaide of Saxe-Meiningen became queen consort.

It does not seem to have been an elevation in rank that she had particularly desired, or one for which she was, perhaps, eminently suited, by upbringing or temperament. In addition, where the king was concerned she had to cope with a peculiarly odd and trying character. She must, however, have found something lovable about her old husband, for she undoubtedly became deeply attached to him, as he had very quickly become attracted to her from their first meeting. As a 'Sailor King', with all the traits of a blaspheming, hot-tempered, and an irascible, though kind-hearted old sea dog, William IV was for ever setting the court and his statesmen by the ears, or, as he might have said, 'wiping the decks with them'. How could they be expected to have the patience to cope with a monarch who would amble about the streets, his umbrella under his arm like any ordinary civilian, publicly rebuking them for providing him with 'a damn bad pen' with which to sign important documents, seeing no need for all the fuss and expense of a coronation, and unceremoniously dropping important visiting sovereigns from his carriage at the door of their hotels! And not caring a darn for their blasted reforms so long as he got a little peace! He certainly seemed to possess all the delightful attributes of as comic a king as was ever conceived by W. S. Gilbert.

No, they could not cope with any patience. But Adelaide could, and did, for all the strain that it put upon her. She could do more. She could take under her wing the king's quiverful of 'bastards', introduce them as respected members of society, arrange suitable marriages for them, and even influence William's youngest son to take Holy Orders.[2] She was, in truth, a born wife and mother, but unfortunately where her own maternal hopes were concerned Adelaide was to lose both her children in infancy.

This early sorrow was, perhaps, an additional reason for her great love of children, and the special tenderness she always displayed towards the only child of Edward, Duke of Kent, who had died before this child, Victoria, was twelve months old.

The following letter was written by Adelaide, when she was Duchess of Clarence, to her little niece, on the princess's third birthday.

May 24th.

Uncle William and Aunt Adelaide send their love to *dear little Victoria* with their best wishes on her birthday, and hope that she will become a *very good Girl*, being now *three years old*.

Uncle William and Aunt Adelaide also beg *little Victoria* to give dear Mama and to dear Sissi a Kiss in their name, and to Aunt Augusta, Aunt Mary, and Aunt Sophia[3] too, and also to the *big Doll*. Uncle William and Aunt Adelaide are very sorry to be absent on that day, and not to see their *dear dear* little Victoria, as they are sure she will be very good and obedient to Dear Mama on that Day, and on many many others.

They also hope that dear little Victoria will not forget them, and know them again when Uncle and Aunt return.

To dear little Xandrina Victoria.

To Princess Victoria, 1829

On the death of her second daughter, Princess Elizabeth of Clarence, in 1821, Adelaide had written to her sister-in-law, the mother of Princess Victoria, 'My children are dead, but your child lives, and she is mine too.' This sincere remark shows something of greatness of spirit, expressed, as it was, from an anguished heart, and more especially as Princess Elizabeth had been the potential heiress to the throne.

Unfortunately for Adelaide the bad feeling that existed between her husband and his sister-in-law was to prevent her from enjoying as much of the companionship of Princess Victoria as she had obviously hoped. William had frankly avowed that he wished to see more of the child, 'but much less of her mother', while the Duchess of Kent, for her part, seemed to fear his 'corrupting' influence on her daughter. As a result, the young Victoria was debarred by her mother from taking part in many of the entertainments that the kindly Adelaide was for ever arranging for the children of her immediate circle of relations.

In acknowledging a birthday present from her niece, the Duchess of Clarence words her letter delicately so that the child shall not realise the tension that exists between her uncle and her mother, although Adelaide does admit to being 'deprived' of seeing her niece.

August 14th.

A thousand thanks to you, dear Victoria, for your very nice and well-written letter full of good wishes, which I had the pleasure to receive yesterday; and many thanks more for the pretty gifts your dear Mamma has sent me in your name. I wore them last night for your sake, dearest child, and thought of you very often.

It gives me great satisfaction to hear that you are enjoying the sea air ... I wish I could pay your Mamma a visit there and see you again, my dear little niece, for I long to have that pleasure, and must resign myself at being deprived of it for some time longer.

Your Uncle desires to be most kindly remembered to you, and hopes to receive soon also a letter from you, of whom he is as fond as I am. We speak of you very often, and trust that you will always consider us to be amongst your best friends ...

God bless you, my dear Victoria, is always the prayer of your most truly affectionate

Aunt Adelaide

When queen consort, to Mrs Fitzherbert, 1831

Although Adelaide had married an outstandingly eccentric husband, there are many instances of William IV's honest intentions as a man, however such actions might have been interpreted in the light of his happening to be king.

Shortly after his accession he and Adelaide went to stay at the Royal Pavilion at Brighton – that fabulous residence of George IV's – and almost his first visit was to Mrs Fitzherbert, his late brother's morganatic wife. This highly esteemed woman, whom, public opinion considered, has been most scandalously treated by George IV, was now reaching her eightieth year. The generous-hearted William, determined to atone to Mrs Fitzherbert for her wrongs, promised to renew her grant and invited her to court. He would have made her marriage lines public had he not been prevented from doing so by his brother's executors.

The old lady was somewhat overpowered by the kindness poured upon her in her declining years, and evidently showed to the observant Adelaide the oppression she felt on her first visit to the royal couple at the pavilion. The day after the visit the queen consort wrote the following kindly note to Maria Fitzherbert.

When Mrs Fitzherbert died a few years later there closed one of the saddest chapters in George IV's disgraceful career.

Dear Madam,

I hope you have passed a good night after your first going out, and have not suffered from it. This fine day will enable you to take a drive, which I am certain will do you much good.

According to my promise, I send you the Litography after my drawing of my niece Louisa.[4]

I was delighted to see you looking so well yesterday, and trust we shall meet oftener next winter than we have done this year.

Accept my best wishes for your health and happiness.

Yours sincerely,

Adelaide

When queen dowager,
to Queen Victoria, 1837

The king's short reign of seven years was fast drawing to a close. In his rapid decline he might vacillate in matters of state, but his fixed determination to remain alive until his niece and heir, Princess Victoria, had attained her majority, stood firm. So unrestrained was his dislike of his sister-in-law, the Duchess of Kent, that on the occasion of his seventy-first birthday, in responding to the toast to his health, the king had angrily and loudly announced before a gathering of 100 guests that he trusted in God that his life might be spared for nine months longer, after which period, in the event of his death, no regency would take place. 'I should then have the satisfaction,' he continued, 'of leaving the royal authority to the person of that young lady' – pointing to Princess Victoria – 'the heiress to the crown, and not in the hands of a person now near me,' who is herself incompetent to act with propriety in the station in which she would be placed.'

In the awe-inspiring hush that followed the queen consort showed pronounced consternation, Princess Victoria burst into tears, and the Duchess of Kent ordered her carriage.

William IV's desire, however, was realised, for he succeeded in living just long enough to see Princess Victoria's eighteenth birthday.

Although requested by her niece and sovereign to take anything she cared for, when departing from Windsor Castle, all the widowed consort selected was a silver cup, which the late king had used at her hand during his illness, and a family painting by Hayter. It is to be wondered if ever any departing queen, when relinquishing her crown, had furnished herself with less in the way of *lares* and *penates*.

The evening before she left Windsor Castle the queen dowager sat for the last time at her desk and wrote the following letter to the young queen regnant.

Windsor Castle,
July 9th.

My dearest Niece,

I must, before I leave this dear Castle, once more express to you the grateful sense I entertain for the kind treatment I have experienced from you since it has pleased our heavenly Father to put you in possession of it. You have contributed much to my comfort under all the painful and distressing circumstances of this time of woe, and I assure you that I ever shall remember it with sincere gratitude.

I hope that you continue quite well, and do not suffer from the exertions and duties of your new position.

My best wishes and Prayers attend you on all occasions, for I shall be to the rest of my life devoted and attached to you as

Your most affectionate
Aunt and Subject,
Adelaide

To Queen Victoria, 1838

The queen dowager was only forty-four years of age when Victoria ascended the throne. She had been in indifferent health for some time, and the nursing of the late king, which she had personally undertaken throughout his last weeks, had proved a considerable strain on her. The rest of her years were to be spent mainly under invalid conditions, with occasional travel in search of health. Yet at any and all times, Adelaide never relaxed her charitable interests. It is said that her public subscriptions alone amounted to over £20,000 a year.

As queen she had concerned herself with the welfare of her old husband, to whom she had given unremitting care, and in the happiness and futures of the royal children in her circle. Despite her peace-loving and retiring character, however, she had not escaped public censure or the imputations of slanderous tongues.

At the time of the Reform Bill, during the political upheavals and rioting that took place, Queen Adelaide had been wrongfully accused of influencing the king. In fact, she held no political views at all, as her letters clearly show. She had, however, an inherent distrust – almost a fear – of change in any form, and a dread of the consequences of rebellion. It was, perhaps, for this reason that her attitude was misinterpreted. Her undisguised preference for her Chamberlain, Earl Howe, also gave opportunity at this time for the uncharitably minded to seek to cast a slur on the relationship, but they failed to destroy one of the many sincere friendships that Adelaide maintained to the end of her days.

After she had become queen dowager her popularity with the nation at large was very great. The queen regnant herself had a deep attachment to her aunt, and wrote on her death in 1849, 'We have lost the kindest and dearest of friends, and the universal feeling of sorrow, of regret, and of real appreciation of her character is very touching.'

Before she died the queen dowager wrote, in her own hand, her instructions as to her funeral. She desired 'not to be laid out in State', for the funeral to take place 'by Daylight', and her coffin, with no procession or ceremony, 'to be carried by Sailors to the chapel at Windsor. I want,' she added, 'to give as little trouble as possible.'

The gentle Queen Adelaide had never consciously given any trouble.

On the day of the coronation of Queen Victoria the dowager queen wrote the following devout and tender-hearted letter to her niece.

> Marlboro' House,
> 28th June, 1838.
> (at a quarter before twelve o'clock on Coronation Day)
> My dearest Niece,
> The guns are just announcing your approach to the Abbey, and as I am not near you and cannot take part in the Sacred

Ceremony of your Coronation, I must address you in waiting to assure you, that my thoughts and my whole heart are with you, and my Prayers are offered up to Heaven for your happiness and the prosperity and glory of your reign. May our heavenly Father bless and preserve you, and His Holy Ghost dwell within you, to give you that Peace which the world cannot give. Accept of these my best wishes, and the Blessing of

Your most devoted and attached aunt,

Adelaide

20

Victoria

(1819–1901)

When princess, to her uncle, Leopold, King of the Belgians, 1837

There exists a deep-rooted and an age-old conviction that women make better monarchs than men. It was unquestionably true in the case of Elizabeth I. It was equally accurate where Queen Victoria was concerned, more especially if one reviews the reigns of her immediate predecessors.

Destined to become queen regnant at eighteen years of age, Alexandrina Victoria – only child of Edward, Duke of Kent (fourth son of George III) by his marriage to Victoria Mary Louisa, daughter of the Duke of Saxe-Coburg-Saalfeld – was to reign on the throne of England for well over sixty years.

Up to the time of her accession she had been so jealously and strictly guarded by her mother – never having been permitted out of her presence or that of the governess, Fräulein Lehzen, by day or night – that practically nothing whatsoever was known as to the young queen's character, capacities, or potentialities. She was, however, to disclose, in course of time, marked abilities as a constitutional sovereign, independence of thought and judgement, wide humanity, and outstanding skill in handling the panoramic procession of prime ministers that passed in and out of office during her long reign. Indeed, 'the little woman who knew her own mind' was to prove something of a phenomenon among crowned heads in the eyes of the world, and to exhibit a vein of steel in administering her regal duties which caused no minister ever to disregard her advice without the fear that he had incurred a dangerous responsibility.

A prodigious letter writer, Victoria's early correspondence reveals her abounding vitality and love of life, her gay, frank and affectionate character, and her zest for all and everything taking place around her. At the same time it is very evident how seriously she regarded her duties as a reigning monarch, combined with how determined she was for it to be understood that her conception, like that of Elizabeth I, of the majesty of kings was high.

On her father's death when she was only a few months old, her mother's brother, Leopold, the unfortunate husband of the Princess Charlotte, became her self-appointed guardian, and was to serve, as she wrote on his death, 'ever as a father' to her.

One of the queen's first acts of personal independence on her accession was to free herself from the dominating influence of her mother – much to the duchess's annoyance and wrath. Her next was very tactfully to discourage her much-loved uncle, Leopold, from any attempts to interfere in matters relating to England's politics and international policy.

The following letter was written by Princess Victoria when the news of William IV's death was hourly expected. Stockmar, to whom she refers, was Baron von Stockmar, her uncle's wise and astute adviser for many years, whom King Leopold had sent over from Belgium to be at hand with help and guidance when Victoria should ascend the throne.

19th June, 1837.

My dearly beloved Uncle,
    Your *kind* and dear letter, containing *most wholesome, prudent, sound* and *excellent* advice, was given me by our good

and *invaluable honest* friend, Stockmar, and I beg you to accept my best thanks for it. Before I say anything else, let me tell you how happy and thankful I am to have Stockmar here; he has been, and is, of the greatest possible use, and be assured, dearest uncle, that he possesses my *most entire confidence.*

The King's state, I may fairly say, is *hopeless*; he may *perhaps* linger a few days, but he cannot recover *ultimately.* Yesterday the physicians declared he could not live till the morning, but to-day he is a little better; the great fear is his *excessive* weakness and no *pulse* at all. Poor old man! I feel sorry for him; he was always personally kind to me, and I should be ungrateful and devoid of feeling if I did not remember this.

I do look forward to the event which it seems is likely to occur soon, with calmness and quietness; I am not alarmed at it, and yet I do not suppose myself quite equal to all; I trust, however, that with *good-will, honesty* and *courage* I shall not, at all events, *fail.* Your advice is most excellent, and you may depend upon it I shall make use of it, and follow it, as also what Stockmar says. I *never showed* myself *openly*, to belong to any party, and I do not belong to any party. The administration will undoubtedly be well received by me, the more so as I have *real* confidence in them, and in particular in Lord Melbourne;[1] who is a straight-forward, honest, clever and good man.

I need not add much more, dearest Uncle, but that I trust that the All-Powerful Being who has so long watched over my destinies will guide and support me, in whatever situation and station it may please Him to place me ...

When queen regnant, to the Prime Minister, Viscount Melbourne, 1839

As a youthful and an inexperienced sovereign, Victoria was to find no lack of candidates eager to act as counsellors in her administration of affairs. In addition, Uncle Leopold's letters, containing wise advice, continued to pour in; Baron von Stockmar stood steadfastly at her elbow, ready with his guidance; and her governess, daughter of a Hanoverian clergyman and now Baroness Lehzen, having temporarily supplanted her mother in Victoria's affections, had taken over the management of the royal household.

There was, however, to be one paramount influence over the new queen, in the person of her prime minister, William Lamb, Viscount Melbourne, then in his fifty-eighth year. From the beginning Victoria was fascinated by her courtly minister, with his supple intellect, fine sensitive nature, and great personal charm. Further, his reverential affection and solicitous attitude as of a parent completely won the queen's heart. So much did she become attached to Melbourne that she saw no necessity for herself to marry so long as she could reign with him at her side.

Her great dread, in the happiness that their unusual but delightful association gave her, was that the trend of political events might necessitate the resignation of Melbourne and his ministry. When this threatened in 1839, the queen wrote to her very dear prime minister the following letter. Reading between the lines one can sense the note of deep affection and of the despair that had descended upon the little queen at the prospect of her adviser and friend being replaced by a new counsellor of state.

Buckingham Palace,
8th May.

The Queen thinks Lord Melbourne may possibly wish to know how she is this morning; the Queen is somewhat calmer; she was in a wretched state till nine o'clock last night, when she tried to occupy herself and tried to think less gloomily of this dreadful change, and she succeeded in calming herself till she went to bed at twelve, and she slept well; but on waking this morning, all – all that had happened in one short eventful day, came most forcibly to her mind, and brought back her grief; the Queen, however, feels better now; but she couldn't touch a morsel of food last night, nor can she this morning. The Queen trusts Lord Melbourne slept well, and is well this morning; and that he will come precisely at eleven o'clock.

To Prince Albert of Saxe-Coburg-Gotha, 1840

Probably one of the reasons for the young queen's reluctance to marry was the fear of being once more dominated and restrained by an influence similar to that which her mother, the Duchess of Kent, had exercised over her. It was for this same reason, perhaps, that both before and for some time after her marriage to her cousin, Prince Albert of Saxe-Coburg-Gotha, that she made evident her views as to the distinction between the duties of a wife, and those of a ruling sovereign.

As prince consort – although he was never actually created so until 1857, and then the title was bestowed by the queen's initiative only, never by Act of Parliament – Prince Albert was to know, and withstand, many humiliations as only the husband of the queen regnant. Somewhat staid, and reserved of temperament, with no particular liking or attraction for the opposite sex, the young prince was really the 'creation' of his uncle, King Leopold, and of Baron von Stockmar. These two men could be said to have moulded him for the difficult part he was to play.

That Prince Albert was not to contemplate any easy task in his marriage to his cousin Victoria in her regal position and new-found independence must have been more than clear to him from the following letter that she wrote shortly before their wedding in February, 1840.

Buckingham Palace,

31st January.

… You have written to me in one of your letters about our stay at Windsor, but; dear Albert, you have not at all understood the matter. *You forget, my dearest Love, that I am the Sovereign, and that business can stop and wait for nothing. Parliament is sitting, and something occurs almost every day, for which I may be required, and it is quite impossible for me to be absent from London; therefore two or three days is already a long time to he absent. I am never easy a moment, if I am not on the spot, and see and hear what is going on, and everybody, including all my Aunts (who are very knowing in all these things), says I must come out after the second day, for, as I must he surrounded by my Court, I cannot keep alone. This is also my own wish in every way.*

Now as to the Arms: as an English Prince you have no right, and Uncle Leopold had no right to quarter the English Arms, but the Sovereign has the power to allow it by Royal Command; this was done for Uncle Leopold by the Prince Regent, and I will do it again for you. But it can only be done by Royal Command …

Farewell, dearest Albert, and think often of thy faithful

Victoria R.

To Leopold, King of the Belgians, 1841

The year previous to her marriage had proved a very trying one for the young queen. There had been public and political storm over the 'Bedchamber Question';[2] she had been hissed at as she drove on the course at Ascot; and serious Chartist riots had broken out in the north and midlands of England, and had in Birmingham to be put down by armed force.

These troublesome happenings had the effect of hastening the queen into matrimony, a state which she frankly said she had had no desire to entertain 'for at least four years'.

As a concession to the prevalent mood of the country the royal bride was clad from head to foot in articles of solely British manufacture. Attired in dress of Spitalfields silk, veil of Honiton lace, London-made gloves of English kid, and ribbons from Coventry, the queen regnant was married to Prince Albert of Saxe-Coburg-Gotha in the Chapel Royal, St James's, on 10 February 1840.

Her second child – a son – the 'blue-eyed' boy referred to by the queen in the following letter to Uncle Leopold, was sixty years later to ascend the throne as Edward VII. From the queen's postscript it is clear that 'Pussy' – the first-born Victoria Adelaide – resented a rival claimant to parental adoration. A few years later she was – not unreasonably, perhaps – to take a dislike to her pet name, angrily asserting that she was not 'Pussy' but 'The Princess Royal'.

Buckingham Palace,
29th November, 1841.

My dearest Uncle,

I would have written sooner, had I not been a little bilious, which made me very low, and not in spirits to write. The weather has been so exceedingly relaxing, that it made me at the end of the fortnight quite bilious, and this, you know, affects the spirits. I am much better, but they think that I shall not get my appetite and spirits back till I can get out of town; we are therefore going in a week at latest. I am going for a drive this morning, and am certain it will do me good. Our little boy is a wonderfully strong and large child, with very large dark-blue eyes, a finely formed but somewhat large nose, and a pretty little mouth; I *hope* and pray he may be like his dearest Papa. He is to be called *Albert*, and Edward is to be his second name. Pussy, dear child, is still *the* great pet amongst us all, and is getting so fat and strong again ...

I beg you to forgive this letter being so badly written, but my feet are being rubbed, and as I have got the box on which I am writing on my knee, it is not easy to write quite straight – but you must not think my hand trembles.

> Ever your devoted Niece,
> Victoria R.

Pussy is not at all pleased with her brother.

To Miss Florence Nightingale, 1856

Reports by newspaper correspondents of the terrible condition of the Army, and the appalling sufferings of the sick and wounded in the Crimean War, roused the strongest indignation throughout Great Britain.

Having long interested herself in improving the standard of nursing in this country, which indeed was at an unspeakably low level, Florence Nightingale – through the influence of the statesman, Sydney Herbert[3] – set sail for Scutari with a band of trained and capable nurses. The wonderful work undertaken by 'The Lady with the Lamp' to alleviate the conditions of the ill and maimed, and the reforms she introduced into the military hospitals soon caused her praise to be widely acclaimed.

The queen herself was deeply impressed by the success of what must have been an audacious experiment for those times, and under such dangerous conditions. In the following letter to Florence Nightingale she shows her personal appreciation of the 'great and blessed work' of that courageous and remarkable woman. Despite her self-imposed hardships, however, Florence Nightingale lived to be ninety years of age, and on her death in 1910 her coffin was borne by scarlet-coated guardsmen, for whose regimental fellows she had 'fought the good fight' half a century earlier.

Windsor Castle,
(January) 1856.

Dear Miss Nightingale,

You are, I know, well aware of the high sense I entertain of the Christian devotion which you have displayed during this great and bloody war, and I need hardly repeat to you how warm my admiration is for your services, which are fully equal to those of my dear and brave soldiers whose sufferings you have had the *privilege* of alleviating in so merciful a manner. I am, however, anxious of marking my feelings in a manner which I trust will be agreeable to you, and therefore send you with this letter a brooch,[4] the form and emblems of which commemorate your great and blessed work, and which, I hope, you will wear as a mark of the high approbation of your Sovereign.

It will be a great satisfaction to me, when you return at last to these shores, to make the acquaintance of one who has set so bright an example to our sex. And with every prayer for the preservation of your valuable health, believe me, always, yours sincerely,

Victoria R.

To the Earl of Clarendon, 1857

Both the queen and the prince consort warmly approved the proposal to unite the royal houses of England and Prussia by a marriage between their eldest daughter, Victoria Adelaide, and Frederick William, Crown Prince of Prussia.[5] The betrothal took place in 1856 at Balmoral when the princess royal was fifteen years of age and the crown prince in his twenty-fourth year.

Shortly before the date of the wedding two years later an unexpected difficulty arose as to where the ceremony should take place, it being customary for princes of royal blood to be married in Berlin. The suggestion of any alteration of plan exasperated the queen, and she wrote the following angry letter to the Foreign Secretary, the Earl of Clarendon, which not only expresses her feelings without restraint, but also makes it perfectly clear that her decision in the controversy is final.

The princess royal – now known as 'Vicky' – was her father's favourite, and probably Prince Albert more than anyone was to suffer most at parting with his sympathetic, intelligent, and artistic daughter, with whom he had so much in common.

The wedding took place with brilliant ceremonial, accompanied by national rejoicings, at the Chapel Royal, St James's, on 25 January 1858.

Windsor Castle,
25th October, 1857

... It would be well if Lord Clarendon would tell Lord Bloomfield[6] not to *entertain* the *possibility* of such a question as the Princess Royal's marriage taking place in Berlin. The Queen *never* could consent to it, both for public and private reasons, and the assumption of its being *too much* for a Prince Royal of Prussia to *come* over to marry the *Princess Royal of Great Britain* IN England is too *absurd*, to say the least. The Queen must say that there never was even the *shadow* of a *doubt* on Prince *Frederick William's* part where the marriage should take place, and she suspects this to be the mere gossip of the Berliners. Whatever may be the usual practice of Prussian Princes, it is not *every* day that one marries the eldest daughter of the Queen of England. The question therefore must be considered as settled and closed ...

To Leopold, King of the Belgians, 1861

The year 1861 was to open – and alas! close – as a tragic one in the personal life of the queen.

The estrangement that had existed between herself and her mother, the Duchess of Kent, after Victoria's accession to the throne, had been brought to a happy termination through the harmonising influence of Prince Albert, who had won the Duchess's confidence and respect.

In the early part of the year the Duchess of Kent, then seventy-four years of age, had had an operation for an abscess on her arm. Medical reports, however, were satisfactory, and on 15 March the queen went to visit her mother at Frogmore. The following day, to the queen's consternation and grief, her mother died.

This was Victoria's first experience of intimate loss, and in the appended letter written on the same day to the duchess's brother King Leopold, she unrestrainedly gives vent to her emotional distress. Later, finding among her mother's personal papers 'in a little desk I have never seen' keepsakes relating to Victoria's father and to her own childhood, which the duchess had secretly treasured through the years, she was thrown into a state of deepest morbidity, of which she wrote unsparingly to Uncle Leopold.

Frogmore,
16th March, 1861.

My darling beloved Uncle,

On this, the most dreadful day of my life, does your poor brokenhearted child write one line of love and devotion. *She* is gone! That *precious, dearly beloved tender Mother*, whom I never was parted from but for a few months – without whom I can't *imagine life* – has been taken from us! It is too dreadful! But she is at peace – at rest – her fearful sufferings at an end! It was quite painless – though there was very *distressing*, heartrending breathing to witness. I held her dear, dear hand in mine to the very last, which I am truly thankful for! But the watching that precious life going out was fearful! Alas! she never knew me! But she was spared the pang of parting! How this will *grieve* and *distress* you!

You are now doubly precious to us! ... Dear Albert is dreadfully overcome – and well he may be, for *she* adored him! I feel so truly *verwaist*. God bless and protect you. Ever your devoted and truly unhappy Niece and Child,

Victoria R.

To Leopold, King of the Belgians, 1861

Queen Victoria had scarcely had time to recover from the sudden death of her mother before there was to be yet another – and more vital – blow in store for her.

The prince consort, who had been displaying signs of worry and fatigue for some time, took to his bed with what was assumed to be a serious chill. His physician, Sir James Clark, was satisfied that the prince's condition warranted no particular anxiety. In this confidence the queen wrote to her uncle, King Leopold, saying that she did not sit up with Prince Albert at night as she could be of no use, and 'there is nothing to cause alarm'. It proved, however, to be a case of wrong diagnosis, a second opinion disclosing that the prince was suffering from typhoid fever. It was then too late to save his life, and on 14 December,[7] as the distraught and horrified queen knelt by his bedside, he drew his last breath. 'She shrieked – one long wild shriek that rang through the terror-stricken Castle – and understood that she had lost him for ever.'[8]

In spite of any early forebodings that the queen might have had, the prince consort had proved not only an exemplary husband and father, but had exhibited such exceptional abilities as consort to the queen regnant that his death was regarded as a calamitous happening, nationally and internationally. He was only forty-two when he died, but he had literally worn himself out in his efforts to fulfil his task honourably, and, conscientious to the end, had never spared himself in his attempts to serve the country he had been fated to adopt.

In her terrible loneliness and grief, Victoria was now to realise to the full the high-mindedness and fine qualities of the husband she had learned to love so deeply, and in the following letter she gives way, for the second time that fatal year, to her uncontrollable despair.

Osborne,
December 20th.

My *own* Dearest, Kindest *Father*,

For as such have I *ever* loved you. The poor fatherless baby of eight months is now the utterly broken-hearted and crushed widow of forty-two! My *life* as a *happy* one is *ended*! the world is gone for *me*! If I *must live* on (and I will do nothing to make me worse than I am), it is henceforth for our poor fatherless children – for my unhappy country, which has lost *all* in losing him – and in *only* doing what I know and *feel* he would wish, for he is near me – his spirit will guide and inspire me! But oh! to be cut off in the prime of life – to see our pure, happy, quiet domestic life, which alone enabled me to bear my *much* disliked position, CUT OFF at forty-two – when I *had* hoped with such instinctive certainty that God *would never* part us, and would let us grow old together (though *he* always talked of the shortness of life) – is *too awful*, too cruel! And yet it *must* be for *his* good, his happiness! His purity was too great, his aspiration *too high* for this poor, *miserable* world! His great soul is *now only* enjoying that for which it *was* worthy! And I will *not* envy him – only pray that *mine* may be perfected by it and for to be with him eternally, for which blessed moment I earnestly long. Dearest, dearest Uncle, *how* kind of you to come! It will be an unspeakable *comfort*, and you *can do* much to tell people to do what they ought to do. As for my *own good*, *personal* servants – poor Phipps in particular – nothing can be more devoted, heartbroken as they are, and anxious only to live as *he* wished!

Ever your devoted, wretched Child,
Victoria R.

To Mrs Abraham Lincoln, 1865

When that famous statesman, Abraham Lincoln, who had brought a great people through the perils of a mighty revolution, died on 15 April 1865 as a result of a fanatic's bullet, consternation was worldwide. Lincoln's nobility of character, vast humanity, and courage in freeing his nation from slavery were to establish his name as that of one of the greatest benefactors of his fellow-kind in history.

Queen Victoria was very moved by the tragedy, and sent the following letter of sympathy to Mrs Lincoln. Her own personal sorrow was vividly revived, and she records in her journal that such sad and striking events had convinced her more and more of the utter nothingness of this world, of the terrible uncertainty of all earthly happiness, and the utter vanity of all earthly greatness.

Osborne,
29th April, 1865.

Dear Madam,

Though a stranger to you, I cannot remain silent when so terrible a calamity has fallen upon you and your country, and must express personally my deep and heartfelt sympathy with you under the shocking circumstances of your present dreadful misfortune.

No one can better appreciate than I can, who am myself utterly broken-hearted by the loss of my own beloved husband, who was the light of my life, my stay, my all, what your sufferings must be; and I earnestly pray that you may be supported by Him to Whom alone the sorely stricken can look for comfort, in this hour of heavy affliction!

With the renewed expression of true sympathy, I remain, dear Madam, your sincere friend,

Victoria R.

To the Earl of Granville, 1881

For some years following Prince Albert's death the queen, absorbed in her sorrow, withdrew herself from public life to the extent that she became known to her subjects as little more than 'The Widow at Windsor'.[9] All the same, despite her retirement, she was continuing her conscientious administration and guidance in the affairs of the nation, and, in due course, she was to emerge once more from her self-imposed seclusion.

The one who had the most right to claim credit for effecting this revival of the queen's public interests was her prime minister, Benjamin Disraeli,[10] and their personal friendship was a remarkable chapter in the lives of both of them. Where Gladstone, the previous prime minister, had, as Disraeli trenchantly remarked, 'treated the Queen like a public department', he himself had 'treated her like a woman'. None of his predecessors or successors succeeded in approaching the intimate relationship that Disraeli established with his sovereign, whom she openly acknowledged as a valued friend. On his death in April 1881, she wrote, 'My grief is great and lasting.'

In respecting Disraeli's desire, referred to by the queen in the following letter, to be buried at Hughenden, where he had his Buckinghamshire estate, she knew full well his great love for that county, and his admiration of the place it had filled in history.

The funeral was attended by Edward, Prince of Wales, as well as cabinet ministers, ambassadors, and a throng of eminent persons. But perhaps the greatest tribute to Disraeli's memory was paid by the queen herself when, a few days later, she privately visited Hughenden churchyard to lay a wreath of camellias on the grave of 'My dear, great friend'.

Osborne,
21st April, 1881.

The Queen thanks Lord Granville[11] for his words of sympathy. She is overwhelmed with the loss of one of the kindest, truest, and best friends and wisest counsellors she ever had – who had the welfare and comfort of his Sovereign in private affairs as entirely at heart as he had the honour and welfare of the nation.

Well may Lord Granville dread the loss, for he did not follow the example of the late Opposition in trying to lower the Prime Minister of the day and in abusing all his acts, as alas! to the Queen's great grief many of them did.

The country has shown and will show still more now that they have lost him, how much they owed to him. May his example be followed by the rising generation!

The Queen, on being referred to, decided that his wishes to be laid by the side of his devoted wife should be considered as sacred, and that he should rest at Hughenden, of which he was so fond.

To Augusta, Empress of Germany, 1882

The great spiritual courage that the queen possessed was remorselessly tested during her long life, in which she suffered an endless series of personal bereavements and trials. The abundance of physical courage, which she could also claim, was challenged on more than one occasion when attempts were made on her life, the last and seventh such event being in 1882, as she was walking from the train at Windsor station to her carriage, and was shot at from the crowd.

In her diary, which the queen kept for over seventy years, she records simply, 'There was a sound of what I thought was an explosion from the engine, but in another moment I saw people rushing about and a man being violently hustled ... I then realized that it was a shot, which must have been meant for me.'

Shortly after this attempted assassination, Queen Victoria wrote to her great friend the Empress of Germany (whose son, the Crown Prince Frederick had, it will be remembered, married

Victoria's eldest daughter). From the letter one would suppose that the happening had been little more than a 'thrill' as far as the intended royal victim was concerned. It did, however, cause a great outcry, as the queen's popularity was very much in the ascendant, not only in this country but abroad. The youth responsible, a Robert Maclean, was tried for high treason, and the somewhat curious verdict of 'not guilty, but insane' was brought in, causing much comment and controversy. The queen herself, as she mentions in this letter, considered her assailant 'not insane'.[12] However, the verdict remained, and Maclean was sent to an asylum 'during her Majesty's pleasure'.

> Windsor Castle,
> 7th March.

Dearest Augusta,

A thousand thanks for your two dear letters and for your congratulations concerning the incident on March 2nd. Thank God that no one was injured! As I saw nothing and even with the noise of the shot I was not conscious of anything at the time itself, I was not frightened or affected in the very slightest degree … But the sympathy, the interest and the indignation which it has aroused are indeed touching and comforting. Moreover, everywhere abroad people have shown the keenest and most flattering sympathy. I had no idea that I was so popular in other countries. I can swear from the bottom of my heart that I have always wished and endeavoured to do my best for the welfare and happiness of the world, as you yourself can testify, dearest friend. But such recognition during one's lifetime is very rare, and I feel deeply moved by it. Please let this be known when and wherever you see an opportunity! I have sent Vicky a drawing of the criminal which she can show to you. He is a thoroughly bad and eccentric type, but *not* insane …

I enclose a very good article and also several press reports from the newspapers.

> V.R.

To Augusta, Empress of Germany, 1883

The queen's private life by personal choice, as far as her position would allow, was one of extreme simplicity and homeliness, and her motherly sympathy extended to the humblest of her subjects. She did not, as has been commonly supposed, live in an atmosphere of gloom from the time of the prince consort's death to the end of her days. On the contrary, her wide interests and vital force caused the queen, even after the invigorating spirit of Disraeli had been withdrawn, to fling herself wholeheartedly into a multitude of public duties and activities.

When, in 1852, a gentleman by the name of Neild, who lived at North Marston, in Buckinghamshire, had left the queen a handsome fortune on his death, he unwittingly contributed to one of the greatest interests and pleasures of the queen's life: for with this personal fortune she bought Balmoral. One of her factotums there from earliest days was John Brown, who combined the offices of groom, footman, page, and, as she said herself, 'maid'. Nowhere, she confessed to Uncle Leopold, had she found such a 'good, *faithful*, attached servant'. In her later years, to serve her personal amusement and relief from the tedium of affairs of state, she rejoiced in the companionship of this same John Brown, who, in the nature of her court jester, was permitted a liberty of speech and an intimacy of approach which was the privilege of all good servants of his calling.

Following an accident that befell the queen at Windsor Castle in 1883, John Brown's strong Scottish arm was the first to her aid. To her sorrow, however, it was the last act he was to perform for his sovereign, for he died in his sleep while she was still incapacitated from her fall. The following letter that she wrote to her old friend the Empress of Germany shortly afterwards shows how sadly the queen missed Brown's aid and companionship.

Osborne,
5th May,

Dear Augusta,

I am very grateful for your kind letters, and for your ever ready sympathy. My leg is recovering slowly, but only very slowly. The last few days I have been able to get about my room on two sticks, but I still have to be carried up and down stairs ...

Apart from this I feel terribly depressed, and get more so instead of less, for I miss my faithful, kind friend and constant companion more and more at every turn, especially just now, when I so greatly need his care and his strong arm. I enclose a photograph of him but will send more later, as I think you would like to have them as reminders of so many happy hours spent together ... What you say about my peculiar isolation, due to my lofty station with its heavy burdens, and how, for that very reason, the loss of so loyal and esteemed a friend as my never to be forgotten and quite irreplaceable Brown, is doubly, or rather I might say a thousand times heavier, is only too true. My sufferings are indeed cruel, and I feel weighed down with them.

I am sending the photograph unframed, as it is easier to pack. Perhaps you will have it framed and put up where you can sometimes look at it ...

Popular faith in sovereigns had been considerably on the wane in England when Queen Victoria came to the throne, for she had been the innocent inheritor of a crown tarnished by the ineptitude and vice of her Hanoverian forebears. In addition, conditions in Europe were, to say the least, unstable; tumults and upheavals were imminent, and the coming years were to see the breaking up of kingdoms and the overthrow of potentates.

Yet, with the aid of a succession of able ministers – for did ever wise monarch choose foolish advisers? – this great constitutional sovereign brought the British throne, unscathed, through those dynamic times and handed on to her successor a burnished crown which was the symbol of private virtue and public honour. It is significant to record that when Queen Victoria died, 1 square mile in 4 of the land of the world was under the British flag, and probably one person in every five alive was a subject of the Queen of England.

Crystal clear in judgment, iron-willed in character, the queen regnant's policy was exclusively her own, nor, in her regal self-dependence, would she permit any partnership. In this respect she was particularly rigid in excluding her son and heir, Edward, Prince of Wales, from her political duties, an exclusion which she maintained until the end. This circumspect attitude towards the successor, however, was by no means uncommon throughout England's history, and was markedly true in the case of the Hanoverian monarchs.

In the first month of the first year of the new century Queen Victoria died at Osborne in her eighty-second year, and was buried at Frogmore, Windsor. Her passing was a most memorable and revealing event. In the course of the long, long years Victoria had become the Mother of her People, and a safe and sure link between all parts of a democratic empire. Because of this she had won not blind homage, but the passionate loyalty of her subjects, far and wide. Her death was to bring the solemn realisation that the greatest of English constitutional sovereigns, whose name, like that of Elizabeth, would mark an age in history, had laid aside her crown at last and gone to her well-earned rest.

And so, with the departure of the last of the monarchs of the House of Hanover, we end this selection of intimate letters of England's queens. The interest of the letters is in their human quality. The keynote of the personalities, as revealed by their private correspondence, is their essentially human characteristics.

In retrospect, the letters of the queens may be said to serve as a series of 'spotlights' cast on what one must remember were living characters, each striving to play her destined part in the dark and crowded amphitheatre of life.

Which of these queens was most to be admired? Which was most impeccable? Which was most wronged? Which most to be despised? The conclusion must surely depend upon the qualities in a royal sovereign that one personally chooses most to venerate.

While far from being an Iliad of woes, this correspondence as a whole is saddening and curiously chastening, revealing mainly the writer's difficulties, insoluble problems, heartaches and despairs. All the same, the letters contain little more than expressions of the inner feelings of the average human being. Yet should not each of these royal scribes have felt and acted beyond the understanding of the ordinary individual? For her lot was cast in a high estate: she was a queen!

Yes, she was a queen! And if the compiler be permitted to adapt a well-known quotation, had not that queen eyes? Had she not hands, organs, dimensions, senses, affections, passions? She was hurt by the same weapons, subject to the same diseases, healed by the same means, warmed and cooled by the same summer and winter, as was any commoner. If she was pricked, she bled. If she was tickled, she laughed. If she was poisoned, she died. And if she was wronged, should she not seek to be revenged?

In the opinion of the compiler at least, recognition of the undeniable truth of the foregoing passage suitably and sufficiently disarms intolerant criticism of anyone of these royal correspondents.

In considering the solely personal aspects presented in each queen's life story by the evidence of these letters, it is probable that the reader will feel more than inclined to subscribe to the sentiment expressed by Queen Elizabeth I shortly after her accession to the throne: 'They who know what cares I bear, would not think I took any great joy in wearing a crown.'

Elizabeth of York

(1466–1503), Queen Consort of Henry VII

To Isabella, Queen of Castile and wife of Ferdinand of Aragon, 1497

To the most serene and potent princess the Lady Elizabeth [*sic*], by God's Grace Queen of Castile, Leon, Aragon, Sicily, Granada, etc. our cousin and dearest relation, Elizabeth, by the same Grace Queen of England and France, and Lady of Ireland, wishes health and the most prosperous increase of her desires:

Although we before entertained singular love and regard to Your Highness above all other queens in the world, as well for the consanguinity and necessary intercourse which mutually take place between us, as also for the eminent dignity and virtue by which Your Majesty so shines and excels that your most celebrated name is noised abroad and diffused everywhere; yet much more has this our love increased and accumulated by the accession of the most noble affinity which has recently been celebrated between the most illustrious lord Arthur, Prince of Wales, our eldest son, and the most illustrious princess the Lady Catherine, the Infanta, your daughter. Hence it is that, amongst our other cares and cogitations, first and foremost we wish and desire from our heart that we may often and speedily hear of the health and safety of your serenity, and of the health and safety of the aforesaid most illustrious Lady Catherine, whom we think of and esteem as our own daughter, than which nothing could be more grateful and acceptable to us. Therefore we request your serenity to certify of your estate, and of that of the aforesaid most illustrious Lady Catherine our common daughter. And if there be anything in our power which would be grateful or pleasant to Your Majesty, use us and ours as freely as you would your own; for, with most willing mind, we offer all that we have to you, and wish to have all in common with you. We should have written you the news of our state, and of that of this kingdom, but the most serene lord the King, our husband, will have written at length of these things to Your Majesties. For the rest may Your Majesty fare most happily according to our wishes.

From the Palace of Westminster, 3rd day of December, 1497.

Elizabeth R.

To the most serene and potent princess the Lady Elizabeth [*sic*], by God's Grace Queen of Castile, Leon, Aragon, Sicily, Granada, our cousin and dearest kinswoman.

APPENDIX B

Mary, Queen of Scots

(1542–1587)

In the following moving but dignified last letter to Queen Elizabeth it will be noticed that the Queen of Scots avoids any expression which might be interpreted as a plea for mercy. Her request that she should not be put to death privately was solely because she feared that her enemies would say that she had taken her own life. As a Roman Catholic she would, in such circumstances, be known to have died without receiving the rites of the Catholic Church.

On witnessing Queen Elizabeth's distress on receiving this letter, Leicester hastily wrote to Walsingham,[1] 'There is a letter from the Scottish queen that hath wrought tears; but, I trust, shall do no further herein, albeit the delay is dangerous.' From this remark it is obvious that Leicester was determined to hasten the execution of the Queen of Scots before Elizabeth had had time to change her mind.

(Fotheringhay, Northants).

Madame,

Having, with difficulty, obtained leave from those to whom you have committed me to open to you all I have on my heart, as much for exonerating myself from any ill-will or desire of committing cruelty, or any act of enmity against those with whom I am connected in blood, as also kindly to communicate to you what I thought would serve you, as much for your weal and preservation as for the maintenance of the peace and repose of this isle, which can only be injured if you reject my advice, you will credit or disbelieve my discourse as it seems best to you.

I am resolved to strengthen myself in Christ alone, who to those invoking him with a true heart, never fails in His justice and consolation, especially to those who are bereft of all human aid – such are under His holy protection; to Him be the glory! He has answered my expectation, having given me heart and strength, *in spe contra spem* [in hope against hope], to endure the unjust calumnies, accusations and condemnations (of those who have no jurisdiction over me), with a constant resolution to suffer death for upholding the obedience and authority of the apostolical Roman Catholic Church.

Now since I have been on your part, informed of the sentence of you; last meeting of Parliament, lords Buckhurst[2] and Beale having admonished me to prepare for the end of my long and weary pilgrimage I beg to return you thanks, on my part, for these happy tidings and to entreat you to vouchsafe to me certain points for the discharge of my conscience. Sir A. Paulet[3] has informed me (though falsely) that you have indulged me by having restored to me my almoner[4] and the money that they had taken from me, and that the remainder would follow; for all this, I would willingly return you thanks and supplicate still further, as a last request, which I have thought, for many reasons, I ought to ask of you alone, that you will accord this ultimate grace, for which I should not like to be indebted to any other, since I have no hope of finding aught but cruelty from the puritans, who are at this time, God knows wherefore! the first authority,[5] and the most bitter gainst me. I will accuse no one: may I pardon with a sincere heart everyone, even as I desire every one may grant forgiveness to me, God the first. But I know that you, more than anyone, ought to feel at heart the honour or dishonour of your own blood, and that, moreover, of a queen, and the daughter of a king.

Then madame for the sake of that Jesus to whose Name all powers bow, I require you to ordain, that when my enemies have slaked their black thirst for my innocent blood, you will permit my poor desolate servants altogether to carry away my corpse to bury it in holy ground with the other queens of France, my predecessors, especially near the late queen, my mother;[6] having this in recollection, that in Scotland the bodies of the kings my predecessors have been out-raged, and the churches profaned and abolished, and that, as I shall suffer in this country, I shall not be given place with the kings your predecessors,[7] who are mine as well as yours; for, according to our religion, we think much of being interred in holy earth. As they tell me that you will in nothing force my conscience nor my religion and have even conceded me a priest,[8] refuse me not this my last request that you will permit me free sepulcher to this body when the soul is separated, which, when united, could never obtain liberty to live in repose such as you would procure for yourself – against which repose, before God I speak, I never aimed a blow; but God will let you see the truth of all after my death.

And because I dread the tyranny of those to whose power you have abandoned me, I entreat you not to permit that execution be done on me without your own knowledge, not for fear of the torment, which I am most ready to suffer, but on account of the reports which will be raised concerning my death without other witnesses than those who would inflict it, who, I am persuaded, would be of very different qualities from those parties whom I require (being my servants) to be spectators, and, withal, witnesses of my end in the faith of our sacrament, of my Saviour, and in obedience to His church. And after all is over, that they together may carry away my poor corpse (as secretly as you please), and speedily withdraw without taking with them any of my goods, except those which, in dying, I may leave to them ... which are little enough for their long and good services.

One jewel[9] that I received of you, I shall return to you with my last words, or sooner if you please. Once more I supplicate you to permit me to send a jewel and a last adieu to my son, with my dying benediction; for of my blessing he has been deprived since you sent me his refusal to enter into the treaty, when I was excluded by his wicked councillors. This last point I refer to your favourable consideration and conscience, as the others; but I ask them in the name of Jesus Christ, and in respect of our consanguinity, and for the sake of King Henry VII, your grandfather and mine; and by the honour of the dignity we both held, and of our sex in common, do I implore you to grant these requests.

As to the rest, I think you know that in your name they have taken down my dais [canopy and raised platform], but afterwards they owned to me that it was not by your commandment, but by the intimation of some of your privy council. I thank God that wickedness came not from you, and that it serves rather to vent malice than to afflict me, having made up my mind to die. It is on account of this, and some other things that they debarred me from writing to you, and after they had done all in their power to degrade me from my rank, they told me 'that I was but a mere dead woman, incapable of dignity.' God be praised for all!

I would wish that all my papers were brought to you without reserve, that, at last, it may be made manifest to you, that the sole care of your safety was not confined to those who are so prompt to persecute me. If you will accord this my last request, I would wish that you would write for them; otherwise they do with them as they choose. And moreover I wish that, to this my last request, you will let me know your last reply.

To conclude, I pray God, the just Judge, of His mercy, that He will enlighten you with His holy spirit; and that He will give me His Grace to die in the perfect charity I am disposed to do, and to pardon all those who have caused or who have co-operated in my death. Such will be my last prayer to my end, which I esteem myself happy will precede the persecution which I foresee menaces this isle, where God is no longer seriously feared and revered, but vanity and worldly policy rule and govern all – but I will accuse no one, nor give way to presumption. Yet while abandoning this world and preparing myself for a better, I must remind you, that one day you will have to answer for your charge, and for all those whom you doom, and I desire that my blood and that of my country may be remembered in that time. For why? From the first days of our capacity to comprehend our duties, we ought to bend our minds to make things of this world yield to those of eternity.

From Forteringhay [Fotheringhay], this 19th December, 1586

Your sister and cousin, prisoner wrongfully,

Marie, *Royne* [*sic*].

Notes

1 Catherine of Aragon

1. Her governess, or first lady.
2. De Puebla.
3. Her establishment for the service of her chamber, as ladies and chamber women.
4. The jewels were valued at 20,000 crowns, and the plate at 15,000 crowns.
5. Her Spanish ladies and the household remaining with her.
6. The debts.
7. From Spain.
8. In Spain.
9. Seemingly, Lord Edmund Howard, father of Henry VIII's fifth wife, Catherine Howard.
10. Father of Edmund Howard, Surrey had the dukedom of Norfolk, which had been confiscated by Henry VII, restored to him after his victory at Flodden Field.
11. The shrine of Our Lady at Walsingham, founded in 1061 and favourite place of devotion of Catherine of Aragon and Henry VIII. Henry later ordered this famous chapel to be demolished.
12. State governess to Mary.
13. i.e. 'cheerful'.
14. i.e. 'careful not to offend Him.'
15. To prevent the introduction into her writing desk of incriminating papers by unsuspected persons.
16. That is 'whosoever keeps her keys'.
17. Mary's best friend next to her mother.
18. Mary.
19. i.e. any suggestion that Catherine might flee the country with her daughter.

2 Anne Boleyn

1. Certain authorities declare this pedigree to be false, and suggest it was purchased by Anne Boleyn when she became Marchioness of Pembroke.
2. Anne's French governess, Simonette.
3. Catherine of Aragon.
4. The authenticity of this letter has been questioned by some authorities, chiefly because the handwriting differs from the well-known autograph of Anne Boleyn, and the document is not signed, as would be expected, 'Anna the Quene'. The letter is said to have been found among the chancellor Thomas Cromwell's papers some years after Anne Boleyn's death. Strickland believes it to have been written by Anne Boleyn, the tone of the letter being perfectly consistent with her character in its reckless disregard as to consequences.
5. Henry VIII had created Anne Boleyn Marchioness of Pembroke in 1532. This royal marquisate had last been borne by his uncle, Jasper Tudor.
6. Jane Seymour.
7. The gentlemen Anne refers to were her brother George, Viscount Rochford; Henry Norris, Groom of the Stole; Sir Francis Weston and William Brereton, gentlemen of the Privy Chamber; and Mark Smeaton, a musician. Sir Thomas Wyatt, the poet, was under suspicion, but escaped the fate of the others, all of whom were executed with the exception of Smeaton, who, holding no rank, was hanged. Anne herself, as is perhaps known, was executed with a sword, the executioner coming over from France.

4 Anne of Cleves

1. A parallel example of royal discourtesy is instanced on the occasion of the first meeting between George IV, when Prince of Wales, and Caroline of Brunswick.
2. Anne of Cleves, a Lutheran, had become converted to the Roman Catholic faith.

5 Catherine Howard

1. History relates that this first lover was one Henry Manox, a musician, and that the intimacy took place while Catherine was under the guardianship of the Dowager Duchess of Norfolk.
2. Lady Rochford's evidence against her husband had led to his execution for adultery with his own sister, Anne Boleyn.

6 Catherine Parr

1. Catherine Parr, who had sincerely embraced the doctrine of the Reformation, had ventured to protest on Henry VIII issuing a proclamation forbidding the use of a translation of the scriptures that he had previously licensed.

2. Edward VI.
3. The title of Princess, which Henry VIII had withdrawn from both Mary and Elizabeth, was now restored to them.

7 Lady Jane Grey

1. Sion House, at Isleworth, presented by Henry VIII to the Duke of Northumberland. After Northumberland's execution, Mary I restored this historic convent to the Bridgetine nuns, from whom it had been wrested.
2. The Duke of Suffolk, for whose insane ambition his daughter and son-in-law had been sacrificed, was executed eleven days later on Tower hill.

8 Mary I

1. Such instructions were: 'At seasons convenient, [she was] to use moderate exercise, taking open air in gardens, sweet and wholesome places and walks – which may conduce unto her health, solace, and comfort ... At other seasons, to dance, and among the rest to have good respect to her diet, which is ... to be pure, well-prepared, dressed and served with comfortable, joyous, and merry communication ... Likewise, the cleanliness and well-wearing of her garments and apparel, both of her chamber and person, so that everything about her be pure, sweet, clean, and wholesome, as to so great a princess doth appertain: all corruptions, evil airs, and things noisome and unpleasant to be eschewed.'
2. Of humble origin, Cromwell, before his execution for corrupt practices in 1540, had virtually become vice regent. A nephew assumed his name, and was the great-grandfather of Oliver Cromwell, the Protector.
3. Wife of the Lieutenant of the Tower, Lady Kingston had previously been in the service of Catherine of Aragon.
4. Jane Seymour.
5. Jane Seymour.
6. Gossip: godmother, or relative in God.
7. Refers to Edward VI, Seymour's nephew.
8. William Parr, Marquis of Northampton, Catherine Parr's only brother.
9. Charles V, Emperor of the Holy Roman Empire, and Mary's cousin.
10. Elizabeth was at Ashridge at the time, and had proposed going to her other establishment, Donnington Castle, Newbury.
11. Philip of Spain was the son of Charles V, Mary's cousin.
12. The Spanish ambassador.
13. Philip's confessor.

9 Elizabeth I

1. The original letter was written in 'elegant Italian'. (Wood.)
2. These may have been due only to 'hoydenish' spirits on Elizabeth's part, but nevertheless she had a pronounced feminine streak in her character. For example, although demure in dress in early years,

towards the end of her reign she possessed a wardrobe of 'three thousand gowns, and eighty wigs of divers coloured hair'.

3. Advise.

4. 'Not without suspicion of poison.' Ballard's *Memoirs of Celebrated Ladies of Great Britain*, 1752. The fate of her infant daughter, Mary Seymour, is obscure, but she appears to have died young.

5. Katharine Ashley, her governess.

6. A request made to Thomas Seymour by Elizabeth on behalf of one of her chaplains.

7. That Durham Place was appointed to be a mint. Formerly the property of Elizabeth's mother before Anne Boleyn's marriage to Henry VIII, Elizabeth considered she had a right to it as a town house.

8. Elizabeth often spoke of her governess in this familiar way.

9. Refers to Catherine Parr's death.

10. Meaning 'that the Admiral should come'.

11. That is, try to effect the marriage.

12. Elizabeth's historic remark, on hearing of Thomas Seymour's execution in March of that same year – 'This day died a man with much wit, and very little judgment' was possibly made with the intention of baffling her enemies. All the same, it shows her astuteness in estimating the character of her fellow-beings.

13. Northumberland and his party.

14. The will of Henry VIII.

15. The gravity of Edward VI's illness, and news of his death, were kept secret from Elizabeth, as they were from Mary.

16. Evidently refers to their last interview, when Elizabeth had been commanded to Mary's presence.

17. Thomas Seymour.

18. Sir Thomas Wyatt, son of the poet, her mother's great friend. He was later executed for his part in the rebellion.

19. Henry II of France. By seeking to implicate Elizabeth, his hope was that she would be put to death by Mary, and his future daughter-in-law – afterwards Queen of Scots – would be recognised as prospective Queen of England.

20. Sir John Brydges, afterwards created Baron Chandos.

21. According to the English chronicler, Holinshed, while at Woodstock Manor Elizabeth 'wrote these verses with a diamond in a glasse window verie legible as followeth:
"Much suspected, of me
Nothing proved can be,
Quoth Elizabeth, Prisoner."'

22. It is not without interest to note that when in her teens she declined an offer of marriage with the King of Sweden's eldest son. Elizabeth declared to the Swedish ambassador 'that if left to her own free will, she would always prefer a maiden life'.

23. Lord Darnley was the grandson of Margaret of Scotland – Henry VIII's sister – by her second husband, the Earl of Angus.
24. Mary was at this time virtually a state prisoner in England, and had complained of ill health through 'rigorous treatment'.
25. Heir to the King of France.
26. The royal family of France.
27. One of Queen Elizabeth's maids-of-honour.
28. As Lord Robert Dudley, he had been imprisoned in the Tower at the same time as Elizabeth, for aiding and abetting his father Northumberland and brother Guildford Dudley in their attempt to place Jane Grey on the throne.
29. See Appendix B.
30. i.e. 'learn'.
31. In using the above quotation from Shakespeare's *Henry IV*, it is interesting to recall that *The Merry Wives of Windsor* is said to have been written by Shakespeare at the desire of Elizabeth I, who was so delighted with the character of Falstaff in *Henry IV* that she wished to see him represented as a lover.
32. That is, meaning 'harmless' in Elizabeth's day.
33. Vicar in Christ: an allusion to Elizabeth's position as head of the Church.
34. Oddly enough, the Norris crest was a raven.
35. 'Let this bitterness be valued; let melancholy go to Hades!'
36. After her accession, Elizabeth had a silver coin struck, with the phrase *Posui Deum adjutorem meum* ('I have chosen God as my helper').

10 Anne of Denmark

1. Anne of Denmark greatly appreciated Ben Jonson as a poet, and he was the author of most of the wonderful masques with which the queen consort amused her court.
2. The queen consort's private residence was Somerset House, which after her coronation was named Denmark House, and on which she expended a fabulous sum in improvements and embellishments.
3. George Heriot held accounts against Anne of Denmark for £40,000, and died in 1624 worth a fortune. He was the 'Jingling Geordie' of Sir Walter Scott's Fortunes of Nigel.
4. Anne of Denmark was probably only too pleased to broadcast this amusing piece of news, as she had no liking for Margaret Stuart. After the latter's marriage, their differences rose to a great height, it being rumoured that Margaret Stuart had said 'her child belonged to her aged husband, as none of those the Queen had borne belonged to the king'. As a consequence, she was banished from the outraged queen consort's court.
5. Carr was a Scottish adventurer, whom James I loaded with wealth and honours. He was promoted to the post of Lord Chamberlain, and became Earl of Somerset.

6. i.e. Overbury. Curiously enough, he was destined to die by poison secretly administered through the agency of Somerset and his countess.

7. 'Never any man in any age, nor, I believe, in any country or nation, rose in so short a time to so much greatness of honour, fame, and fortune, upon no other advantage or recommendation than the beauty and gracefulness of his person.' (Clarendon, *History of the Rebellion*.) Buckingham was assassinated at the age of thirty-six.

11 Henrietta Maria

1. 'Mamangat' was a term of endearment.

2. Jonchets, a set of small sticks, in the form of rushes, used to play with in a similar manner to the game of spillikins. Poule, probably some card game.

3. That is, Parliament's.

4. Van Tromp, the Dutch admiral in charge of Henrietta Maria's convoy.

5. Born at Geneva, Mayerne was first physician to four monarchs: Henry IV of France, James I, Charles I, and Charles II. He considered cookery as an important branch of healing, and wrote the best cookery book of his era. A noted *bon vivant*, he died in 1655 at the age of eighty-two.

6. Jermyn was her confidential secretary, and Father Philip her confessor.

7. Claude de Lorraine, Duke of Chevreuse.

8. Abraham Cowley, the Cavalier poet, was assistant to Jermyn, Henrietta Maria's confidential secretary.

9. Both Houses of Parliament.

10. Mazarin, Prime Minister of France.

11. Sir Thomas Fairfax, negotiator between the Army and Parliament.

12. An intimate friend of Henrietta Maria in the court of Anne of Austria, Madame de Motteville in her memoirs gave many particulars of the history of Charles I's consort personally recounted to her by Henrietta Maria.

13. Scoundrel.

14. The convent, habitual retreat of Henrietta Maria, to which she had always gone when under pressure of sorrow or ill health.

12 Catherine of Braganza

1. In Pepys's opinion, 'She hath a good, modest, and innocent look, which is pleasing.' He adds that the first English words he ever heard Catherine of Braganza utter were: 'You lye!' They were addressed to Charles II.

13 Mary Beatrice of Modena

1. Refers to defeat at La Hogue.

2. An ardent Catholic and supporter of the Jacobite cause, Melfort died at St Germains in 1714, leaving his family in a state of destitution. Mary Beatrice of Modena took him under her protection.

3. A fortnight later Mary Beatrice of Modena gave birth to a daughter at the palace at St Germains. The child was christened Louisa Mary.

4. See Princess Anne's letters.

5. Refers to her son, 'The Pretender', who had also been attacked by smallpox.
6. One of the nuns.
7. 'And now there is my expectation! Nothing but God!'

14 Mary II

1. Son of William II of Orange, and Mary, daughter of Charles I.
2. Mary's chaplain and almoner.
3. The second husband of Lady Bellasyse.
4. The Hague.
5. The Prince of Wales.
6. Nottingham was Mary's Lord Chamberlain.
7. English admiral, of valiant memory, who had risen from the position of cabin boy. His mother lived in All Saints' Street, in the ancient Cinque Port of Hastings, where he often visited her. A portion of the house, built in 1570, still stands.
8. Lord Portland William's minister and confidant; M. Overkirk, Mary's Dutch official; Lady Derby, Mary's first lady.
9. i.e., at Whitehall.
10. i.e., at Kensington.
11. i.e., she and the king.
12. Their household.
13. Anne was pregnant.
14. The queen did not intend to sit down to the card table with Lady Marlborough present.
15. Meaning 'by coming to court'.

15 Anne

1. Originally built by Henry VIII for the purpose that its name denotes, The Cockpit later became a theatre attached to the court. Charles II had it converted into a residence for Anne.
2. Sunderland was president of the council, and in 1687 became a Catholic. At the same time he was corresponding with William of Orange. His treachery was discovered by James II, and he was dismissed office. Sunderland later became one of William III's confidential advisers.
3. Charles II.
4. Lady Sunderland.
5. James II's daughters had nicknamed their father and his consort 'Mansell' and 'Mansell's wife'.
6. Lady Sunderland.
7. According to Evelyn's diary, she had been one of Charles II's 'concubines'.
8. Mrs Robarts and Mrs Turine were bedchamber women to the queen.
9. i.e., 'being about to return to town'.
10. Princess Mary's letters to Princess Anne on this subject do not appear

to have been preserved.

11, 12, 13. Mrs Dawson and Mrs Bromley were bedchamber women to the queen; Dr Waldgrave and Sir Charles Scarborough were the queen's regular physicians; and 'Roger's daughter' was the daughter of Sunderland.

14. Mary de la Baudie, the queen's seamstress.

15. Lady Powis, state governess to the Prince of Wales.

16. Mrs Dawson had been in the household of Anne Hyde when both Mary and Anne were born. At a subsequent period she solemnly attested that the Prince of Wales was as much a child of the queen as Princess Anne was of the Duchess of York.

17. Her husband, Prince George of Denmark.

18. George of Denmark.

19. James II.

20. Mary Beatrice of Modena.

21. Anne was pregnant.

22. This retreat of the Bridgetine nuns, which had originally been presented to them by Henry V in 1420, had once more been wrested from that community by Elizabeth I. In Anne's day, the possessor of this historical palace was the Duchess of Somerset, who 'was pleased to place Sion House entirely at her [Anne's] service' during the crisis between Anne and Mary II.

23. Their uncle, 1st Earl of Rochester.

24. The Bishop of Worcester.

25. The household of Anne.

26. Naval victory of La Hogue, which saw the end of James II's hopes of regaining his throne.

27. George of Denmark.

28. i.e., of her household.

29. William and Mary.

30. James II.

31. Her household.

32. Her husband, George of Denmark.

33. Anne's nickname for William III.

34. The 'signal scratch' was a court refinement introduced from France, a knock being considered importunate, and even boding ill, whereas the 'scratch' was like the pawing of an affectionate animal, attached not to the sovereign power, but to the sovereign's person.

35. Seemingly refers to his request for captaincy general.

36. Later known to English history as the Duchess of Kendal and the Countess of Darlington.

16 Caroline of Brandenburg-Anspach

1. The contemporary translations of Caroline's letters have here been transcribed into correct English, as will be gathered.

2. The electress Sophia.
3. Frederick William, grandson of the electress. The Queen of Prussia hoped Caroline would marry him, as she did not share her husband's views regarding the archduke Charles.
4. One of the final utterances of this remarkable queen on her deathbed (at which her brother, afterwards George I, was present) was, 'I am at last going to satisfy my curiosity about the origin of things, which even Leibnitz could never explain to me; to understand space, Infinity, being, and nothingness.'
5. Refers to Queen Anne.
6. The electress Sophia, who enjoyed being styled 'Princess of Wales' in her own circle.
7. When Caroline became queen consort, her favourite's husband – a manager of the Duke of Marlborough's estates – was created Viscount Sundon.
8. Amelia.
9. George II.
10. It is amusing to record that George II is reputed to have said (though it seems more attributable to the wit of his queen):
   England was ruled by Elizabeth;
   James I was ruled by his gross appetites;
   Charles I by his wife;
   Charles II by his whores;
   James II by his priests;
   Mary II by William III;
   And Anne by her women favourites.
   'But who,' he finished boastfully, 'do they say rules me?' Had his hearers made answer to his rhetorical question they would with one accord have cried: 'Caroline!'

17 Charlotte Sophia of Mecklenburg-Strelitz

1. In this connection, the opinion of that astute observer of his fellow-men Dr Johnson, after a long discourse with George III, is worthy of note: 'Sir, they may talk of the King as they will; but he is the finest gentleman I have ever seen.'
2. At one period, malicious gossip, never to be restrained, reached supreme absurdity when it strove to link the name of Charlotte Sophia with that of the Chevalier d'Eon. Ambassador and diplomat, the Chevalier had an amazing personal history, and dual nature, which were to occupy the public mind, unconcerned with his political services, to no small degree when, in 1777, an action was brought in the King's Bench, the decision on which depended upon establishing the sex of d'Eon.
3. Evidently a birthday present, as the letter is written on the young prince's birthday.
4. The Harcourt's estate at Nuneham, Oxfordshire.

5. 'Selfishness'?

6. Among his severest critics were such men of broad outlook as Lord Byron, Leigh Hunt, Thackeray and Thomas Moore. The last described George IV as a 'sick epicure's dream, incoherent and gross'.

7. It would, perhaps, be difficult to find more faithful pen sketches of Charlotte Sophia than those provided by this keenly observant and lively minded diarist.

8. Charlotte Sophia's fifth son, Ernest Augustus, afterwards King of Hanover.

9. The queen consort's seventh son, Adolphus Frederick.

10. The reader may be interested in the appended list of the children of George III and Charlotte Sophia.

    George Augustus Frederick, Prince of Wales (1762–1830) afterwards George IV.

    Frederick, Duke of York (1763–1827).

    William, Duke of Clarence (1765–1837), afterwards William IV.

    Charlotte Augusta (1766–1828).

    Edward, Duke of Kent (1767–1820), father of Queen Victoria.

    Augusta Sophia (1768–1840).

    Elizabeth (1770–1840).

    Ernest Augustus, Duke of Cumberland (1771–1851), afterwards King of Hanover.

    Augustus Frederick, Duke of Sussex (1773–1843).

    Adolphus Frederick, Duke of Cambridge (1774–1850).

    Mary (1776–1857).

    Sophia (1777–1848).

    Octavius (1779–1783).

    Alfred (1780–1782).

    Amelia (1783–1810).

11. i.e., 'than had the king died'.

12. Princess Charlotte, then sixteen years old.

13. Sir Henry Halford, the King's physician.

14. Refers to his wife, Caroline of Brunswick.

15. Afterwards king of the Belgians.

16. Princess Charlotte's establishment at Claremont, near Esher.

18 Caroline of Brunswick

1. By this Act, passed in 1772 by direction of George III, any unions of heirs apparent or presumptive to the crown were rendered null and void if they had been contracted without royal consent before the age of twenty-five. After that age, members of the royal family were free to marry without such consent, provided they gave notice of their intention to the Privy Council and obtained the approval of both Houses of Parliament.

2. The preceding letters by Caroline of Brunswick were obviously drafted

by her advisers, for her signature.

3. Sir William Gell, her lord chamberlain.

4. Sydney Smith, wit and litterateur.

5. Matthew Gregory Lewis. The monk was among his many literary successes, although strongly offending contemporary taste.

6. Lady Anne Hamilton, sister of the Duke of Hamilton, remained a staunch friend to Caroline of Brunswick throughout her trials. Caroline nicknamed her 'Joan of Arc'. She was the anonymous author of *The Secret History of the Court of England*.

7. 'My mother has led a bad life, but she would not have done so badly if my father had not led even a worse.' This remark is wittily substantiated by a similar one made by Caroline of Brunswick herself: 'I am not altogether blameless, for I have committed adultery – with Mrs. Fitzherbert's husband.'

8. The Prime Minister.

9. Probably refers to John, brother of the Emperor of Austria, Francis II.

10. Her banker at Milan, Giuseppe Marietti.

11. Frederick William, of whom Byron wrote, he 'rushed into the field and foremost fighting, fell'. He was killed at Quatre Bras, 1815.

12. See *The Trial at Large of Her Majesty, printed from the Journals of the House*, 1821.

13. Her father, the Duke of Brunswick, one of Frederick the Great's generals, was killed in 1806, fighting valiantly against the French, at the Battle of Jena.

14. If any proof were required of Princess Charlotte's devotion to her mother, and Caroline of Brunswick's power to inspire deep affection in the heart of her daughter, it will be found in a letter which Princess Charlotte wrote to her mother shortly before her confinement. It is clear that she had a presentiment that she would not survive the coming ordeal, and she longs for her mother's presence at this time. In the course of this same letter she writes – '... I now feel the bitterness of your absence. You have no substitute in this heart; there is none to occupy your place in my sinking eyes. Even the affectionate attentions of my amiable consort are insufficient to supply the chasm in my bosom, but leave it unsatisfied. By a refinement of cruelty we may be separated on earth, and I as well as yourself may be doomed the victims of malignant persecution. But in a better world, our congenial spirits will rush to meet each other, where no envious and hating friends can intervene ... Death would obliterate no image of delight from my heart, save that which, in the portrait of a beloved mother, nature has still left to the hoping, devoted yet fearing Charlotte.' (Aspinall: *Letters of George the Fourth*, 1938)

19 Adelaide of Saxe-Meiningen

1. Mrs Jordan had died some years previously, at St Cloud.

2. Somewhat to his sire's dismay, Augustus became rector of Mapledurham, near Reading.
3. 'Sissi,' Princess Victoria's half-sister. The Duchess of Kent, her mother, had been previously married to Charles, Prince of Leiningen.
   'Aunt Augusta', wife of Adolphus, Duke of Cambridge.
   'Aunt Mary', wife of William Frederick, Duke of Gloucester.
   'Aunt Sophia', Princess Sophia, youngest surviving daughter of George III. She remained unmarried, although reputed to have borne a son by a General Garth, one of her father's suite.
4. The paralysed daughter of Adelaide's sister, the Duchess of Saxe-Weimar, whom the queen consort had adopted. She died in 1833.
5. Victoria's mother, the Duchess of Kent, who sat immediately next to the king at dinner.

20 Victoria

1. The Prime Minister.
2. As succeeding prime minister when the Melbourne Cabinet went out of office, Sir Robert Peel had requested that the queen should no longer retain her Ladies of the Bedchamber, who were all wives or sisters of the Whig opposition. The queen obstinately refused to part with any one of her ladies, however, and the dispute between the sovereign and Peel became a political issue. Long and violent discussions, in and out of Parliament and throughout the country, took place as a consequence. On the whole, sympathy was with the queen, but, at the same time, no little public alarm was felt at the possibility of the queen having fallen into the hands of an intriguing coterie. Victoria was adamant, however, in her determination to retain her household without any changes (she herself was a staunch Whig) and, as a result, Lord Melbourne and his party remained in power.
3. Afterwards Lord Herbert of Lee.
4. The brooch was more in the nature of a badge, the design being a St George's Cross in red enamel and the royal cypher surmounted by a crown of diamonds. Encircling the badge was the inscription 'Blessed are the merciful', and it also bore the word 'Crimea'.
5. Afterwards Frederick III, Emperor of Germany. A dying man when he ascended the throne in 1888, he reigned for ninety-nine days only and was succeeded by his eldest son and Victoria's grandson, William II.
6. Prussian ambassador.
7. This date was to be a significant one for the queen. On 14 December 1878, her second daughter, Princess Alice of Hesse, died at the age of thirty-five from diphtheria, while nursing her children. On 14 December 1895, one of her numerous great-grandchildren was born. With an assurance almost akin to mystic vision, the aged queen recorded the event on that date in her diary as 'a gift from God'. Destined to reign as George VI, the boy was christened Albert, after

the prince consort, and Queen Victoria was delighted, as she wrote to his father, then Duke of York, to be godmother.

8. Lytton Strachey, Queen Victoria, 1948.
9. Immortalised by Rudyard Kipling in his *Barrack-Room Ballads*.
10. Created Earl of Beaconsfield in 1876.
11. A member of Gladstone's ministry.
12. As a result of the general discussion that arose on the verdict, a short Act of Parliament was passed in 1883 by which a jury is directed to bring in a special verdict when it is satisfied that the accused person is insane at the time of the crime. This verdict is commonly known as 'Guilty but insane' and today is regarded as tantamount to an acquittal of the crime.

Appendix B: Mary Stuart, Queen of Scots

1. Sir Francis Walsingham. There is corroborative evidence that Walsingham employed the services of an expert to forge Elizabeth's signature to the death warrant.
2. Thomas Sackville. He and Robert Beale, clerk of the council, announced to Mary the death sentence that had been passed by Parliament, adding 'that she must not hope for mercy'.
3. Sir Amias Paulet, a rigid Puritan, selected by Leicester to be one of the Queen of Scots' keepers.
4. Dr Preau. He remained at the castle, but was forbidden to see the royal prisoner.
5. Mary is clearly inferring here that Elizabeth is dominated by the Puritan faction.
6. Mary of Lorraine or Guise, married to James V of Scotland In 1538.
7. i.e., that she will not be buried in Westminster Abbey, as she would wish. James I afterwards observed his mother's request.
8. In this the Queen of Scots was to find herself deceived. Her chaplain was not permitted to see her.
9. Presumably refers to the diamond ring that Elizabeth had at one time sent her as a token of friendship. It was an English custom to give a diamond, to be returned in time of distress as a request for aid. In this case, Elizabeth had had two diamonds set in two rings, which when laid together formed the shape of a heart. She had sent one ring to Mary and had kept the other herself.

Acknowledgements

I have to acknowledge the gracious permission of Her Majesty the Queen to make use of material from the Royal Archives, Windsor.

The letters, or excerpts from letters, used in this compilation have been gathered from various sources, to be found in the index.

I hereby express my thanks, and acknowledge indebtedness to:

Cassell & Co. Ltd, Publishers, and Curtis Brown Ltd, Literary Agents, for permission to make use of certain letters from *The Letters of Queen Anne*, 1935, by Beatrice Curtis Brown.

Longmans Green & Co., for permission to quote letters from Wilkin's *Caroline The Illustrious*, 1904.

Cambridge University Press, for permission to quote letters from Aspinall's *Letters of George IV*, 1938 (Crown copyright).

John Lane, The Bodley Head, for permission to quote letters from Clerici's *Queen of Indiscretions*, 1907 (Translated by Frederick Chapman).

John Murray Ltd, for granting permission to include letters from Benson and Esher's *Letters of Queen Victoria*, 1908, George Earle Buckle's *Letters of Queen Victoria*, 1926 and 1932, and Mary Hopkirk's *Queen Adelaide*, 1946.

Mr Hector Bolitho for his permission to make use of two letters from *Further Letters of Queen Victoria*, Butterworth, 1938.

The Cresset Press and H. van Thal for permission to include letters from *The Royal Letter Book*, 1937.

A suggested list of books for further reading will be found at the end of this volume.

In compiling these letters I am indebted to public and private libraries for ready facilities offered. I also desire to record my appreciation of the help given by Mr R. C. Mackworth-Young (Royal Archives).

My thanks are likewise due to Mollie Crichton-Gordon and Dr George Wendel for aid in necessary translation work.

Margaret Sanders

List of Letters and Sources

Adelaide of Saxe-Meiningen to Princess Victoria, p. 196, Royal Archives, 37135/6, p. 197, Hopkirk: *Queen Adelaide* (1946). To Mrs Fitzherbert, p. 198, Hopkirk: *Queen Adelaide* (1946). To Queen Victoria, p. 199, Royal Archives, 37173, p. 201, Royal Archives 37241. **Anne** to Princess of Orange, p. 139, Strickland: *Lives of the Queens of England*, Vol. V (1884 edition), pp. 140, 142, 143 Curtis Brown: *Letters of Queen Anne* (1935), p. 144, Strickland: *Lives of the Queens of England*, Vol. V (1884 edition), p. 145, Curtis Brown: *Letters of Queen Anne* (1935), p. 146, Strickland: *Lives of the Queens of England*, Vol. V (1884 edition) Curtis Brown: *Letters of Queen Anne* (1935). To Prince of Orange, p. 149, Strickland: *Lives of the Queens of England, Vol. V* (1884). To Mary Beatrice of Modena, p. 150, Strickland: *Lives of the Queens of England, Vol. V* (1884). To James II, p. 152, Strickland: *Lives of the Queens of England, Vol. VI* (1884). To Mary II, pp. 152, 154 *Conduct of* the Duchess of Marlborough. To Lady Marlborough, pp. 155, 156 *Conduct of* the Duchess of Marlborough. To Duchess of Marlborough, p. 158, Curtis Brown: *Letters of Queen Anne* (1935). To Duke of Marlborough, p. 159 Curtis Brown: *Letters of Queen Anne* (1935). **Anne Boleyn** to Sir Thomas Boleyn, p. 13, Ellis: *Royal Letters*. To Henry VIII, p. 14, Wood: *Letters of Royal and Illustrious Ladies* (1846). To Cardinal Wolsey, pp. 15, 16, Wood: *Letters of Royal and Illustrious Ladies* (1846). To Henry VIII, p. 18, Strickland: *Lives of the Queens of England, Vol. II* (1884). **Anne of Cleves** to Henry VIII, p. 23, Wood: *Letters of Royal and Illustrious Ladies* (1846). To Duke of Cleves, p. 24, Strickland: *Lives of the Queens of England, Vol. II* (1884). To Mary I, p. 25 Strickland: *Lives of the Queens of England, Vol. II* (1884). **Anne of Denmark** to George Heriot, p. 88, Strickland: *Lives of the Queens of England, Vol. IV* (1884). To James the First, pp. 89, 90, Strickland: *Lives of the Queens of England, Vol. IV* (1884). To Earl of Salisbury, p. 91, Strickland: *Lives of the Queens of England, Vol. IV* (1884). To Sir George Villiers, p. 92, Strickland: *Lives of the Queens of England, Vol. IV* (1884). To James I, p. 92, Strickland: *Lives of the Queens of England, Vol. IV* (1884). To Duke of Buckingham, p. 93, Strickland: *Lives of the Queens of England, Vol. IV* (1884). **Caroline of Anspach** to

List of Letters and Sources

Gottfried Wilhelm Leibnitz, pp. 162, 163, 165, Wilkins: *Caroline The Illustrious* (1901). To Mrs Clayton, pp. 166, 167, Royal Archives, Geo. Addl. MSS. 28 (57) and (24). To Duchess of Kendal, p. 168, Wilkins: *Caroline The Illustrious* (1901). To Princess of Wales, p. 170, Royal Archives, Geo. 52823. **Caroline of Brunswick** to Prince of Wales p. 182, Huish: *Memoirs of George IV*. To queen consort, p. 184, Fitzgerald: *Good Queen Charlotte* (1899). To a friend, p. 186, Van Thal: *Royal Letter Book* (1937). To Lady Charlotte Campbell, p. 187, Clerici: *Queen of Indiscretions* (1907). To Princess Charlotte, p. 189, Royal Archives, Geo. 49977 and 49985. To George IV, p. 191, Clerici: *Queen of Indiscretions* (1907). **Catherine of Aragon** to King Ferdinand of Castile, pp. 2, 3, Wood: *Letters of Royal and Illustrious Ladies* (1846). To Henry VIII, p. 5, Strickland: *Lives of the Queens of England, Vol. II* (1884). To Princess Mary, pp. 6, 7, Strickland: *Lives of the Queens of England, Vol. II* (1884). To an unnamed friend, p. 9, Wood: *Letters of Royal and Illustrious Ladies* (1846). To Dr John Forest, p. 10, Wood: *Letters of Royal and Illustrious Ladies* (1846). To Henry VIII, p. 12, Chatterton: *Royal Letters*. **Catherine of Braganza** to Duke of Ormond, p. 111, Strickland: *Lives of the Queens of England, Vol. IV* (1884). Catherine Howard, p. 27, Strickland: *Lives of the Queens of England, Vol. IV* (1884). **Catherine Parr** to Henry VIII, p. 30, Strickland: *Lives of the Queens of England, Vol. II* (1884). To Thomas Seymour, pp. 31, 32, Strickland: *Lives of the Queens of England, Vol. II* (1884). **Charlotte Sophia of Mecklenburg-Strelitz** to Prince of Wales, p. 172, Royal Archives, Geo. 36346-7. To Lady Harcourt, p. 173, Fitzgerald: *Good Queen Charlotte* (1899), p. 174, Fitzgerald: *Royal Dukes and Princesses of the Family of George III*. To Prince of Wales, p. 175, Royal Archives, 36431. To Lady Harcourt, p. 176, Fitzgerald: *Good Queen Charlotte* (1899). To Lord Harcourt, p. 176, Fitzgerald: *Royal Dukes and Princesses of the Family of George III*. To the prince regent, p. 178, Taylor: *Taylor Papers*, p. 180, Aspinall: *Letters of George the Fourth* (1938) (Crown copyright). **Elizabeth I** to Anne of Cleves, p. 60, Strickland: *Lives of the Queens of England, Vol. III* (1884). To Catherine Parr, p. 60, Wood: *Letters of Royal and Illustrious Ladies* (1846). To Thomas Seymour, p. 61, Wood: *Letters of Royal and Illustrious Ladies* (1846). To Princess Mary, p. 62 Wood: *Letters of Royal and Illustrious Ladies* (1846). To Catherine Parr, pp. 64, 65, Strickland: *Lives of the Queens of England, Vol. III and Vol. II* (1884). To the Protector Somerset, pp. 66, 68, 69, Strickland: *Lives of the Queens of England, Vol. III*. To Duke of Northumberland, p. 70, Wood: *Letters of Royal and Illustrious Ladies* (1846). To Mary I, p. 72, Strickland: *Lives of the Queens of England, Vol. III* (1884). To Philip of Spain, p. 74, Wood: *Letters of Royal and Illustrious Ladies* (1846). To Mary, Queen of Scots, p. 76, Strickland: *Life of Mary Queen of Scots*, p. 77, Strickland: *Lives of the Queens of England, Vol. III* (1884). To Dr Richard Cox, p. 78, Strickland: *Lives of the Queens of England, Vol. II* (1884). To John Harington, p. 78, Strickland: *Lives of the Queens of England, Vol. II* (1884). To Earl of Leicester, p. 79, Strickland: *Lives of the Queens of England, Vol. II* (1884). To Mary, Queen of Scots, p. 80, Strickland: *Lives of the Queens of England, Vol.*

II (1884). To Henry III of France, p. 81, Strickland: *Lives of the Queens of England, Vol. II* (1884). To James VI of Scotland, p. 82 Strickland: *Lives of the Queens of England, Vol. II* (1884). To Lady Paget, p. 83, Van Thal: *Royal Letter Book* (1937). To Lady Norris, p. 84, Fuller: *Worthies of Oxfordshire.* To Lord Mountjoy, p. 85, Strickland: *Lives of the Queens of England, Vol. III* (1884). **Henrietta Maria of France** to Mme de Montglat, p. 95, Green: *Letters of Henrietta Maria* (1857). Mme de St George, p. 96, Green: *Letters of Henrietta Maria* (1857). To her son, Charles, p. 97 Green: *Letters of Henrietta Maria* (1857). To Charles I, p. 98, Green: *Letters of Henrietta Maria* (1857). To Mme de St George, p. 98, Green: *Letters of Henrietta Maria* (1857). To Charles I, pp. 100, 101, Green: *Letters of Henrietta Maria* (1857). To Sir Theodore Mayeme, p. 103 Green: *Letters of Henrietta Maria* (1857). To Charles I, pp. 104, 105 Green: *Letters of Henrietta Maria* (1857), p. 106, Strickland: *Lives of the Queens of England, Vol. IV* (1884). To M. de Grignan, p. 106, Green: *Letters of Henrietta Maria* (1857). To Mme de Motteville, p. 108, Green: *Letters of Henrietta Maria* (1857). To Charles II, p. 109, Green: *Letters of Henrietta Maria* (1857). **Jane Grey** to Mary I, p. 37, Wood: *Letters of Royal and Illustrious Ladies* (1846). To Duke of Suffolk, p. 40, *Historians' History of the World*, Vol. XIX (1926). **Mary I** to Cardinal Wolsey, p. 43, Wood: *Letters of Royal and Illustrious Ladies* (1846). To Henry VIII, p. 44, Strickland: *Lives of the Queens of England, Vol. II* (1884). To Thomas Cromwell, p. 45, Strickland: *Lives of the Queens of England, Vol. II* (1884). To Henry VIII, pp. 46, 47 Strickland: *Lives of the Queens of England, Vol. II* (1884). To Duchess of Somerset, p. 48, Strickland: *Lives of the Queens of England, Vol. II* (1884). To Thomas Seymour, p. 49, Strickland: *Lives of the Queens of England, Vol. II* (1884). To Catherine Parr, p. 50, Strickland: *Lives of the Queens of England, Vol. II* (1884). To Edward VI, pp. 50, 52 Strickland: *Lives of the Queens of England, Vol. II* (1884). To Princess Elizabeth, p. 53, Strickland: *Lives of the Queens of England, Vol. II* (1884). To Philip of Spain, p. 55, Wood: *Letters of Royal and Illustrious Ladies* (1846), p. 56, Strickland: *Lives of the Queens of England, Vol. II* (1884). To the Lord Admiral, p. 57, Wood: *Letters of Royal and Illustrious Ladies* (1846). **Mary Beatrice of Modena** to the Pope, p. 113, Strickland: *Lives of the Queens of England, Vol. V* (1884). To Princess of Orange, p. 114, 115, Strickland: *Lives of the Queens of England, Vol. V* (1884). Louis XIV, p. 115, Strickland: *Lives of the Queens of England, Vol. V* (1884). To Angelique Priolo, p. 116, Strickland: *Lives of the Queens of England, Vol. V* (1884). To Princess Anne, p. 118, Strickland: *Lives of the Queens of England, Vol. V* (1884). To Angelique Priolo, pp. 119, 120 Strickland: *Lives of the Queens of England, Vol. V* (1884). **Mary II** to Lady Churchill, p. 123, *Conduct of* the Duchess of Marlborough. To Lady Bellasyse, p. 124, Strickland: *Lives of the Queens of England, Vol. V* (1884). To James II, p. 125, Strickland: *Lives of the Queens of England, Vol. V* (1884). William III, pp. 126, 127, Strickland: *Lives of the Queens of England, Vol. VI* (1884). To William III, pp. 128, 130, 131, 132, 133, Strickland: *Lives of the Queens of England,* Vol. VI. To Princess Anne, p. 135, *Conduct of* the Duchess of Marlborough, p. 139, Strickland: *Lives of the Queens of England,* Vol. VI. (1884). **Victoria** to King Leopold, p. 203, Benson and Esher: *Letters of Queen Victoria* (1908). To Viscount Melbourne, p. 205, Benson and Esher: *Letters of Queen Victoria* (1908). To Prince Albert of Saxe-Coburg-Gotha, p. 206, Benson and Esher: *Letters of Queen Victoria* (1908). To King Leopold, p. 207, Benson and Esher: *Letters of Queen Victoria* (1908). To Florence Nightingale, p. 208, Benson and Esher: *Letters of Queen Victoria* (1908). To Earl of Clarendon p. 210, Benson and Esher: *Letters of Queen Victoria* (1908). To King Leopold, pp. 211, 212, Benson and Esher: *Letters of Queen Victoria* (1908). To Mrs Lincoln, p. 213, Buckle: *Letters of Queen Victoria* (1926). To Earl of Granville, p. 214, Buckle: *Letters of Queen Victoria* (1930). To Augusta, Empress of Germany pp. 215, 216 Bolitho: *Further Letters of Queen Victoria* (1938).

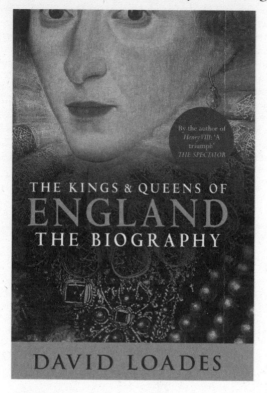